MEDIA, FEMINISM, CULTURAL STUDIES

Liv Tyler: Star In Ascendance
by Thomas A. Christie

John Hughes and Eighties Cinema
by Thomas A. Christie

The Cinema of Richard Linklater
by Thomas A. Christie

The Christmas Movie Book
by Thomas A. Christie

The Cinema of Hayao Miyazaki
by Jeremy Mark Robinson

The Sacred Cinema of Andrei Tarkovsky
by Jeremy Mark Robinson

Jean-Luc Godard: The Passion of Cinema / Le Passion de Cinéma
by Jeremy Mark Robinson

Julia Kristeva: Art, Love, Melancholy, Philosophy, Semiotics
by Kelly Ives

Luce Irigaray: Lips, Kissing, and the Politics of Sexual Difference
by Kelly Ives

Helene Cixous I Love You: The Jouissance *of Writing*
by Kelly Ives

Disney Business, Disney Films, Disney Lands
The Wonderful World of the Walt Disney Company
Daniel Cerruti

Stepping Forward: Essays, Lectures and Interviews
by Wolfgang Iser

Andrea Dworkin
by Jeremy Mark Robinson

Wild Zones: Pornography, Art and Feminism
by Kelly Ives

Global Media Warning: Explorations of Radio, Television and the Press
by Oliver Whitehorne

'Cosmo Woman': The World of Women's Magazines
by Oliver Whitehorne

Cixous, Irigaray, Kristeva: The Jouissance of French Feminism
by Kelly Ives

Sex in Art: Pornography and Pleasure in Painting and Sculpture
by Cassidy Hughes

The Erotic Object: Sexuality in Sculpture
From Prehistory to the Present Day
by Susan Quinnell

Women in Pop Music
by Helen Challis

Feminism and Shakespeare
by B.D. Barnacle

FORTHCOMING CINEMA BOOKS

Mel Brooks
Hayao Miyazaki: Pocket Guide
Akira: The Movie and the Manga
Cowboy Bebop
Ghost In the Shell
Legend of the Overfiend
Fullmetal Alchemist
Donald Cammell
Ken Russell
Tim Burton
George Lucas
Francis Coppola
Orson Welles
Pier Paolo Pasolini
Ingmar Bergman
The Pirates of the Caribbean Movies
The Twilight Saga
The Harry Potter Movies

the james bond movies
of the 1980s

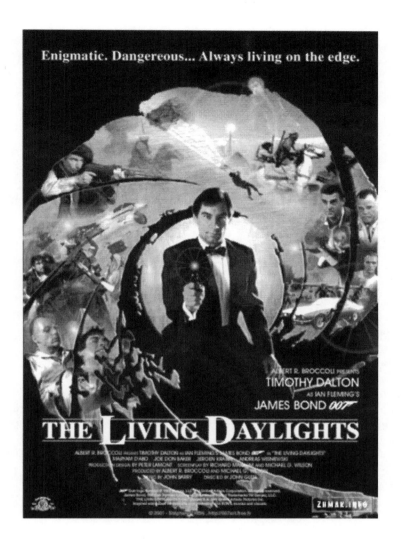

the james bond movies
of the 1980s
Thomas A Christie

Crescent Moon

First edition 2013.
© Thomas A. Christie 2013.

Printed and bound in the U.S.A.
Set in Book Antiqua 10 on 14pt and Gill Sans.
Designed by Radiance Graphics.

British Library Cataloguing in Publication data available for this title.

ISBN-13 9781861714503 (Pbk)

Crescent Moon Publishing
P.O. Box 1312
Maidstone, Kent
ME14 5XU, Great Britain
www.crmoon.com

Contents

Appendices

Acknowledgements

I would like to thank the following people for their fellowship and support during the compilation of this book:

Douglas J. Allen, Dr Colin M. Barron, Eddy and Dorothy Bryan, Julie Christie, Sarah Fletcher, Denham and Stella Hardwick, Margaret Job, Dr Elspeth King, Ivy Lannon, Rachael J. McClure, Raymond McFadyen, Michael McGinnes, Ian McNeish, Mary Melville, Dr Scott Hames, Alex and Kelley Tucker, and Professor Rory Watson.

Particular appreciation goes to Berwick-upon-Tweed Library and Morpeth Film Library for their kind assistance with research materials for this book.

Special thanks to Jeremy Mark Robinson of Crescent Moon Publishing for his thoughts and suggestions.

This book is dedicated to
Mr J. Denham Hardwick MBE
"This never happens to James Bond."

and
Mr Douglas J. Allen
who was there when it all began.

007 HAS STARTED SHOOTING AT CHECKPOINT CHARLIE

Photography began at Checkpoint Charlie in West Berlin, to be followed by filming at Pinewood Studios, England and other locations in India, Germany, and the U.K.

ALBERT R. BROCCOLI presents

ROGER MOORE as IAN FLEMING'S
JAMES BOND 007™ in

Produced by ALBERT R. BROCCOLI   Directed by JOHN GLEN
Executive Producer MICHAEL G. WILSON

FOR RELEASE 1983

DIE JAMES BOND *007* COLLECTION

ALBERT R. BROCCOLI präsentiert ROGER MOORE als IAN FLEMMING's JAMES BOND *007*

OCTOPUSSY

HAS JAMES BOND FINALLY
MET HIS MATCH?

ALBERT R. BROCCOLI Presents

ROGER MOORE

as IAN FLEMING'S

JAMES BOND 007

A VIEW TO A KILL

Starring TANYA ROBERTS · GRACE JONES · PATRICK MACNEE
and CHRISTOPHER WALKEN Music by JOHN BARRY Production Designer PETER LAMONT
Associate Producer TOM PEVSNER Produced by ALBERT R. BROCCOLI and MICHAEL G. WILSON
Directed by JOHN GLEN Screenplay by RICHARD MAIBAUM and MICHAEL G. WILSON

SEAN CONNERY
is JAMES BOND in

NEVER
SAY
NEVER
AGAIN

JACK SCHWARTZMAN and KEVIN McCLORY Present
a TALIAFILM production a IRVIN KERSHNER Film

SEAN CONNERY
"NEVER SAY NEVER AGAIN"

Also starring
KLAUS MARIA BRANDAUER · MAX VON SYDOW · BARBARA CARRERA · KIM BASINGER · BERNIE CASEY · ALEC McCOWEN and EDWARD FOX as "M"
Director of Photography DOUGLAS SLOCOMBE B.S.C. Music by MICHEL LEGRAND Executive Producer KEVIN McCLORY Screenplay by LORENZO SEMPLE, JR.
Based on an Original Story by KEVIN McCLORY, JACK WHITTINGHAM and IAN FLEMING Directed by IRVIN KERSHNER Produced by JACK SCHWARTZMAN
Title song by LANI HALL Music by MICHEL LEGRAND Lyrics by ALAN and MARILYN BERGMAN

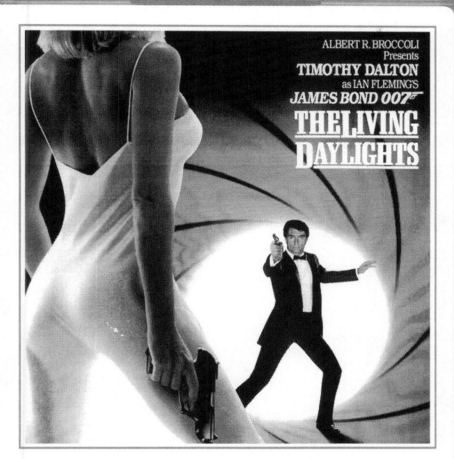

His bad side is
a dangerous
place to be.
TIMOTHY DALTON
JAMES BOND 007
LICENCE TO KILL
COMING JULY '89

I

INTRODUCTION

Few would dispute that Eon Productions' *James Bond* series has become the longest running and most profoundly successful, in both financial and cultural terms, of all British film franchises. Based upon author Ian Fleming's (1908-64) widely-read range of spy thrillers, the films have proven to be extremely popular with audiences immediately from their inception in the early 1960s, and continue to draw massive box-office figures in the present day. James Chapman, in his landmark 1999 text *Licence to Thrill: A Cultural History of the James Bond Films*, cites the remarkable fact that anywhere between 25% and 50% of the global population has watched at least one entry in the *Bond* cycle via the medium of cinema or television[1], and – as its landmark fiftieth anniversary has amply proven – the series' popularity and appeal shows no sign of waning in the foreseeable future.

However, the *Bond* films are remarkable for more than their broad audience appeal. From the earliest days of the franchise, the series has proven to be of intense interest to critics and cultural commentators who have determined its relevance as an acute socio-political barometer of British cultural attitudes. For although the series has its fair share of frequently re-used archetypal elements – futuristic gadgetry, larger-than-life villains and increasingly fantastic chase sequences, to name only a few – it is the means and manner in which these fundamental components have been employed which has proven to be of most interest to observers. This is because the series has been filmed in the midst of radical changes not only to fashions and social attitudes during its duration of almost half a century; the geopolitical makeup of the planet has changed almost beyond recognition since the first screenings of Terence Young's *Dr No* in 1962, and to maintain audience interest the *Bond* franchise has constantly adapted to meet expectations and to remain relevant to the issues of the day.[2]

There can be few periods of global political realignment more profound than that of the 1980s, a decade that began with bitter brinkmanship between the Soviet and American superpowers when *détente* wavered dangerously, and which was ultimately to end with the USSR on the brink of total collapse and the world facing an uncertain future. Given the intense public interest in such historic international changes, it was only to be expected that the *Bond* series would need to take these considerable adjustments in global politics into account throughout the narrative of its films in order to maintain the continuing success of their box-office performance. Yet as we will see, the producers faced a new, additional challenge; although the franchise had adapted to changes in the 'temperature' of the Cold War over the years, it had not – until this point – anticipated the possibility of the replacement of a bipolar superpower system in the world order with a new, unipolar one.[3] Thus as the 1980s progressed, the custodians of the *Bond* series would need to contend with the radical redevelopment of a character who had become the very epitome of Cold War intrigue into a hero for a new era, where the old constants of containment and mutually assured destruction were being briskly swept away.

One key element of the series' success lay in the inventiveness and flexibility of Eon Productions, the custodians of the *Bond* franchise since its inception in the early sixties. Led by American producer Albert R. 'Cubby' Broccoli (1909-96) from the very beginning of the cycle, often in collaboration with his long-time colleague Harry Saltzman (1915-94) until the mid-1970s, by the eighties Broccoli had been joined in his production responsibilities by Michael G. Wilson (1942-), a highly adaptable screenwriter and producer (also a legal expert and electrical engineer). Wilson's scriptwriting talents were drawn on no less than five times throughout the 1980s, for his collaborations with veteran screenwriter Richard Maibaum (1909-91) were called upon for all of the Eon *Bond* films which were produced throughout the course of that decade. Maibaum, whose experience of writing for the screen stretched back to the mid-1930s, had been responsible for the scripts of almost every *Bond* film in the series up to that point; with the exceptions of just three entries – *You Only Live Twice* (1967), *Live and Let Die* (1973) and *Moonraker* (1979) – his screenwriting talents had become virtually synonymous with the cycle. Rounding off the central creative team was John Glen (b. 1932), a veteran of the British film industry who would helm all five *Bond* films produced by Eon Productions in the 1980s. The only director ever to oversee five successive *James Bond* films, Glen's tenure was an often controversial one which would bear witness to dramatic changes in the films' tone and content led by the production team, the substitution of the (highly popular) leading actor for the first time since 1973, and considerable fluctuation in audience figures as the eighties progressed.

The decade has also become known for an interesting oddity in the *Bond* oeuvre in the form of *Never Say Never Again* (1983), an independently-produced film based upon Ian Fleming's 1961 novel *Thunderball* which formed the end result of a long-running legal battle which had involved Fleming and one of his literary collaborators, Kevin McClory. Although generally successful with critics, the film, directed by experienced Hollywood director Irvin Kershner (1923-2010), is in most respects a modern, technically refined update of the 1965 Eon Production *Thunderball*, even going so far as to re-employ Sean Connery as Bond – the first time that the actor had assumed the role since 1971's *Diamonds Are*

Forever. Yet *Never Say Never Again* was not an Eon Production, and although produced independently of the main cycle it seems anachronistically much closer in tone to the earlier *Bond* films than the (arguably even more politically conscious) official productions of the 1980s.[4] It remains, however, an peculiarity of no small significance, although – as will be discussed later in this book – it is one which is perhaps best viewed in isolation from the series at large.

In evaluating the importance and effectiveness of the 1980s *Bond* films released under the Eon Productions banner, it is important to note that they must be assessed with respect to the wider context of the series as a whole. As Chapman has perceptively suggested, the *Bond* series' relevance to the world of cinema – and its socio-cultural contribution in general terms – cannot be fully considered while the cycle remains in progress, which still remains the case in the present day.[5] Indeed, it is not only the series' immediate past that must be examined in this context. Now, a full two decades after the conclusion of the 1980s, the *Bond* franchise continues to prove that it is still very much in operation, having retained its prevalent status in popular culture and its long-standing success with the cinemagoing public in spite of various (often profound) production difficulties over the years. Thus we must examine the particular manner in which the radical change in direction that the series took in the 1980s – in an attempt to shore up its then-depleting viewership figures – would come to affect latter-day reception of the *Bond* films, both critically and in terms of box-office returns.

This book will attempt to chart the creative path of the *James Bond* series through one of the most tumultuous decades of the late Twentieth Century by examining all five 1980s entries which were to take their place within the annals of the Eon *Bond* films: *For Your Eyes Only* (1981); *Octopussy* (1983); *A View to a Kill* (1985); *The Living Daylights* (1987), and *Licence to Kill* (1989). As will be discussed, the conditions of their production and the perceived necessity to provide the audience with an increasingly relevant, contemporary approach to the pre-existing 'Bond formula' ultimately provides an interesting view not only of British attitudes towards the Cold War as it reached its conclusion, but also of the more wide-reaching implications of Britain's changing role in geopolitics at that period in time.

Although the *Bond* films have been subject to intense academic scrutiny throughout virtually the entire lifespan of the cycle, ideological studies tend to encompass the whole of the series to date in order to pinpoint specific and/or universal themes emerging from the series when seen as an unfolding text. Many others have centred upon the disparity between Fleming's Bond and the development of the filmic Bond, who over the years has gradually evolved into a very different character from the gritty post-War protagonist of the novels. However, by centring on one specific decade of the series' development it is my hope that this study will ultimately investigate the manner in which the political themes of the *Bond* films were specifically adapted to a volatile and often unpredictable era in world history.

Primarily, the following chapters discuss the manner in which the *Bond* film series was to develop throughout the eighties. Among the issues considered are the production team's views on the strategies which had come to underpin the format of the *Bond* cycle, particularly the manner in which these approaches could be equated to the Cold War of the past as well as to meet the rapidly developing geopolitical situation of the 1980s in a suitably effective manner. Bond's literary and historical foundations are also engaged with, particularly in terms of their influence over the series' ideological development as the decade progressed. Yet in geopolitical terms, it is also necessary to examine the changing nature of the Cold War throughout the duration of the 1980s, developing from renewed nuclear brinkmanship at the beginning of the decade to *glasnost* and a later weakening of the Soviet position on the world stage. Eon Productions were culturally proactive in elaborating on Bond's Cold Warrior persona, first by restating the series' explicit Cold War credentials, and then by gradually redeveloping the series' format as the decade progressed in order to adapt to the evolving global political situation. In this way, the creative team attempted to maintain the films' relevance to world audiences, and their approach was to be reflected in the balanced treatment of Bond's Soviet counterparts. Conversely, it is essential to consider the manner in which influences from the United States, both in terms of politics and audience expectation, were to affect the *Bond* productions during the decade. A number of the films featured scenes set in American locations, or were to include United States involvement of one kind or another, which was to run in parallel with an engagement with issues antithetical to Soviet communism, including free-market capitalism, the global arms trade, and the supremacy of corporate interests. America's changing world role, from superpower confrontation to fledgling unipolar superstate, is also discussed with regard to the latter entries in the eighties canon of *Bond* films.

The *Bond* cycle's audience reception underwent several changes in fortune throughout the course of the 1980s; its audience figures were to fluctuate considerably as the decade progressed, most notably at the American box-office where consistently strong competition from Hollywood studios was to prove progressively more damaging to the series' financial prosperity. Using statistical data of each film's box-office performance, both worldwide and on a country-by-country basis, this book also discusses the numerous contributing factors which were to affect the series' income from audiences at home and abroad. But beyond a consideration of the films' respective production lies the far-reaching cultural and creative influence of the *Bond* series; although the immensely popular Eon movies had always proven to be inspirational to the wider film industry, particularly during the sixties, the 1980s would bear no less witness to the ongoing prominence of the cycle, with many well-known films of the decade drawing some of their inspiration (sometimes in subtle ways) from the creatively fertile *Bond* legacy.

Ultimately, the conclusion of the book draws from the findings of previous sections in order to provide final deductions about the *Bond* series' relevance to the Cold War climate of the 1980s, and vice-versa. The views of critics and commentators, both contemporary and retrospective, will be discussed in order to evaluate the manner in which the eighties Bond films mirrored the anxieties of a changing world, and the uncertainties of a post-Cold War international environment. Having examined the cultural and political implications of the eighties Bond canon, the book then comes to a close with a scene-by-scene analysis of *The Living Daylights*, one of the most significant of all of the contributions to the Eon Productions stable to be released during the decade under discussion.

REFERENCES

1. James Chapman, *Licence to Thrill: A Cultural History of the James Bond Films* (London: I.B. Tauris, 1999), p.14.
2. Janet Woollacott, 'The James Bond Films: Conditions of Production', in *The James Bond Phenomenon: A Critical Reader*, ed. by Christoph Lindner (Manchester: Manchester University Press, 2003), 99-117, pp.99-100.
3. John Cork and Bruce Scivally, *James Bond: The Legacy* (London: Boxtree, 2002), p.233; pp.236-37.
4. Jeremy Black, *The Politics of James Bond: From Fleming's Novels to the Big Screen* (London: Greenwood Press, 2001), pp.145-46.
5. James Chapman, 'A Licence to Thrill', in *The James Bond Phenomenon: A Critical Reader*, ed. by Christoph Lindner (Manchester: Manchester University Press, 2003, 91-98, p.91.

2

SHAKEN AND STIRRED: EON PRODUCTIONS, COLD WAR GEOPOLITICS AND THE 1980s

Looking back at the world stage of the 1980s, it is difficult to imagine a more eventful period in recent global history. The Soviet occupation of (and later retreat from) Afghanistan; the Falklands War; Ronald Reagan's 'Star Wars' Satellite Defence Initiative and the fall of the Berlin Wall are all events which have become indelibly etched into the modern consciousness. It was against this chaotic backdrop of world affairs that the then-twenty year old *James Bond* film franchise was to witness one of the most dramatic shifts in its long history.

Retrospectively, it seems almost odd to reflect that a deepening of Cold War tensions would necessitate a change in direction for the *James Bond* motion picture series. After all, Fleming's novels of the 1950s depicted a protagonist who was to become virtually synonymous with the acute ideological gulf between East and West – as Jeremy Black observes in *The Politics of James Bond* (2001), initial entries in Fleming's canon of novels were very much the product of their time, addressing the ideological and practical conflicts of the Cold War in a world still witnessing the geopolitical aftermath of the Second World War.[1]

Yet the Cold War of the 1950s had become a very different kind of conflict three decades later, its complexion having been altered by the perilous depths of the Cuban Missile Crisis and the constructive optimism of *détente* before descending, once more, into firm entrenchment by the time of the early 1980s. Likewise, the *James Bond* series of films had also displayed long-term stylistic development since its inception in 1962; the movies had taken a divergent course (sometimes markedly so) from the plots of the original Fleming novels since the concluding years of the sixties. Chapman suggests that this creative departure had decisively occurred by the early 1970s, when the only similarity to the Fleming novels eventually became the titles of the books being shared by the films, and the names of some central characters mirroring those of their literary counterparts – even if their personalities and modus operandi differed markedly in the translation.[2]

Thus by the time of the release of *For Your Eyes Only* in 1981, Eon Productions' *Bond* franchise had already deviated manifestly from the source material of the Fleming novels for a decade. The fact that few in the viewing public would by now be expecting an adaptation of Fleming's work in anything but the loosest sense had come to lend the producers considerable creative latitude in guiding the artistic direction of the series, with no particular obligation to revise and modernise Fleming's now-increasingly outmoded plotlines. This was not to say, however, that the general tone and style of Fleming's original stories were to be entirely abandoned. Indeed, the kind of narrative realised so effectively in the earliest films in the series, those considered closest to Fleming's original source material, have long been considered the series' creative zenith by many. This is particularly true of *Goldfinger* (Guy Hamilton, 1963), perceived by numerous critics to be the most refined of all the *Bond* films in its delicate balance of technical skill, narrative drama and relative faithfulness to the initial text.[3]

Furthermore, although Fleming's novels had long since been eclipsed by the film series in terms of commercial popularity and cultural significance by the 1980s, the *Bond* author continued to cast a long shadow over the creative objectives of the film producers for many years after his death in 1964. In part, the desire to remain faithful to the style if not the content of Fleming's original texts arose from an acknowledgement of the author's growing recognition among critics – the original Fleming works were to receive considerably more analytical interest from a historical perspective than they ever had at the time of their original release. As John G. Cawelti and Bruce A. Rosenberg observe in their analytical study *The Spy Story* (1987), the character of James Bond captivated readers and moviegoers alike, elevating Fleming's novels beyond other spy thrillers of the same vintage through their compelling adherence to the principles and configuration of the genre.[4]

Given this affirmation of Fleming's novelistic skill as the progenitor of the Bond character and general ethos, it is interesting to note that after a decade of marked divergence from the original source material – most notably evidenced in Lewis Gilbert's high-profile films *The Spy Who Loved Me* (1977) and *Moonraker* (1979), neither of which contain any ostensible similarity to the source texts beyond their titles – it was to be the early 1980s which were to display a tentative shift back towards the content of the original *Bond* texts. The beginning of the decade was to witness the *Bond* films drawing significant inspiration for their plotlines from those of the Fleming works for the first time since *On Her Majesty's Secret Service* (Peter Hunt, 1969). As director John Glen observed in his 2001 autobiography *For My Eyes Only*, the 1980s were to see the *Bond* producers working to make a conscious break from the fantastical world-domination scenarios of many previous entries, particularly the grandiose science fiction excesses of *Moonraker*, by basing 1981's *For Your Eyes Only* on Fleming's unambiguously Cold War-oriented short story of the same name as well as another of his short fiction works, *Risico*.[5] This premeditated swing back towards the style and content of Fleming's source texts can be seen as more than a knee-jerk reaction to the often-harsh critical reception of the overly ostentatious *Bond* films of the late 1970s. As Lee Pfeiffer and Dave Worrall remark in *The Essential James Bond* (2003), accusations that *Moonraker* had diverged too radically from the recognised structural conventions of the series led the Eon Productions creative team to seek a return to realism which would elevate themes of espionage and Cold War tension over any previous predisposition toward spectacle and whimsy.[6]

Although the desire to depart from the more blatant fantasy elements of the late 1970s films was undoubtedly one contributing factor to this return to the basics of the *Bond* filmic 'blueprint', there may have been other additional influences. It can be argued that the resumption of Cold War friction at the time offered the production staff an opportunity to restore Bond's relevance to the geopolitical situation in which contemporary Britain found itself – a very different Britain, and a very different Cold War, from that which had been experienced by Fleming. Yet in spite of the vast social and political upheaval which had resulted in the cultural aftermath of the 1950s and 60s, the paradigmatic Cold War threat itself remained unaltered beyond obvious semantic changes. Thus a moral as well as ideological polarity was increasingly being perceived which was to give way to a distinctive mode of political rhetoric specifically tailored to the nature of the conflict – as exemplified by Ronald Reagan's infamous 'Evil Empire' speech, for instance – which was to have obvious parallels with the long-established Bondian formula. Umberto Eco, in his ground-breaking analysis of the *Bond* novels 'The Narrative Structure in Fleming' (1966), identifies just such a Manichean ideology, which closely mirrors the polarisation between the two competing superpowers; although society and technology may have moved on, Fleming's powerfully-employed interplay of archetypes retained a kind of common collective significance which remained as relevant, recognisable and immediate to modern filmgoers in the latter years of the Cold War as it had at the time of the conflict's inception.[7] Thus by equating Bond with the traditional virtues of liberal democratic freedom, and his enemies with the perceived brutality and repression of the totalitarian Communism of the Eastern Bloc, a clear ethical and ideological polarity is evident – though, it must be said, it may be impulsive to equate the power of the Bond character defined in Eco's summation with mythology in the Levi-Straussian sense. Although Bond is undoubtedly a champion of established Western freedoms, his mythic quality can also be seen as appreciably constrained by the character's ingrained cultural attitudes and some manifest imperfections in the makeup of his personality: a fact which was emphasised most clearly at the end of the eighties. The Bond of the novels is most certainly no paragon of virtue, and the depiction of his character in the films – though considerably streamlined and often less world-weary in comparison to its literary forebear – is likewise a complex mix of honour and ruthlessness. David Giammarco, for instance, has posited the view that the actors succeeding Sean Connery in the role of Bond had gradually moved away from Fleming's cold-blooded, melancholic character, embracing wit, charm and skilled proficiency to the point that this enigmatic figure had begun to appear, to all intents and purposes, more or less incapable of error and thus virtually unbeatable in the eyes of his enemies and audiences alike.[8]

This dichotomy in Bond's character was particularly potent in the 1980s films, where there was first an intentional attempt by producer Albert R. Broccoli and screenwriters Richard Maibaum and Michael G. Wilson to reinforce the proficiency and mercilessness of Roger Moore's Bond[9] – a somewhat awkward fit, given Moore's amiably charming, at times almost avuncular approach to the role – and then an even more deliberate effort to reassert the disillusionment and ruthlessness of the literary Bond throughout the course of Timothy Dalton's portrayal.[10] As Mike Storry and Peter Childs observe in their book *British Cultural Identities* (1997), James Bond has joined a number of prominent characters in literature and film – including Sherlock Holmes, Allan Quatermain and Richard Hannay – who are identifiably British and uphold a robust sense of patriotism, but who do not, in and of themselves, embody or exemplify the United Kingdom itself.[11] Indeed, the very cross-media nature of Bond has made a definitive interpretation of the character impossible. As Scott Murray so succinctly notes in his 1987 article 'The Bond Age', there no longer remains a single 'authentic' James Bond, but rather a wide variety of different possible readings of the character: 'there is no one James Bond; there are many'.[12]

Given the eighties' general shift back to the traditional core values of the series – namely, a return to the style of the earliest *Bond* films – the assignment of John Glen as director can be seen as a logical choice on the part of the Eon producers, who were seeking a restoration of the grittier style and more substantial ideological content of the formative entries in the cycle. Glen's association with the *Bond* series was long established, having served as editor and second-unit director for *On Her Majesty's Secret Service*, *The Spy Who Loved Me* and *Moonraker* before assuming the mantle of director for all five officially-produced *Bond* films produced throughout the 1980s.[13] In addition to his work with Eon, Glen had considerable experience with both the television and film industries reaching back as far as Carol Reed's legendary *The Third Man* (1949), where he had served as assistant sound editor.[14] Therefore he seemed eminently well-placed to steer the series through the uncharted waters of the new decade ahead, particularly as *Moonraker* – the immediately preceding entry in the series – had garnered the most enthusiastic response at the box-office since the series began (grossing $202.7 million worldwide)[15], indicating that interest in the series remained healthy even if many critical appraisals had begun to cool discernibly. Broccoli's assignment of screenwriter Michael G. Wilson to collaborate with series stalwart Richard Maibaum would similarly prove inspired, the younger partner in the writing team having an immediate effect on the tried-and-tested *Bond* formula by constraining the humorous excesses of Roger Moore's immediately preceding entries in the series and energetically steering the films' plotlines back along more earnest, socially-relevant lines. With Maibaum's proven experience and Wilson's creative dynamism, the creative collaboration behind the series' screenplays throughout the eighties was to provide the foundation for some dramatic shifts in the stylistic presentation of the *Bond* cycle as the decade progressed. Broccoli's conscious attempts to shift the series' tone in the eighties were shared by his creative team, and considerable effort was expended by Eon Productions to recreate the Cold War relevance of the sixties' *Bond* films while simultaneously maintaining the series' meteoric commercial success. Writing in 2001, director Glen appeared to be somewhat philosophical about the direction of the film series that he had been contracted to oversee from the early 1980s onwards. He noted that he had studied earlier entries in the cycle with great care and had eventually drawn the conclusion that, for the *Bond* franchise, a liberal infusion of compelling action sequences and a vigorous sense of momentum was at least as important as a persuasive and credible plotline.[16] Yet balancing this observation is the fact that screenwriters Wilson and Maibaum would, in fact, pen a number of *Bond* screenplays throughout the eighties which have since come to be considered amongst the most substantial of the Eon canon in terms of storyline complexity. Critics such as Michael Di Leo, for instance, have ventured the opinion that *For Your Eyes Only* can be considered the most plausible and intense of the seven *Bond* films which featured Roger Moore,[17] whereas the *Screen International* review of *The Living Daylights* praised the film for its 'relentless action [and] labyrinthine plot'.[18] Indeed, four of the five Eon films throughout the eighties are influenced by Cold War issues to a greater or lesser extent. While *For Your Eyes Only* focuses on a very traditional East-West conflict over weapons technology, *Octopussy* was to put a different complexion on the issue through Bond's attempts to avert a catastrophic shift in the balance of global power, but the following two entries – *A View to* a *Kill* and *The Living Daylights* – would instead concentrate on the efforts of rogue factors attempting to accrue material gain beyond the jurisdiction of authorities on either side of the Iron Curtain.

Eon Productions' decision to rework the series in an attempt to regain a harder-edged approach for the latter-day Cold War era – in addition to an attempt to reverse the trend of depicting Bond more as an invincible hero than a real-world intelligence operative[19] – must be balanced against a perceived danger that excessive tampering with the archetypal structure of films in the series ran the risk of upsetting its virtually unbroken run of success at the box-office. Broccoli's distinctive approach to the series he made famous has been noted, retrospectively and concisely, by the observation that while no-one (including Broccoli himself, Glen has suggested) seemed able to exactly define the winning combination of generic and structural characteristics that had made the cycle so monumentally successful, as a producer he had no particular appetite to risk deviating too far from a formula that had been responsible for creating a global cinematic phenomenon.[20]

This observation appears all the more germane when considered in light of the bravest – and ultimately ill-starred – experiment with the series which was to take place during the eighties. The most radical departure from the traditional *Bond* formula during his tenure, 1989's *Licence to Kill*, performed poorly at the American box-office, only just breaking even – albeit in competition with a variety of top-grossing Hollywood blockbusters released during the same year which included Steven Spielberg's *Indiana Jones and the Last Crusade* and Tim Burton's *Batman* (which, as Alan Barnes and Marcus Hearn attest, was almost certainly the decade's most heavily promoted feature film).[21] *Licence to Kill's* sharp deviation from audience expectations of a traditional Bondian plot structure, and the film's decidedly lukewarm commercial reception, have been perceived as contributing factors towards the complex six-year hiatus which beset the production of the series before the release of Martin Campbell's *Goldeneye* in

1995.[22] Paul Simpson's summation of *Licence to Kill*'s performance was largely representative of critical opinion when he noted that, had the film been a blockbuster success, the trajectory of the franchise may have looked dramatically different from that point onwards... but instead, its lacklustre response amongst the filmgoing public (in the United States, at least) made further such marked departures in style and structure from the accepted *Bond* formula highly unlikely.[23]

It may be argued that Eon had already laid much of the groundwork for this thematic digression with the narrative of *A View to a Kill*, a film which featured as its lead villain a lethal renegade who proved to be beyond the control of both the KGB and the CIA: a psychotic industrialist with truly global ambitions who regards the political climate of the Cold War as little more than a mildly-aggravating irrelevance. But with the radical step of replacing Bond's usual mission-based approach with a personal vendetta to drive the plot, the later *Licence to Kill* formed something of an endpoint in Broccoli's attempts to reform the *Bond* franchise in the eighties. In the early part of the decade, with nuclear tensions mounting and international relations between the superpowers at an all-time low, the emphasis had centred on adapting Roger Moore's Bond from the urbane, jet-setting spy of the 1970s into a much more ruthless, dangerous character who – whilst more recognisably human – had a far harder edge and tangible sense of vulnerability. (It is difficult to reconcile, for instance, Moore's alligator-hopping antics in Guy Hamilton's *Live and Let Die*, 1973, with the tense nuclear defusion sequence during the circus finale of *Octopussy* a decade later.) By the end of the 1980s, the Cold War was all but over, and public interest had drifted towards the coming era which American President George H.W. Bush had famously termed the 'New World Order'. Thus Dalton's Bond, who was a far more severe and unpredictable character than Moore's portrayal had ever been, was shifted from the role of Cold War hero to rogue agent – a move which, in its perceived failure to draw audiences, was ultimately to prompt a major revision in creative attitudes. New strategies would need to be engendered in order to avoid anachronism in the films of the following decade, in which the producers had no choice but to adjust the *Bond* framework once again in order to introduce innovative modern scenarios for the post-Cold War world. Opinions differed on the success of *Licence to Kill,* however; Glen, for instance, considered his final entry in the *Bond* series to be his finest work of all five films that he had directed for Eon Productions throughout the decade,[24] and he echoed the opinions of contemporary critics who had praised Dalton's performance as being much closer to the Fleming source texts than his immediate predecessor had been. Yet it has also been observed that the pitiless brutality of the international drugs trade, though a topic that was certainly contemporary and relevant to the time, may ultimately have moved the film too far from the scenarios of previous entries in the *Bond* series, even though it also allowed for a more evocative incorporation of the uncompromisingly dark tone which had permeated so many of Fleming's original novels.[25]

By the end of the decade, Bond had come full circle from international playboy spy back to the world-weary agent of Fleming's early texts, and – as has been suggested by a number of commentators – the gradual removal of the Soviet Union as a threat to the security of the West had led to a search for an appropriate new nemesis to replace the looming totalitarian menace of international Marxist-Leninist Communism. In striving to formulate a response to the changing geopolitical climate and shifting cultural tastes, the Eon Productions creative team had drawn on various aspects of the series' history to craft a compelling social environment for Bond. As the decade unfolded, this included an evocation of the heightened sense of danger hailing from the series' Cuban Missile Crisis period, a hint of the Fleming novels' melancholic ennui, and an acknowledgement of the increasing encroachment of digital technology into everyday life in a manner that could only have been guessed at in the series' early days. But just as audience expectations of Bond were changing, so too was the depiction of the international milieu in which the character operated. As the following chapters will discuss, the role of Soviet Russia in the film series was a far from straightforward one, and even Bond's traditional allies, the Americans, were to have an increasingly complex role in the series' representation of international relations as the Bond cycle progressed through the 1980s.

REFERENCES

1. Jeremy Black, *The Politics of James Bond: From Fleming's Novels to the Big Screen* (London: Greenwood Press, 2001), p.5.
2. James Chapman, *Licence to Thrill: A Cultural History of the James Bond Films* (London: I.B. Tauris, 1999), p.150.
3. Michael Di Leo, *The Spy Who Thrilled Us: A Guide to the Best of Cinematic James Bond* (New York: Limelight Editions, 2002), pp.1-2.
4. John G. Cawelti and Bruce A. Rosenberg, *The Spy Story* (Chicago: University of Chicago Press, 1987), p.154.
5. John Glen, *For My Eyes Only: My Life with James Bond* (London: Brassey's, 2001), p.110.
6. Lee Pfeiffer and Dave Worrall, *The Essential James Bond: The Revised AuthorisedGuide to the World of 007* (London: Boxtree, 2003), p.123.
7. Umberto Eco, 'The Narrative Structure in Fleming', in *The Bond Affair*, ed. by Oreste Del Buono and Umberto Eco (London: Macdonald, 1966), p.59.
8. David Giammarco, *For Your Eyes Only: Behind the Scenes of the Bond Films* (London: ECW Press, 2002), p.195.
9. Alan Barnes and Marcus Hearn, *Kiss Kiss Bang Bang: The Unofficial James Bond Film Companion* (London: B.T. Batsford, 1997), p.139.
10. Sebastion Ffolkes, 'Timothy Dalton is James Bond', *Starburst*, August 1987, pp.42-43.
11. Mike Storry and Peter Childs, *British Cultural Identities* (London: Routledge, 1997), pp.18-19.
12. Scott Murray, 'The Bond Age', *Cinema Papers*, Issue 66, 1987, p.21.
13. Glen, pp.225-30.
14. ibid., p.233.
15. John Cork and Bruce Scivally, *James Bond: The Legacy* (London: Boxtree, 2002), pp.301-02.
16. Glen, pp.110-11.
17. Di Leo, p.12.
18. 'QSF', '*The Living Daylights*', *Screen International*, 608, 4 July 1987, p.38.
19. Giammarco, p.197.
20. Glen, p.222.
21. Barnes and Hearn, p.186.
22. ibid., pp.187-89.
23. Paul Simpson, *The Rough Guide to James Bond* (London: Penguin, 2002), p.120.
24. John Glen, cited in Giammarco, p.221.
25. ibid.

3

COMING IN FROM THE COLD: JAMES BOND AND ANGLO-SOVIET RELATIONS IN THE 1980S

As I have observed in the previous chapter, it seems somewhat ironic in hindsight to note that the filmic James Bond – one of the single most archetypal of Cold War heroes – actually came to have a far more ambivalent relationship with his Russian counterparts than any reader of the Fleming novels could have anticipated. But with global politics changing rapidly throughout the course of the eighties, it seemed only fitting that Bond's dealings with the representatives of the Soviet Union would likewise be forced to adapt and evolve in order to better suit the social and cultural turbulence of the decade.

Although the *Bond* films were often characterised as Cold War thrillers, particularly during the stylistic reinvention of the early 1980s films, the Soviet Union tended to be more of an implied threat within the narrative rather than the specific antagonist. Such was the profusion of criminal masterminds and organised terrorist syndicates offered up by the series during its history, prior to the 1980s critics would be forced to return to near the very beginning of the series – *From Russia with Love* (Terence Young,

1963) – to find a truly orthodox Cold War fable. Young's film was significant in that its central plot featured agents of the Soviet Union who formed a direct adversarial role against Bond rather than an ancillary threat. As *From Russia with Love* was considered to be one of the most critically successful entries in the series (and, indeed, continues to be so), it is perhaps unsurprising that the Eon production team would choose to emulate the film's stark, uncompromising depiction of Cold War brinkmanship during their portrayal of the glacial geopolitical climate of the 1980s: an attempt to get back to basics in the most uncertain of times. There is no small amount of evidence to show the high regard which many in the Eon Productions creative team held *From Russia with Love*, only the second of the *Bond* films to be produced by Albert R. Broccoli. In his autobiography, John Glen has observed that although Young's *Dr No* had made an immediate and significant impression on him, *From Russia with Love* was to make even more of an impact,[1] and certainly the screenplays at the beginning of the decade in particular can be seen to reflect a desire by Michael G. Wilson and Richard Maibaum to steer the *Bond* films away from the larger-than-life spectacle of the seventies entries in the series back to a leaner, more starkly-drawn storytelling style. This is underscored by the fact that, during the screen tests for *For Your Eyes Only* in 1980 – when it was thought that Roger Moore would not be reprising the role of Bond for a fifth time – the production team chose to recreate a scene from *From Russia with Love* to test the abilities of prospective candidates for the part, with director Glen noting that he drew particular creative inspiration from Young's approach to the scene from years beforehand.[2] However, the perceptive Broccoli demonstrated a clear awareness of the fact that a direct restitution of the content and style of the early *Bond* films would not, in and of itself, be adequate for the increasingly sophisticated audiences of the new decade. The Cold War of the 1980s was at once both similar and very different in nature compared to that of two decades previously, and the challenge facing Eon Productions was how to replicate the vivid depiction of bitter international tension and Soviet antipathy while remaining aware of new technological developments and a vastly altered social environment.

It is perhaps relevant to observe the manner in which Soviet Russians themselves were to view Eon's development of the *Bond* series throughout the eighties. Writing during the theatrical release of *The Living Daylights* in 1987, *Daily Telegraph* journalist Trevor Fishlock considered the reaction of then-prominent Russian newspaper *Komsomolskaya Pravda*, which declared that 'the film deals in outdated attitudes, that people in Western Europe no longer believe that the Russians are the big bogy, the source of threat and intrigue'.[3] This admission from the approved voice of the declining Soviet regime, acknowledging that the balance of the Cold War was indeed starting to tilt, does somewhat anticipate the major change of direction that would take place in the next film in the cycle, *Licence to Kill*, where Cold War references were to be dropped almost entirely from the narrative. It also highlights a major paradigm shift in Soviet critical attitudes towards the *Bond* series. As Fishlock observed:

> Over the quarter century of Bond's cinematic career, the official Moscow view was for some time extremely frosty. The authorities here did not much care for Bond's role as the singlehanded superman representative and saviour of Western democracy. They did not like films in which Russians were always the black hats. In recent times, however, the attitude has been more relaxed and Bond films have been seen as the hokum they really are.[4]

Fishlock's analysis that the Soviet view of the *Bond* films had softened by the 1980s is echoed by the views of Eon's production staff at the time. Certainly the screenwriting team of Maibaum and Wilson were to shift the focus of the antagonist's role from Soviet agents and sympathisers (in the first half of the decade) to rogue factors and autonomous adversaries, acknowledging the sentiment that the USSR's role as a global threat to democracy was becoming overly familiar to audiences. Likewise, when discussing the filming of *Octopussy* in 1982, Glen's retrospective observations also reveal that in spite of the identity of the film's central aggressor, a renegade Soviet general, he and the creative team had nonetheless strived to portray a balanced interpretation of the Russians throughout the film. He notes that during filming near the Berlin Wall, security personnel from the Communist regime were seen photographing the production team from over the Wall in East German territory, and he reflected that at the time (not least as he had been informed that some top-ranking Soviet political staff were reputedly secret admirers of the *Bond* films) he had hoped they would clandestinely approve of Eon's attempts to provide a sympathetic view of some of the Russian characters – such as shrewd KGB chief General Anatol Gogol – whenever it was appropriate to do so.[5]

Despite this acknowledgement of the Eon team's desire to portray the Soviets as believable, understandingly-rendered foes rather than as a faceless menace, it is also important to note that – at the start of the decade, at least – the shadow of the Cold War was more clearly perceptible in the *Bond* films than at any time since the aftermath of the Cuban Missile Crisis. James Chapman notes that with *For Your Eyes Only*, there was a very deliberate intent to distance the production from the unrestrained science fiction extremes of its immediate predecessor, *Moonraker* (Lewis Gilbert, 1979)[6], meaning that the film was very much a self-consciously contemporary spy thriller, eschewing the usual globe-trotting *Bond* travelogue in favour of a European-set production with obvious Cold War concerns.[7] He also observes that the following entry in the series, *Octopussy*, continues this pre-meditated departure from the over-the-top special effects and unabashed technological spectacle of the late seventies entries in the series, retaining contemporary relevance and the same emphasis upon Cold War brinkmanship.[8]

There is little doubt, then, that Broccoli's desire to reinvigorate the filmic Bond's status as a Cold Warrior was successful, at least at the beginning of the decade. Yet even here, it must be noted that the antagonists of the above films are not the Soviet military itself; at least, not directly. *For Your Eyes Only* centres around a confrontation between malign proxies working on behalf of the Russians, in which Bond eventually becomes embroiled, whereas the principal adversary of *Octopussy* is a rogue Soviet general who is operating independently of his superiors. These antagonists were to suggest the threat of Soviet domination in a much more direct manner than the larger-than-life Bond villains of the late 1960s and 1970s. It is particularly relevant to compare them to the ostentatious SPECTRE organisation (the Special Executive for Counterintelligence, Terrorism, Revenge and Extortion), Bond's long-running opponent during the Sean Connery and George Lazenby era, whose goal was repeatedly to encourage antipathy between the superpowers whilst politically supporting neither.

The *Bond* films of the early eighties are layered with more complexity than the kind of Manichean battle of ideologies that was so often found to be employed in more conventional Cold War narratives. Writing at the time of the film's cinematic release in 1981, *Variety* reviewer 'Cart' praised *For Your Eyes Only* for its realism, noting that 'the more prosaic nature of the weapons and villainy here brings Bond closer to the "real world", if such a thing was ever on view in this series'.[9] This view is reinforced by Chapman, who develops the observation that with *Octopussy*, the previously unambiguous polarity of East-West relations is further blurred by the film's depiction of a political skirmish taking place behind enemy lines: in his opinion, the film was to indicate an ideological dispute that existed between the Politburo and Soviet armed forces, one preferring mediation and effective international relations while the other instead supported unambiguous military strength and coercion.[10] The former is perhaps best epitomised by the canny General Gogol, an effective spymaster and skilled negotiator who is usually impressed by Bond's versatility even when British aims (almost inevitably) conflict with his own. This is particularly well illustrated at the conclusion of *For Your Eyes Only*, when Bond – having spent virtually the entire film risking his life to recover a missile command system – destroys it rather than allowing it to fall into Soviet hands. Gogol, rather than killing Bond (although he has every opportunity to do so), instead shares the British agent's joke that his action was the perfect example of *détente* in action: a textbook stalemate.

Counterbalancing Gogol's humanity and diplomacy, however, is *Octopussy*'s militant General Orlov, the very personification of the Soviet thirst for military conquest. Played with characteristic fervour by acclaimed stage actor Steven Berkoff, Orlov seeks to force Western nuclear disarmament by any means necessary in order to pave the way for a Soviet occupation of Western Europe using conventional mechanised infantry. As Chapman notes, screenwriters Maibaum and Wilson are at pains to emphasise that Orlov's bloodlust is not sanctioned by the Kremlin – he is even rebuked by the Chairman of the Communist Party (Paul Hardwick, very obviously emulating Leonid Brezhnev) for his expansionist ambitions – but nonetheless, his character provides an undeniable undercurrent of intimidation and imperialistic zeal.[11] General Orlov's uncompromising depiction manages to deflect previous criticism that the *Bond* series' newly-pursued sense of realism had rendered some of its villains bland – a particularly damaging allegation when the flamboyant nature of the antagonist had become such an essential ingredient of the Bond formula. Writing in *Films Illustrated* in 1981, for instance, Andrew Rissik notes that 'the villains of *For Your Eyes Only* [...] are dreary, run-of-the-mill hitmen, and they can't scare you because they aren't anything out of the ordinary'.[12] Orlov, on the other hand, provides a much more trenchant critique of perceived Soviet aggression: as Alan Barnes and Marcus Hearn observe, he is the most stereotypically blustering, treacherous 'red menace' imaginable, contemptuous of Western society and thirsting for its conquest by any means – nuclear or conventional – that are available.[13] When Orlov's murderous scheme is uncovered at the film's conclusion, Gogol watches him die not with commiseration but with disdain, making clear that the renegade's internecine efforts to trigger a continent-wide conflict seemed as repellent to the Soviet establishment (by inference) as they were to the West.

True to Eon Productions' intention to maintain equilibrium in their depiction of the Russia of the 1980s, Gogol is set against the ranting, vociferous anti-capitalist militancy of Orlov in much the same way that he had been used as a counterbalance in relation to the scheming of Kristatos, the brutal, Soviet-sympathising Greek magnate of *For Your Eyes Only*. Played by veteran character actor Walter Gotell, Gogol was to regularly appear in every entry in the *Bond* series from *The Spy Who Loved Me* (Lewis Gilbert, 1977) until *The Living Daylights* a decade later. Gogol's role remained similar throughout all of his appearances, in that he came to personify the mutual respect and professional understanding that existed between the intelligence services of the Cold War powers (his natural counterpart being Bond's Secret Service superior, 'M').[14] Although Bond's relations with Gogol were frequently more cordial than with most other Russians in the series, there was never any doubt that Gogol remained entirely loyal to the Soviet cause, just as Bond was to Western democracy. What differentiates Gogol from the more antagonistic Soviet characters, however, is that he consistently proves himself to be more concerned with maintaining parity between the two superpowers than in destabilising the fragile status quo. This is most clearly demonstrated in his angry exchange with the warmongering Orlov, as the latter outlines his plans for the Soviet domination of Europe at a government meeting which takes place at the beginning of *Octopussy*. This duality in the films' approach to Anglo-Soviet relations – depicting the Russians as aggressively expansionistic on one hand, yet providing a complementary ideological balance on the other – is central to Eon's revision of the Bond formula in the early 1980s. The desire to cultivate a more rounded view of Soviet Russia in the films appears to be particularly acute in the largely sympathetic portrayal of Gogol, who – as Jeremy Black judiciously notes – is rendered very much as an authentic human being within Soviet society, rather than simply a faceless cog in a totalitarian machine.[15]

Interestingly, after having refined the *Bond* series' Cold War credentials at the beginning of the 1980s, the Russians were relegated to a relatively subordinate role by the time of *A View to a Kill* in 1985. Although the film's central antagonist, Max Zorin, transpires to be a former KGB agent, his origins are actually revealed to derive from Nazi eugenics experimentation, and ultimately the character is shown to be motivated by neither dominant ideology of the Cold War. A billionaire industrialist, he seeks to destroy America's Silicon Valley via a plot which involves seismic manipulation, thus guaranteeing that his corporation will establish a global gridlock on microchip production. The irony of the capitalistic ruthlessness of a former Soviet was not lost on the critics of the day, with *Monthly Film Bulletin*'s Tim Pulleine drawing specific attention to the 'former KGB agent now more concerned with pursuing independent wealth and power'.[16] This contradictory aspect of Zorin's character is central to the film's Cold War significance, albeit only in the sense that it suggests his transcendence of the traditional premise of *Bond* villains threatening the carefully calculated East-West stalemate. As Black observes, Zorin was an interesting character largely because of the fact that he openly defied the hegemony of both East and West, functioning as a symbol of a postmodern society that may have been affected by the Cold War, but was no longer specifically defined by it.[17]

The central theme in *A View to a Kill* was thus not territorial expansionism, but the importance – and fragility – of world economics. In spite of the film's engagement with the worst excesses of entrepreneurial greed, a subject which was starting to become very topical in the latter years of the Reagan presidency, no attempt was made to link the subject to its contrasting thematic counterpart, the start of the Soviet Union's gradual economic collapse. However, it did lay the groundwork for such a theme to be explored (albeit obliquely) in the following film, *The Living*

Daylights, where the antagonist – General Georgi Koskov – is both a high-ranking Soviet official and an enterprisingly opportunistic capitalist.

Koskov is a very different kind of renegade than the bombastic, ultra-patriotic General Orlov, and he is free of the unrepressed psychoses evidenced in the behaviour of Max Zorin. His motivations are entirely self-serving, and his elaborate scheming – a convoluted plot involving arms dealing and drug smuggling – replaces the more overt themes of geopolitical brinkmanship that had existed in *For Your Eyes Only* and *Octopussy*. However, the film's engagement with the Soviet occupation of Afghanistan, where much of the action takes place, provides topicality to a narrative that is less directly engaged with Soviet aggression, but remains nonetheless pervaded by Cold War themes. Chapman notes that *The Living Daylights* explores Soviet society from different angles – Europe, through the defection scenes in Czechoslovakia, and then Afghanistan, where occupying Russian troops play a prominent part in the plot – to emphasise the ongoing war of espionage between East and West; a conflict in which Britain still had a critical part to play.[18]

Further to this new ambiguity in presenting the opposing ideologies of the Cold War was Eon Productions' introduction of a new leading actor, Timothy Dalton, who portrayed Bond for the first time in *The Living Daylights*. A classically-trained actor of no small repute, Dalton ushered in a different, more solemn portrayal of the protagonist, contrasting considerably with Roger Moore's buoyant, gentlemanly rendering of the Bond character. This was relevant to the film's approach to the depiction of the Soviet threat to the West, as Dalton's Bond had the potential to be a much more brutal, relentless individual than Moore's often mannered portrayal had sometimes tended to suggest. Correspondingly, the Dalton Bond's approach to Russian antagonists was a much less measured one than Moore's character had tended to use, as reflected clearly by Wilson and Maibaum in their screenplay. This change is most noticeable in Bond's interaction with General Leonid Pushkin, Gogol's replacement at the head of the KGB: disinclined to dawdle around with glib pleasantries, Dalton's Bond wastes no time in demanding answers while leaving the alarmed Pushkin staring down the barrel of his gun.[19]

The scene is vivid in its momentum and ferocity, particularly in comparison with the films which had immediately preceded it in the *Bond* cycle. But as Dalton himself has observed, when the film had first been drafted under the assumption that Moore would have been returning to the part for an eighth time, the initial plan had been for Bond and Pushkin to discuss matters cordially over a glass of champagne.[20] Michael Marano has noted that in casting Dalton, Broccoli succeeded in re-establishing Bond as a culturally relevant and functional character in the world of the late eighties precisely because of the way that the actor's approach was able to harness the attitudes and general essence of the spy's time-honoured qualities – which had been circumscribed by the character's Cold War experiences – and then remapping these tendencies in a way that allowed Bond to connect meaningfully with the rapidly changing world around him, where long-held attitudes and political forces were now in flux.[21]

Dalton's uncompromising and sometimes rather bleak take on the Bond role, coupled with Wilson and Maibaum's multifaceted depiction of a world moving beyond bipolar geopolitical certainties, marked a film that was even more unrelenting in its interpretation of the international intelligence community than anything Eon Productions had offered earlier in the decade. As Black has astutely noted, *The Living Daylights* upped the mystery quotient far beyond the level expected from most *Bond* films, with very few of the characters and situations proving to be whom or what they may initially have appeared to be.[22] Yet paradoxically, this was to be the last *Bond* film of the eighties to feature Cold War themes, and – as the flow of history would have it – by the time of Dalton's second and final appearance as Bond in 1989, the superpower conflict between Communism and free-market capitalism was rapidly becoming less relevant to the world at large (and, by extension, to the dynamics of the *Bond* series). Chapman, for instance, has observed that *Licence to Kill* heralded a considerable shift in gear for the cycle, namely that the Cold War anxieties of the earlier 1980s films are not just downgraded in importance, but actually disregarded completely.[23] Indeed, for the first time in the history of the *Bond* films, the geopolitical milieu that had been inherited from Fleming's novels was briskly fossilising due to the fast pace of real world current affairs. For the series' final entry of the decade, the Eon creative team were to move on to other threats facing global stability, and the only reference to the East-West conflict appears when 'M' orders Bond to report to Istanbul – a front line in the Cold War – for an assignment.[24] Due to the personal vendetta which is driving the film's plot, it is an order which Bond promptly refuses.

Therefore, by the end of the 1980s the *Bond* series had reached the end of an interesting decade-long cycle with regard to its relationship with the Soviet Union. After an attempt at the beginning of the eighties to reinforce the series' Cold War credentials, the decade's rapid changes in international politics had ultimately reshaped the films in an entirely unforeseen way. *For Your Eyes Only* had reversed the trend of the lavish, globe-trotting extravaganzas of the late 1970s by containing all of the action within Europe, heightening the sense of Cold War tension by focusing on the interplay of Western and Eastern Bloc agents within (by Bondian standards) a relatively confined area. All location filming took place in European countries, with the exception of some underwater scenes which had been filmed on location in the Bahamas.[25] By the end of the decade, however, *Licence to Kill*'s location shooting was filmed entirely in Mexico and the USA, with the only European filming taking the form of interior shooting at Pinewood Studios.[26] The Cold War had been firmly relegated to the background, and by the time the series would next be concerned with a depiction of Russia – in *GoldenEye* (Martin Campbell, 1995) – the film's action would be based within a post-Communist democracy, while demonstrating an even more concentrated attempt to redefine the series in order to bolster its relevance with contemporary audiences.

Although historical progress appeared to have pacified Bond's greatest foe, the victory was neither conventional nor clear-cut, and the challenges faced by Bond and the intelligence community were portrayed as greatly altered and complicated, rather than ameliorated, by the passing of Soviet Communism. For in *Licence to Kill*, evidence can be seen of an early interpretation of the unipolar world which was in the nascent stages of formation around the United States of America, the sole remaining super-power, and the Eon films provide indications throughout the 1980s that although an analysis of Bond's enemy reveals much about the series during this decade, so too can an examination of his closest allies.

REFERENCES

1. John Glen, *For My Eyes Only: My Life with James Bond* (London: Brassey's, 2001), p.44.
2. ibid., p.115.
3. Trevor Fishlock, 'Russians Dismiss "Silly" Bond Film', in*The Daily Telegraph*, 8 August 1987, p.6.
4. ibid.
5. Glen, p.137.
6. James Chapman, *Licence to Thrill: A Cultural History of the James Bond Films* (London: I.B. Tauris, 1999), p.204.
7. ibid.
8. ibid., p.211.
9. Cart, '*For Your Eyes Only*', in *Variety*, 24 June 1981, p.23.
10. Chapman, p.214.
11. ibid., pp.214-15.
12. Andrew Rissik, 'Where Can James Bond Possibly Go from Here?', in*Films Illustrated*, Volume 10, Issue 119, 1981, 413-16, p.414
13. Alan Barnes and Marcus Hearn, *Kiss Kiss Bang Bang: The Unofficial James Bond Film Companion* (London: B.T. Batsford, 1997), pp.153-54.
14. Andy Lane and Paul Simpson, *The Bond Files: The Unofficial Guide to Ian Fleming's James Bond* (London: Virgin Books, 1998), p.206.
15. Jeremy Black, *The Politics of James Bond: From Fleming's Novels to the Big Screen* (London: Greenwood Press, 2001), p.100.
16. Tim Pulleine, '*A View to a Kill*', in *Monthly Film Bulletin*, Volume 52, Issue 618, July 1985, p.228.
17. Black, p.172.
18. Chapman, p.234.
19. ibid., p.237.
20. Timothy Dalton, cited in Chapman, p.237.
21. Michael Marano, 'Who is the Best James Bond?: Dalton's Gang', in *James Bond in the 21st Century: Why We Still Need 007*, ed. by Glenn Yeffeth (Texas: BenBella Books, 2006), 101-12, p.108.
22. Black, p.150.
23. Chapman, p.240.
24. Black, p.152.
25. Hoyt L. Barber and Harry L. Barber, *The Book of Bond, James Bond* (Nipomo: Cyclone, 1999), p.216.
26. ibid., p.217.

4

COLD WARRIOR: JAMES BOND AND ANGLO- AMERICAN RELATIONS IN THE 1980s

In the previous chapter, I discussed some of the ways in which James Bond's relationship with his traditional Russian adversaries changed greatly (if gradually) over the course of the 1980s. Progressing from a renewed attempt to stress Bond's role as a Cold Warrior in the wake of the Soviet invasion of Afghanistan during Jimmy Carter's Presidency, by the time of *The Living Daylights* in 1987 the series had slowly begun to embrace the concept of *glasnost*. This was symbolised most fully in the retirement of long-running character Anatol Gogol, who was to make his final appearance in this film, the general having been transferred from the executive of the KGB to the Soviet foreign affairs bureau.[1] Although the Soviet Union would not officially cease to exist as a political entity until the beginning of the following decade, the world of the late 1980s was fast approaching a unipolar geopolitical model, with the United States of America at its heart. Yet this development, and the prelude to it, can be seen as having been anticipated by several of the *Bond* films produced by Eon during the course of the eighties.

In 1987, on the event of the series' 25th anniversary, Alexander Cockburn observed in *American Film* magazine the manner in which 'Bond became the embodiment of Western discourse on the Cold War. The men who would later construct the Reaganite view of the universe turned, time and again, to Bond for their edification'.[2] Yet interestingly, if the series came to prove influential (even tangentially) in the policy decisions of early 1980s America, other fascinating areas of intersection can be witnessed even earlier in the cycle's history. The 'Star Wars' Strategic Defence Initiative, for instance, was pursued by the Reagan administration to employ orbital laser emplacements to destroy incoming Soviet nuclear warheads – a concept which was very similar to the space-based laser weapon deployed by Ernst Stavro Blofeld in Guy Hamilton's earlier entry in the series, *Diamonds Are Forever* (1971).[3] However, Ronald Reagan's controversial 'Evil Empire' speech, in which he identified Soviet Russia as 'the focus of evil in the modern world'[4], actually appeared somewhat outmoded and unsophisticated in comparison to the Eon films' less Manichean approach to the conflict between East and West which was crafted by writers Michael G. Wilson and Richard Maibaum during the eighties. For although there was absolutely no ideological sympathy, explicit or implicit, to be found with the Marxist-Leninist cause in the *Bond* films of the 1980s, Broccoli (and, later, Wilson when he began to share production duties) had presented a largely balanced, even-handed view of Bond's Russian opponents in order to enhance the series' sense of realism throughout the decade. However, just as the Soviets were not demonised en-masse by the series, but instead treated objectively and – in the main – impartially, the films' treatment of Britain's American allies was likewise measured in its approach, particularly as the decade progressed.

For Your Eyes Only did not feature America or its part in the

Cold War, being solely concerned with the race to keep British defence technology out of the hands of the Soviets. As James Chapman observes, the lack of American influence within the film allows for a particularly British aspect to emerge as the narrative explores the United Kingdom's role on the world stage at the time, emphasising a kind of immediacy and awareness of current events (such as the cameo appearance of Janet Brown and John Wells as Margaret and Denis Thatcher) which was comparatively rare for the series as a whole.[5] In a manner of speaking, then, America's specific absence from the plot is almost as significant as its presence, allowing Britain's own (arguably subordinate) Cold War function to occupy centre stage. After the overwhelming involvement of American organisations in the immediately preceding entry in the series, *Moonraker*, which had prominently included NASA and the CIA, the effect of shifting emphasis so firmly away from the United States and its growing influence in world affairs in *For Your Eyes Only* seemed almost jarring. Indeed, the switch of focus onto the British Cold War role is particularly interesting at this latter-day point in the series' history precisely because, as Chapman notes, it is actually quite unusual for the central threat of a *Bond* film to be focused on Britain alone: the danger tends to be global in scale, or at the very least aimed at the West *en masse*, which better situates Bond as a champion for Western interests writ large, albeit with a specifically English origin.[6] However, the following film in the series – *Octopussy* – was to offer an explicit and pivotal function for the Americans, through an exploration of their defensive role in Western Europe.

The narrative of *Octopussy* was, if anything, even more specifically ideological than *For Your Eyes Only*. Whereas the earlier film had centred around Bond's attempts to keep cutting-edge British military technology out of Russian hands, *Octopussy* upped the ante by considerably broadening the nature of the central threat. Not only British interests were at stake from the Russian General Orlov's plans, but those of all Western Europe and, by extension, North America as well: by setting off a nuclear warhead in West Germany within an American airbase, Orlov's hope is that the rest of Europe will draw the conclusion that the resulting explosion was the accidental responsibility of the US Armed Forces, a tragic technical fault which would most likely trigger the removal of American nuclear weapons from mainland Europe and thus rendering the west of the continent vulnerable to a Soviet invasion not by use of atomic weaponry, but rather through the deployment of traditional mechanised infantry.[7]

Orlov's plan to force the unilateral nuclear disarmament of Western Europe, leaving it susceptible to Russian occupation using conventional weapons,[8] seems considerably more immediate than the implausible fantasy scenarios of the late 1970s Bond films.[9] Ironically, the ostentation of the apocalyptic scheming employed by The Spy Who Loved Me's Carl Stromberg and Moonraker's Hugo Drax suddenly seemed much less far-fetched in a world which existed under the renewed shadow of nuclear annihilation, a fact which Octopussy made all too clear. However, the film also draws particular attention to America's presence in Europe, essential in counterbalancing the threat of the Warsaw Pact countries with the reciprocal positioning of conventional and nuclear weaponry. As Jeremy Black notes, the Bond films were far from the only motion pictures at the time to be discussing, as many other organs of public discourse were exploring, the fact that not all Soviets favoured global conquest at any price: whereas the Politburo sequence at the beginning of the film makes plain the regime's orthodox line on defensive matters, Orlov senses an opportunity to strike at the foundations of the diplomatic bonds which exist between Western Europe and North America, drawing the audience's attention to the practical and strategic realities of living in proximity to nuclear weapons.[10]

Thus the focus shifts from technological espionage to territorial expansionism, with America's interests tied inextricably to the wider collective security of the West. The underlying message of Wilson and Maibaum's screenplay appears to be that the route of diplomacy and negotiation favoured by General Gogol and his allies in the Politburo is the only logical way forward for the Soviet Union, with Orlov's extremist actions being rejected in theory and foiled in practice.[11] Thus American containment of Russian expansionism in Europe is reaffirmed to such a degree that critics were by now beginning to question the efficacy of Soviet antagonism as depicted in the series. As *Variety*'s correspondent 'Lor' conjectured, 'though the Bond formula still works, apparently Ian Fleming's Cold War-era concept of SMERSH making the USSR the official villain is gone forever'.[12]

The next film in the *Bond* series, *A View to a Kill*, is even more specifically concerned with American national interests, though not explicitly in Cold War terms. Previous entries in the series had heavily featured American venues, most notably Guy Hamilton's films *Goldfinger* (1964), *Diamonds Are Forever* (1971) and *Live and Let Die* (1973), but the narrative of *A View to a Kill* was not only closely related to the USA in terms of its geographical setting; the film also exhibited a direct engagement with contemporary developments in technology and the economy, two fields in which America's dominance had continued to grow dramatically during the post-War era. The film also hinted towards a kind of new postmodern internationalism, with its central antagonist – Max Zorin – owing his training to Soviet Russia, his fortune to American consumerism and his heritage to Nazi Germany, whilst making his home in Western Europe. Times appeared to be changing, and Broccoli seemed determined that his creative team would meet the task of maintaining the Eon series' relevance in the face of new configurations which were challenging long-held geopolitical assumptions. Director John Glen's own observations on the making of the film are particularly revealing. He states in his autobiography that *A View to a Kill* marked a determined attempt to keep the *Bond* series in step with contemporary developments in the action cinema of the time – a developing genre which was fast-moving and had become very much in tune with the eighties cultural zeitgeist –

while simultaneously remaining as faithful as possible to the customs and conventions that had been established in previous Eon productions.[13]

The decision of Broccoli and Wilson to situate *A View to a Kill* in the rapidly developing America of the mid-1980s undoubtedly gives the film a contemporary edge, but the subordination of the USA's Cold War role within the plot forces the film to focus on other aspects of America's international function at the time; mainly, the overwhelming importance of its free-market economic supremacy. This, coupled with the general intention to maintain the films' relevance to modern film-going audiences, was counterbalanced by criticism from some quarters that *A View to a Kill*'s narrative did not quite match the creative team's progressive intentions. Paul Simpson gives a fairly representative example of this line of analysis when he notes that while every attempt may well have been made by the producers to keep pace with the action thrillers of the time, the film had little hope of succeeding given the (now all too obvious) advancing years of its star, who appeared ill-placed to match the prominent muscle-bound Hollywood actors who were dominating the box-office at the time.[14]

Not oblivious to these criticisms, Eon Productions' assignment of Timothy Dalton to replace Roger Moore in the following film, *The Living Daylights*, can be seen as a deliberate attempt – in the words of *Independent* journalist Sheila Johnston – to reinvent Bond as 'a mythical hero tailored for modern anxieties'.[15] The loose internationalism of *A View to a Kill* continued in *The Living Daylights*, though in more complex ways. Although its central villain – Georgi Koskov – was a serving Soviet general, his profiteering plans were entirely contingent on the involvement of his criminal partner: an American arms trader named Brad Whitaker.

Although Americans had occasionally been cast as subsidiary villains during the course of the *Bond* films, this was in fact the first time in the series' history that an American character had been elevated to the status of a joint-principal antagonist. (Even Mr Big, leader of the New York-based crime-ring in *Live and Let Die*, had been explicitly revealed to be a Caribbean national – living in the US for diplomatic purposes but presumably not in possession of American citizenship.) Pains are taken within the script of *The Living Daylights* to stress that Whitaker, like Koskov, is operating without the endorsement of his government. They share a single motivating drive – enlightened self-interest – which transcends political and territorial concerns.[16] Furthermore, Bond is made aware of Whitaker and his part in Koskov's schemes during a meeting with Felix Leiter, a CIA agent who had been a recurring character through many of series' earlier entries. Bond's long-running friendship with Leiter, beginning in *Dr No* (Terence Young, 1962), had developed into an oft-referenced metaphor for British and American co-operation throughout the films of the 1960s and early 1970s. Notably, however, Leiter had not featured in the *Bond* films since 1973's *Live and Let Die*. A disciplined and supportive associate of Bond, and by extension British Intelligence, the sharp and witty Leiter contrasts sharply with the egomaniacal, sociopathological excesses of Whitaker who – as Black observes – is ultimately shown to be a psychologically disturbed weapons dealer with a military fixation, a character who is playing out his delusions of world domination in a different manner from many other Bond villains.[17]

In terms of Whitaker's ideological function, juxtaposing military and economic interests, thematic comparisons have been drawn between the character's distinctive martial rhetoric and topical figures of the time such as Oliver North,[18] and furthermore the complexity of the film's intricate international arms-dealing plotline was suggestive of alleged American foreign entanglements during this period of history. However, these observations must be balanced against Chapman's astute reflection that news of the Iran-Contra scandal only broke when *The Living Daylights* was already well into the process of being filmed, meaning that although there are many fascinating parallels between fictional and real-life events, it would be misleading to assume that the artistic impetus of the production team or writers Wilson and Maibaum was being influenced by the specific political situation that was being played out at the time.[19]

An exploration of America's global influence was to return, along with Felix Leiter, in the final eighties entry in the *Bond* series. *Licence to Kill* was also to prove to be the film most influenced by America's emergent post-Cold War international role. With the East-West conflict now eradicated from the narrative completely, the plot and style of the film are much more closely tailored to perceived American action movie conventions than any of the other entries in the *Bond* canon during the 1980s. The film's action was split between Florida and the fictional Central American republic of Isthmus, with *Licence to Kill* being primarily based around the machinations of Franz Sanchez, a powerful and culturally sophisticated drug baron who controls an extensive criminal empire with far-reaching international connections. Black suggests that the American foreign policy connotations of *The Living Daylights* are developed even more explicitly in *Licence to Kill*, with the machinations taking place in Isthmus City forming a very thinly-veiled allegory of Central American politics that would have been all too obvious to the audiences of the time.[20]

Black also posits the view that Sanchez was in some ways suggestive of Panamanian General Manuel Noriega, who had become an extremely controversial individual in American current affairs during the eighties.[21]

Licence to Kill was a determined break from the traditional Bond format in a number of ways. Firstly, its North American (and Central American) focus is enhanced by the fact that Britain itself has little or no relevance to the plot – Bond's mission is one of vengeance, to hunt down and revenge his critically injured friend Leiter and his late wife, who had been murdered by Sanchez. Black perceptively notes that as it would have been next to impossible to shoehorn Britain (or British interests) into the film in any kind of credible way, Bond's errand of revenge becomes all the more important as it is ultimately shown to be the sole reason for his presence in Isthmus.[22] This desire to achieve greater relevance to American audiences was crucially important to the *Bond* franchise's producers, not least given the fact that prominent directors from the United States such as John Landis were actively being courted to helm the project before John Glen was invited by Broccoli and Wilson to resume the *Bond* director's chair for the fifth (and, as it was to prove, final) time.[23]

Secondly, there is the fact that Leiter's near-death marks an important turning point in the series' history. As Bond's longest-serving non-British ally, Leiter (and, by extension, the CIA at large) had, up until this point, proven to be just as resilient and resourceful as Bond himself. That the character is so swiftly and brutally removed from the action at the beginning of the film – and, indeed, his suffering provides the motivation for Bond's subsequent actions in tracking Sanchez to Central America – further emphasises the point that times had indeed changed, both for Bond and for the world, now that the old ideological certainties of the Cold War were promptly being swept away. Furthermore, for the first time in the series Bond was depicted as a renegade factor, functioning against the orders of his superiors and even actively being hunted by them.[24] This was consistent with Eon Productions' intention to move with the times and produce a challenging, contemporary *Bond* film which was in touch with modern audiences. This approach was to have drawbacks, however; as Chapman rightly observes, *Licence to Kill* rapidly moves so far from pre-existing expectations of the *Bond* series' conventional style and makeup that it ultimately ceases to bear much resemblance to a *Bond* film at all.[25]

Ultimately, if these changes had been intended to make the modern *Bond* movie more palatable for American audiences, the result was not entirely successful, even in spite of the film's ideological relevance, gritty realism and heavy use of American locales. *Licence to Kill* performed badly at the box-office, though admittedly the takings recouped in United States cinemas proved to be far fewer (the film only just managed to break even) than its reasonable success elsewhere in the global market, making its financial fortunes appear worse than was in fact the case. Nonetheless, the film's perceived failure as a serious draw at theatres caused major critical speculation about the way ahead for the *Bond* series.[26] There was considerable conjecture amongst commentators with regard to the reasons for *Licence to Kill*'s lack of success with audiences, from the manner in which the film's marketing had been handled to the public perception of its star, with commentators such as Chapman venturing the opinion that although Timothy Dalton may well have been a stage actor of considerable experience, on reflection he may not have had the specific combination of star qualities needed to stand out from the crowd in the increasingly well-populated field of Hollywood action thrillers in the late eighties.[27]

Due to changing world events and audience expectation, the conclusion of the 1980s saw the *Bond* series in a far different position to that which it had occupied at the beginning of the decade. *Licence to Kill* was to mark the final writing collaboration between Wilson and Maibaum, and also the last time that Glen would occupy the director's chair. Although he had firmly indicated in 1989 that he fully intended to direct more films in the series if invited by Eon,[28] the long hiatus which followed the release of *Licence to Kill* was to see this ambition thwarted. There was little doubt, however, that the format of the films had indeed developed and evolved – more drastically in the latter half of the decade than the former – and also that Broccoli and Wilson had indeed attempted to maintain the series' topicality and relevance to current affairs by all possible means. In retrospect, however, the question now had to be raised over the point where audiences – both American and global – considered an acceptable balance to be struck between the newly enhanced level of realism which had emerged within the series, and the sense that the *Bond* films should remain faithful to their tried and tested formula.

REFERENCES

1. James Chapman, *Licence to Thrill: A Cultural History of the James Bond Films* (London: I.B. Tauris, 1999), p.239.
2. Alexander Cockburn, 'James Bond At 25', in *American Film*, Volume 12, Issue 9, 1987, p.28.
3. Jeremy Black, *The Politics of James Bond: From Fleming's Novels to the Big Screen* (London: Greenwood Press, 2001), p.143.
4. Ronald Reagan, cited in Black, p.143.
5. Chapman, p.207.
6. James Chapman, 'A Licence to Thrill', in *The James Bond Phenomenon: A Critical Reader*, ed. by Christoph Lindner (Manchester: Manchester University Press, 2003), 91-98, p.97.
7. Lee Pfeiffer and Dave Worrall, *The Essential James Bond: The Revised Authorised Guide to the World of 007* (London: Boxtree, 2003), p.134.
8. Steven Jay Rubin, *The Complete James Bond Movie Encyclopaedia* (London: Contemporary Books, 2002), p.312.
9. Black, pp.92-93.
10. ibid., p.92.
11. ibid., pp.92-93.
12. Lor, '*Octopussy*', in *Variety*, 8 June 1981, p.23.
13. John Glen, *For My Eyes Only: My Life with James Bond* (London: Brassey's, 2001), p.157.
14. Paul Simpson, ed., *The Rough Guide to James Bond* (London: Penguin, 2002), p.115.
15. Sheila Johnston, 'James Bond: For Your Eyes Mainly', in *The Independent*, 2 July 1987, p.12.
16. Chapman, p.235.
17. Black, p.150.
18. Chapman, p.240.
19. ibid., pp.235-36.
20. Black, p.151.
21. ibid.
22. ibid.
23. Nick Setchfield, 'Heroes and Inspirations: John Landis', in *SFX*, Issue 217, February 2012, 78-81, pp.80-81.
24. Chapman, p.241.
25. ibid., pp.242-43.
26. ibid., p.246.
27. James Chapman, 'Bond and Britishness', in *Ian Fleming and James Bond: The Cultural Politics of 007*, ed. by Edward P. Comentale, Stephen Watt, and Skip Willman (Bloomington: Indiana University Press, 2005), p.139.
28. Mark A. Altman, 'Nobody Still Does It Better', in *Cinefantastique*, July 1989, p.61.

5

WHEN BOND WASN'T BOND: *NEVER SAY NEVER AGAIN*

Never Say Never Again has become one of the great cinematic curios of James *Bond* lore, not least as its genesis has become almost as interesting as the events of the movie itself. It was the only non-Eon *Bond* production to be filmed during the eighties, and one of only two unofficial motion pictures to feature the Bond character to date (the other being *Casino Royale,* 1967, a sprawling but reasonably zeitgeisty parody of the Fleming spy phenomenon which was helmed by no less than six directors: John Huston, Ken Hughes, Val Guest, Robert Parrish, Joe McGrath and Richard Talmadge). Although *Never Say Never Again* is remarkable in that it was forced to create (by necessity) an entirely new take on the *Bond* film ethos which was quite different from the now-familiar Eon Productions format, it has become better-known for the unanticipated return of Sean Connery, after an absence of twelve years, to the role that he had helped to make famous across the globe.

The film was born from the result of a complex and long-running legal dispute between United Artists and film-maker Kevin McClory, who had collaborated with scriptwriter Jack

Whittingham and Bond creator Ian Fleming on a screenplay between 1959 and 1960 – entitled 'James Bond, Secret Agent' – which was to feature the first appearance of the SPECTRE organisation and its nefarious founder, Ernst Stavro Blofeld. A year later, Fleming published his novel *Thunderball* (1961), which contained many elements that were alleged to have been based upon the content of the aforementioned screenplay – a fact that would later be acknowledged during a trial in London's High Court in 1963, which ultimately led to McClory being assigned the copyright of the *Thunderball* screenplay and the film copyright of the novel of the same name.[1] After negotiations with United Artists, McClory co-operated with the Eon Productions film adaptation of *Thunderball* which was released in 1965, with Sean Connery returning to the role of James Bond for the fourth time. However, McClory's legal team ensured that the rights would revert back to him after a ten year period of exclusion, which would enable him to produce his own cinematic remake of the *Thunderball* story at a later period.[2] After a great deal of further legal arbitration, this film eventually came to be made as *Never Say Never Again*, a production which – due to an intricate web of intellectual copyright agreements – could not draw on any of the well-known stylistic tropes of the Eon Productions, while the Eon films of the time were precluded from using SPECTRE or Blofeld as antagonists (a fact which is irreverently alluded to at the beginning of *For Your Eyes Only*).

McClory acted as executive producer on *Never Say Never Again*; the film was produced by Jack Schwartzman and distributed by Warner Brothers. The movie was to be helmed by veteran Hollywood director Irvin Kershner, a film-maker with a diverse back-catalogue of motion pictures. Also occasionally active as an actor, producer and screenwriter, the late Kershner had become well-known at the time for his films *Hoodlum Priest* (1961), *The Luck of Ginger Coffey* (1964), *Up the Sandbox* (1972) and *Eyes of Laura Mars* (1978). He had also worked on episodes for a number of television series in the early part of his career, including *The*

Rebel (1959-61), *Cain's Hundred* (1961) and *Naked City* (1962-63). However, he had become most immediately recognisable to audiences of the time as the director of *The Empire Strikes Back* (1980), the enormously successful first sequel to George Lucas's science fiction blockbuster *Star Wars* (1977). Kershner had won the OCIC Award at the Cannes Film Festival in 1961 for *Hoodlum Priest*, being nominated for the Palme d'Or in the same year. He had also been nominated for the Outstanding Directing in a Special Program (Drama or Comedy) Award at the 1977 Emmy Awards for his historical drama *Raid on Entebbe* (1976), which had screened on NBC. Additionally, he was presented with a Saturn Award for Best Director in 1981 for his work on *The Empire Strikes Back* (1980), and was later conferred the Life Career Award in 2010, the year of his death.

If signing up an eminent American directorial talent like Kershner for the production was a major coup for McClory and Schwartzman, the achievement was dwarfed by the fact that – against all odds – Sean Connery had agreed to reprise the role of James Bond once more. The man who had brought the agent to life on the big screen for the first time in 1962's *Dr No* (only Barry Nelson had portrayed the character in an earlier onscreen incarnation, in CBS's *Climax! Theater* television production of *Casino Royale* in 1954), Connery had played Bond on five occasions before his departure from the franchise, being succeeded briefly by actor George Lazenby in *On Her Majesty's Secret Service* (Peter Hunt, 1969). Following Lazenby's fleeting tenure in the role, Connery was to return to Bond once again in *Diamonds Are Forever* (Guy Hamilton, 1971), but seemed determined at the time that this reprise would be a one-off event – a fact that the later film's title, *Never Say Never Again*, gently teases. Following the release of *Diamonds Are Forever*, Connery had appeared in films as diverse as John Boorman's futuristic fantasy *Zardoz* (1974), John Huston's historical adventure *The Man Who Would Be King* (1975), Richard Attenborough's wartime drama *A Bridge Too Far* (1977), Ronald Neame's science fiction thriller *Meteor* (1979), and Terry

Gilliam's surreal comedy *Time Bandits* (1981), amongst many others. Only a few years before he was to win the Academy Award for Best Supporting Actor in recognition of his role as Jimmy Malone in Brian De Palma's historical drama *The Untouchables* (1987), suddenly Connery was back playing the part that he had made a cultural icon – and under the direction of Kershner, who had previously collaborated with him on the romantic comedy drama *A Fine Madness* (1966), in which Connery had starred as poet Samson Shillitoe. The return of this renowned acting talent to the Bond role after a twelve year absence genuinely surprised the general public and media commentators alike,[3] and there was sincere interest in how he would approach the role after so many years' absence (not least as the Eon Productions, which had starred Connery's long-time friend Roger Moore since the time of his departure in the early seventies, had changed in tone and style several times in comparison with the earlier entries in the *Bond* cycle).[4]

What is perhaps most remarkable about *Never Say Never Again* is the fact that, for the first time, Bond is depicted as ageing, and even – if only occasionally – appears to be slightly out of his depth. The issue of the character's increasing maturity was never dealt with during the Eon films up to this point, where Bond is generally shown to be physically capable and in tune with modern technological developments during every outing (even although Roger Moore was, in actuality, almost three years Connery's senior). In sharp contrast to the character as he had been portrayed in *Thunderball*, Connery plays Bond as a much more seasoned figure, retaining the charm and occasional ruthlessness of his younger self but also making the agent appear rather more comfortable in his own skin. This Bond has been out of the field for an unspecified period of time, assuming an instructional role in middle-age. His superior in the intelligence services, M (Edward Fox), clearly sees him as a relic of bygone days, and only returns him to active duty as a last resort. It soon becomes clear that this older Bond is forced to rely on his wits and improvisational skills much more than his fading physical strength and abilities. Although he sometimes seems to struggle with the cutting-edge technology that he is faced with throughout the film, Bond still manages to win the day through quick-thinking, and his efforts seem to signify the victory of his sharp instincts and droll sense of humour over the cool technocratic disdain of his opponents. Connery appears to be even more comfortable with the role in his fifties than he was in his earlier days, making Bond a more sympathetic figure as a result: this variation of the character is no super-hero, but rather a world-weary spy who merely wants to reach retirement in one piece. Naturally, however, his advancing years do not discourage him from pushing himself to the limit when the full extent of SPECTRE's plot eventually becomes clear.

The film also proves to be an interesting experience in the way that it presents an alternative variation on the Bondian 'universe'. Gone are the familiar conventions such as the famous Monty Norman *James Bond* title theme and Maurice Binder's immediately recognisable gun barrel opening sequence. The dryly witty banter between Bond and his superiors was also heavily downplayed; the Edward Fox iteration of M was a much more self-important, bureaucratic character than the authoritarian father-figures created by Bernard Lee and Robert Brown in the Eon films. Fox's M is very much a government civil servant first and foremost, his role as spymaster seeming almost like a secondary consideration.[5] (The issue of Bond's continued suitability for the modern intelligence community was to be raised by the Eon films several years later, when Judi Dench assumed the role of M in Martin Campbell's *GoldenEye*, 1995.) Consequently Miss Moneypenny (played here by Pamela Salem) is reduced to a mere extended cameo, lacking much of the customary repartee that had existed between Bond and Eon series regular Lois Maxwell. Most striking of all, perhaps, is the reinvention of gadget-master Q as a harried technician who (in a manner that would have been all too familiar to audiences of the eighties) finds his department suffering from chronic budget cutbacks. No longer an avuncular inventor of wildly ostentatious contraptions, Alec McCowen's Q (better-known to Bond as 'Algy') is a down to earth, straight-talking government employee, more likely to complain about his dwindling resources and lack of staff support than to proudly unveil a custom-built Aston Martin with rocket launchers.[6] The character as portrayed by McCowen is perhaps even more of a gently comic figure than the familiar Desmond Llewelyn version, though it should be noted that although his departmental assets are taxed to the limit, his technological prowess remains intact: he still manages to come up with the goods when required, much to Bond's benefit later in the film. Less subtle comic relief is supplied by a brief supporting performance from Rowan Atkinson as a bumbling junior MI6 agent, the amusingly-named Nigel Small-Fawcett.

Never Say Never Again was, of course, also notable for the return of Bond's old antagonists, SPECTRE, and the organisation's enigmatic leader. In *Thunderball*, Ernst Blofeld had appeared in a then-customary cameo role, as had been the case in Terence Young's earlier film *From Russia with Love*. Here, however, he is elevated to a more prominent position within the story, and with a decidedly different portrayal than had been established during the latter days of Connery's tenure in the sixties and seventies: in the hands of Swedish actor Max von Sydow, the ruthless megalomaniac in a Nehru jacket becomes a charming, sharp-suited criminal mastermind very much in the vein of Anthony Dawson's brief appearances as the character early in the Eon cycle's history. Von Sydow brings a cultured refinement to the role, making Blofeld a much more civilised and urbane character than the one which audiences had subsequently become used to. His lack of overt brutality is also neatly contrasted with the savage actions of his subordinates within the ranks of his organisation, emphasising the fact that this is one criminal kingpin who has no desire to dirty his hands unnecessarily. Von Sydow has had an enormously varied acting career since his screen debut in Alf

Sjöberg's *Bara en mor* (1949). Although his immortality has been assured amongst cineastes for his role as Antonius Block in Ingmar Bergman's unforgettable *The Seventh Seal* (1957), his many other appearances have included films such as George Stevens's Biblical drama *The Greatest Story Ever Told* (1965), Michael Anderson's thriller *The Quiller Memorandum* (1966), William Friedkin's horror *The Exorcist* (1973) (and also its sequel, John Boorman's *Exorcist II: The Heretic*, 1977), Stuart Rosenberg's wartime drama *Voyage of the Damned* (1976), Mike Hodges's tongue-in-cheek science fiction adventure *Flash Gordon* (1980), and John Milius's fantasy *Conan the Barbarian* (1982), to name only a few. Von Sydow brings a real touch of class to Blofeld, and it is only regrettable that his role – while somewhat expanded in relation to its original brief manifestation in *Thunderball* – was not developed even further. (Like Connery, Von Sydow would be nominated for an Academy Award later in the eighties – in his case, for Best Actor in a Leading Role for his performance in Bille August's *Pelle the Conqueror*, 1987.)

There are many other differences between *Thunderball* and *Never Say Never Again*, the most obvious being the latter's exploitation of developments in technology since the time of the original film's production including new missile guidance systems and the digital technology revolution. SPECTRE agent Fiona Volpe becomes the equally deadly Fatima Blush, a performance which gained actress Barbara Carrera a Golden Globe nomination for Best Performance by an Actress in a Supporting Role in a Motion Picture in 1984. Bond's mission collaborator Domino Derval is replaced by Kim Basinger's Domino Petachi, though the character's role in the film's events remains largely unchanged. Bond's old ally from the CIA, Felix Leiter (this time played by Bernie Casey), is presented with a rather more prominent role in comparison with the original film. But perhaps the most notable change is the substitution of Adolfo Celi's wealthy, eyepatch-wearing SPECTRE gangster Emilio Largo with the equally prosperous but rather more cultivated Maximillian Largo, as portrayed by Klaus Maria Brandauer. Although this antagonist's function in the storyline was to prove largely the same as that of the Celi version, and Largo remains Blofeld's deputy at the pinnacle of SPECTRE's command hierarchy, the character's sly cunning and criminal proficiency is articulated very effectively by Brandauer. Just as Celi had neatly encapsulated the character's inherent danger and barely-suppressed temper, Brandauer excels in forging a character who is no less treacherous but who conveys that sense of threat from beneath a detached, saturnine facade. Although active as a film actor on continental Europe since the mid-sixties, and in theatrical roles even earlier than that, Brandauer was perhaps most recognisable to Anglo-American audiences of the early eighties for his appearances in films such as András Kovács's *A Sunday in October* (1979) and István Szabó's harrowing drama *Mephisto* (1981). He has also become a noted director for both stage and screen, and would later be nominated for an Academy Award in recognition of his supporting role in Sydney Pollack's *Out of Africa* (1986). (Connery and Brandauer would appear together again, some years later, in Fred Schepisi's adaptation of John Le Carré's *The Russia House*, 1990.)

One thing that is particularly striking about *Never Say Never Again* is the way that it chimes in so perfectly with renewed Cold War tensions in a way that – ironically enough – would not have seemed entirely out of place during John Glen's tenure as the Eon films' director. Although the central danger of the story remains more or less unchanged in comparison to that which had formed the primary threat of *Thunderball* in the mid-sixties, the heightened nuclear paranoia of the eighties made the notion of hijacked atomic warheads more immediate rather than less so.[7]

Largo's state-of-the-art ship, the *Flying Saucer* (an Anglicised version of his predecessor's *Disco Volante*), was very much in line with the kind of bleeding-edge technological fetishism of the Eon series, while his lethal videogame tapped effortlessly into the eighties' fixation with digital electronics and home entertainment. Ultimately, this has led to observations by some commentators –

such as Steven Rubio – that although much was made of *Never Say Never Again*'s non-canonical status within *Bond* lore, the film actually remains fairly faithful to the established plot conventions of the Eon format throughout and ultimately sets itself (perhaps surprisingly) a rather conservative approach.[8] Rather, it is continually emphasised that it is Bond himself who has changed rather than the narrative formula, and the film is generally at its most interesting when it explores the ramifications of the hitherto-invincible 007 grappling with the consequences of growing older. The theme is all the more effective due to the skilful way that Connery deliberately underplays the issue; Bond may no longer be at the peak of physical fitness, but he is also an experienced, practised character who is considerably more at ease with himself. The old charisma is still there in abundance, but the audience is now presented with a Bond who is not only fighting opponents with global ambitions, but also combating his own weaknesses in an intelligence world which seems to be moving more quickly (and diversifying in many different ways) than he is able to comfortably keep pace with. But in the true Bondian spirit, Connery's charm is such that the audience are never left in much doubt that the character will somehow manage to win through in the end, no matter how difficult the struggle to get there.

The critical reception of *Never Say Never Again* has been mixed, both at the time of its release and in retrospect, with commentators divided over the film's perceived merits and shortcomings. While some have praised the performances and the sagacious updating of the prevalent themes of the sixties *Bond* films for a new generation,[9] others have been considerably less enthusiastic, with much of the critical dissatisfaction centring on Connery's advancing years causing him to appear less than credible as the jet-setting man of action that he had popularised so many years previously.[10] There was also considerable press interest in the fact that *Never Say Never Again* was being released in the same year as Eon Productions' official *Bond* production, *Octopussy* (although there was, in fact, several months between the two films' respective premieres, precluding a direct head-to-head battle at the box-office). Despite the fact that *Never Say Never Again* performed strongly, it was unable to beat the Eon film either in terms of domestic gross in the US or the international box-office figures. (At the American box-office, *Never Say Never Again* grossed $55,432,841,[11] falling some way short of *Octopussy*'s total of $67,893,619.[12]) Nonetheless, Connery's return attracted significant media attention at the time of the film's release and, quite in spite of the film's unofficial status alongside the Eon canon, it has retained audience interest over the years, seeing release on VHS, DVD and – more recently – on Blu-Ray disc.

Never Say Never Again presents, in a number of ways, a tantalising alternative version of the Bond story – a world where 007 is allowed to retire in peace, together with the long-term romantic partner he had always been denied, and find rest even in the face of his superiors' fevered pleas for him to return to active duty. This is a Bond who has come to peace with himself in ways that his Eon counterpart never quite seems to have done (in any incarnation), and the character's acceptance of his gradually fading relevance seems in stark contrast to the unwavering attempts at the time by Albert R. Broccoli and his production team to emphasise Bond's continuing significance as a cultural icon by reinventing him to suit changing social and cinematic tastes. Interestingly, McClory did attempt to mount another remake of *Thunderball* in the mid-nineties, tentatively entitled *Warhead 2000*. Although the project became mired in legal entanglements from its inception and ultimately came to nothing,[13] McClory's eventual choice of lead actor (had the production come to fruition) may well have allowed for further dimensions of the character to be explored in ways which diverged still further from the Eon Productions. As it remains, that particular prospective side-step in the Bond mythos must always remain within the realms of speculation. But when all is said and done, *Never Say Never Again* is an appealing filmic curiosity, especially when considered in contrast with the narrative and stylistic conventions of the Eon cycle, and one which offers a fleeting view of what might have resulted if the *Bond* productions had taken a slightly different route. Whether such a direction could possibly have sustained the series for as long as the decades-long Eon franchise has done, however, is another question entirely.

REFERENCES

1. Lee Pfeiffer and Dave Worrall, *The Essential James Bond: The Revised Authorised Guide to the World of 007* (London: Boxtree, 2003), p.45.
2. Anon., 'Kevin McClory, Sony & Bond: A History Lesson', in*Universal Exports.net*, 2007. <www.universalexports.net/00Sony.shtml>
3. Roger Ebert, *'Never Say Never Again'*, in *The Chicago Sun-Times*, 7 October 1983. <http://rogerebert.suntimes.com/apps/pbcs.dll/article?AID=/19831007/RE VIEWS/310070301/1023>
4. Richard Corliss and Richard Schickel, 'Cinema: Raking Up the Autumn Leavings', in *Time Magazine*, 17 October 1989. <www.time.com/time/magazine/article/0,9171,952223,00.html>
5. Jeremy Black, *The Politics of James Bond: From Fleming's Novels to the Big Screen* (London: Greenwood Press, 2001), p.84.
6. Tony Bennett and Janet Woollacott, 'The Moments of Bond', in *The James Bond Phenomenon: A Critical Reader*, ed. by Christoph Lindner (Manchester: Manchester University Press, 2003), 13-33, p.30.
7. William J. Palmer, *The Films of the Eighties: A Social History* (Carbondale: Southern Illinois University, 1993), p.191.
8. Steven Rubio, 'Who is the Best Bond Villain? If I Were a Villain, But Then Again, No', in *James Bond in the 21st Century: Why We Still Need 007*, ed. by Glenn Yeffeth (Texas: BenBella Books, 2006), 93-100, p.99.
9. Jürgen Müller, *Movies of the 80s* (London: Taschen, 2003), p.193.
10. David Denby, 'Movies: Sean is Back and the Shark Has Got Him', in *New York Magazine*, 7 November 1983, pp.100-01.
11. Box-office data from BoxOfficeMojo.com <http://boxofficemojo.com/movies/?=neversayneveragain.htm>
12. Box-office data from BoxOfficeMojo.com <http://boxofficemojo.com/franchises/chart/?id=jamesbond.htm>
13. Michael Cooper, *'Warhead 2000*: The Lost Bond Film', in *Alternative 007*, 2007. <www.alternative007.co.uk/ 73.htm>

6

SO WE MEET AT LAST: BOND VILLAINS OF THE 1980s

It is often said that the success or failure of a *James Bond* film can often lie in the effectiveness of its antagonist. Bond villains have become the stuff of popular cultural legend, from Harold Sakata's iconic henchman Oddjob in *Goldfinger* (Guy Hamilton, 1964) through to the metal-dentured Jaws of Lewis Gilbert's *The Spy Who Loved Me* (1977) and *Moonraker* (1979), and they are often among the most memorable features in any film of the cycle. Sometimes, as in the case of Christopher Lee's charismatic assassin Francisco Scaramanga in Hamilton's *The Man with the Golden Gun* (1973), the compelling performance of an accomplished actor can lift an otherwise lacklustre production out of the realms of patchiness and narrative tedium. But on the other side of the coin lies the fact that on some occasions, even the skills of the most stalwart thespian – such as Jonathan Pryce when portraying the scheming media magnate Elliot Carver in *Tomorrow Never Dies* (Roger Spottiswoode, 1997) – can prove unable to raise an entry in the series from the realms of mediocrity if Bond's adversary is perceived to be lacking in menace or somehow fails to present themselves as a worthy or credible enough opponent. The choice of villain in a *Bond* film, therefore, is a crucially important one for the production team, for it is no exaggeration to say that pitching the movie's enemy correctly is a decision which can either aid a production immensely or else encumber it before it can even reach the first hurdle, much less clear it.

A fact that is often overlooked (outside of *Bond* fandom, at least) is that technically speaking, the first Bond villain of the 1980s was none other than 007's long-time opponent, Ernst Stavro Blofeld, the scheming founder of SPECTRE. The reason that the character is often unobserved – in his eighties incarnation, at least – is because he appears only in the introductory pre-titles sequence of *For Your Eyes Only*, and even then he is not addressed by name. However, this arch-antagonist's prominent interaction with Bond throughout earlier entries in the series makes him instantly recognisable to the general audience, and the sequence is successful in resolving a question which had been raised a decade beforehand, namely whether Blofeld had died as a result of Bond's actions at the conclusion of *Diamonds Are Forever* (Guy Hamilton, 1971). Blofeld had appeared a number of times throughout the series' history, first in Terence Young's *From Russia with Love* (1963) and then later in *Thunderball* (1965), when the character was not listed in the films' credits. (During his brief appearance in those early films, he was portrayed by Anthony Dawson – his features concealed during any scenes that he appeared in – with the voice of Eric Pohlmann dubbing his lines.) The intense secrecy which surrounded the leader of SPECTRE was played very effectively to build suspense throughout most of *You Only Live Twice* (Lewis Gilbert, 1967), where the character's features remained unrevealed until near the film's conclusion. Blofeld's portrayal by actor Donald Pleasence has come to be regarded by many as definitive: with his towering intellect, Nehru jacket, ever-present white cat, facial scar, strangely unplaceable accent and bald head, this incarnation of Blofeld is the one which is most often referenced and/or parodied in popular culture as the archetypal supervillain, perhaps most notably as Dr Evil in Mike Myers's superbly over-the-top spoof of the sixties spy film genre, *Austin Powers: International Man of Mystery* (1997). Later entries of the series were to see Blofeld depicted as a darker, arguably more ruthless antagonist by Telly Savalas in *On Her Majesty's Secret Service* (Peter Hunt, 1969) and, following that, in a performance of witty intelligence from the superlatively arch Charles Gray in the aforementioned *Diamonds Are Forever*.

The latter film gave an explanation for Blofeld's constantly-changing appearance by introducing a plastic surgery subplot during the pre-titles sequence, but also ended on an intriguing question: as *Diamonds Are Forever* was the last Eon Production (to date) that was to feature the SPECTRE organisation in any capacity, did Bond succeed in avenging his wife's death (the result of a revenge attack at the hands of Blofeld's accomplice during the famous conclusion of *On Her Majesty's Secret Service*) when he appeared to thwart Blofeld's escape attempt, or had this most resourceful of criminal geniuses managed to evade justice – and even death – one more time? *For Your Eyes Only* finally resolved this issue by briefly reintroducing the character, who had been injured and seemed dependent on a wheelchair for mobility (presumably as a result of Bond's earlier actions, having caused Blofeld's miniature submarine to collide with the control room of an oil rig). As had been the case with Blofeld's earliest appearances, his face is never clearly visible (he was portrayed by actor John Hollis) and his voice is dubbed (by Robert Rietty). Introduced when Bond visits his wife Tracy's grave in a churchyard – a timely nod to the series' past – Blofeld deceives the agent into boarding a remotely-controlled helicopter and then conspires to murder him. It takes all of Bond's cunning to escape the ruse and turn the tables on his old adversary, eventually sending Blofeld hurtling down an industrial chimney stack – a fate that seems rather less ambiguous than his earlier 'demise' in Hamilton's film. Various theories surround the reintroduction of Blofeld in this film, allowing the character – quite possibly Bond's deadliest and most persistent foe – to be effectively sidelined in a cameo appearance which is never referred to again (either in the film itself or, to date, in any later entry in the series). Some have speculated that, as it was by no means certain that Roger Moore would return to the role of Bond in the eighties, this sequence – establishing the character's relationship to his deceased wife, and emphasising his unresolved vendetta against Blofeld – would have presented an effective way of presenting a new actor in the role, immediately underscoring the role of Moore's successor in the continuation of the Eon Productions' canon of films. Others instead suggest that the sequence was a subtle reference to the ongoing legal situation which existed between Eon and Kevin McClory over the latter's attempt to produce an independent *James Bond* film of his own, stressing the fact that the official productions were in no way adversely affected by McClory's use of Blofeld or SPECTRE (neither of which are referred to by name in *For Your Eyes Only*) and casually dispatching them by use of a relatively short sequence in order to make exactly that point. But there is, of course, yet another interpretation. Blofeld's schemes were inevitably grandiose and global in nature, showing fealty to no government or state but, instead, using blackmail, extortion and deception as an eventual means to achieve world domination (as was the case in *You Only Live Twice*, where he conspires to provoke East and West into nuclear conflagration with the eventual goal of ruling the remnants of society with neither mercy or competition). These objectives were, of course, shared by the antagonists of Lewis Gilbert's *The Spy Who Loved Me* (1977) and *Moonraker* (1979). But as has been observed earlier, the eighties were to see a conscious attempt by Eon to restore some semblance of realism and suspense to the narrative of the *Bond* films, and – in so doing – to re-embrace the tangible threat of the series' Cold War origins. Such a visible refutation of the extravagant global domination strategies of the late sixties' and seventies' entries in the series, therefore, is suggestive of a repudiation of the flamboyant antagonists and over-elaborate masterplans of these films, instead making the point that during the eighties, Albert R. Broccoli and his creative team were actively working to ensure that the series would undergo a tangible gear-change.

This contrast in style was very efficiently met in the casting of Julian Glover as the Greek tycoon Aristotle Kristatos, an antagonist who seemed far removed from many of his ostentatious predecessors. The double-agent Kristatos was far more interested in personal gain than doomsday scenarios, and was highly adept at playing both sides of the Cold War against each other – not for some extravagant geopolitical strategy, as had been the case with Blofeld and his ilk, but solely for the acquisition of profit.[1] In the film, the character is greatly expanded beyond the Kristatos of Fleming's original short story, and the action was moved from Italy to Greece. The only characteristic that the filmic Kristatos shares with his immediate antagonistic precursors is a highly cultured demeanour, which mirrors the Mozart-loving Carl Stromberg of *The Spy Who Loved Me* and the gentrified bird-hunting Hugo Drax of *Moonraker*.[2] Yet his refinement is only skin deep, as is evidenced by his habitual double-crossing, his dealing in illegal narcotics, and indeed his brutish actions at the film's climax (most notably towards his young niece Bibi Dahl).

This baccarat-playing businessman was never entirely what he seemed to be, and the character is excellently fleshed out by classical stage actor Glover, who was a well-known face to British audiences from many television appearances as well as his work with the Royal Shakespeare Company. By the 1980s he had become increasingly active in the world of film too, having appeared as General Veers in Irvin Kershner's blockbuster *The Empire Strikes Back* (1980) and – later in the decade – features such as thriller *The Fourth Protocol* (John Mackenzie, 1987) and as the perfidious Walter Donovan in Steven Spielberg's box-office smash *Indiana Jones and the Last Crusade* (1989). Glover brings both charm and a sense of discernible danger to Kristatos, carefully delineating his skill both as a wealthy entrepreneur and a hard-nosed intelligence informant. Kristatos seems unconcerned by the inherent paradox of revelling in capitalistic glory whilst assisting Communist concerns in a manner that could easily tilt the balance of Cold War fortunes (the ATAC device that he has been ordered to retrieve for the KGB holds the ability to put Britain's entire Polaris fleet in jeopardy), and this aids in his depiction as a man of intense contradictions.

Kristatos is certainly a villain who hearkens back to the earlier days of the *Bond* series, with his connection not only to Soviet Russia but also to the Nazi Germany of decades past (clandestine fascist supporters aid him in his smuggling efforts). Yet he is not entirely without precedent amongst antagonists of latter-day *Bond* films, going to bizarrely elaborate attempts to murder the agent (thus offering Bond the opportunity to disentangle himself from peril) when he is entirely free to simply shoot him at an appropriate juncture.[3] Rather more interesting is the theme of revenge which runs compellingly through Richard Maibaum and Michael G. Wilson's screenplay – not just an exploration of the act of vengeance, but also its costs in the long term. Dr Melina Havelock, desperate to avenge the death of her parents (who had died on Kristatos's orders), seeks to murder the Greek magnate in retaliation. Bond is only just able to talk her out of this action when Columbo – a one-time friend of Kristatos who has subsequently become his bitter rival – ends up killing his old adversary in order to save Bond and Melina's lives. There is a strong motif throughout the film which suggests that treachery breeds vengeance, which in turn encourages further vengeance, thus creating a dangerous but seemingly unavoidable cycle of repetition. It had been rare for the *Bond* films to engage with quite such a pronounced narrative premise, much less one which was so bleakly uncompromising, and yet it would not be the only time during the eighties that the screenwriters would explore the issue of retribution in the series.

If Kristatos was a refined Bond villain, the effortless flair and cultivation of Louis Jourdan's Kamal Khan in *Octopussy* surely comes close to eclipsing him. An Afghan prince living in exile in

India, Khan simply exudes urbane sophistication: a backgammon player of repute with an amassed fortune, he puts his expertise in fine arts to good use as a smuggler in everything from precious jewels to advanced weapons technology. Active in film since the late 1930s, Jourdan's polished performance style had been evident in such films as *Letter from an Unknown Woman* (Max Ophüls, 1948) and most especially *Gigi* (Vincente Minnelli, 1958), which had seen him nominated for a Golden Globe Award. Yet he has also been an actor who is unafraid to experiment, as his appearance in films such as Wes Craven's tongue-in-cheek horror *Swamp Thing* (1982) has proven testimony. He brings charm and erudition to Khan in abundance, succeeding in bringing to the character a sense of believability – as well as a calculating cruelty – in ways that were rarely matched by many earlier films in the *Bond* series.

Khan forms one part of an antagonistic pairing in *Octopussy*, albeit a rather unconventional one.[4] The stylish, classy arts lover is balanced by the thuggish General Orlov, a swaggering, arrogant senior commander in the Soviet armed forces with whom Khan has been negotiating. The blustering Orlov may ostensibly seem like the archetypal Communist 'bad guy', thirsting for the conquest of a decadent, capitalistic West (as he perceives it), but his plan to sidestep the Mutually Assured Destruction scenarios so prevalent in discussions of eighties nuclear deterrence is as ingenious as it was worryingly plausible. Orlov is brought to life with characteristic zeal by Steven Berkoff, a highly respected British actor (also an author, playwright and acclaimed director) who, although perhaps best known for his stage work, had been on cinema screens from the end of the 1950s. He had won praise for his appearances in Stanley Kubrick's notorious *A Clockwork Orange* (1971) and later film *Barry Lyndon* (1975), though he also came to be a fixture of popular eighties film thanks to high-profile performances in commercially significant films such as *Beverly Hills Cop* (Martin Brest, 1984) and *Rambo: First Blood Part II* (George P. Cosmatos, 1985).

Berkoff brings an icy restraint to Orlov which he only occasionally allows to crack, as in the character's opening appearance where he discusses (with ill-disguised fervour) a plan for the Soviet domination of Europe, only to be shot down by his rather more judicious superiors. This forces him to take matters into his own hands, attempting to detonate an atomic bomb in an American airbase situated in West Germany in the hope of turning public opinion against nuclear weaponry in Europe, eventually allowing conventional Soviet military strength to dominate the continent. Orlov's rejection of the practicalities of the Warsaw Pact in providing equilibrium of power between East and West is counterbalanced by the diplomacy that had become the watchword of *détente*, and ultimately trumped by it in such a way that the renegade's lethal schemes seem not just homicidal but also hopelessly outmoded. Nowhere is this more amply demonstrated than in his brinkmanship with the KGB's General Gogol, the latter an equally patriotic Soviet who believes that the preservation of the geopolitical status quo is the only thing saving the planet from potential nuclear devastation. Gogol's principled opposition to Orlov's conspiracy (he is not a Soviet 'dove' so much as a well-disposed individual with civilised, humanitarian concerns) emphasised Eon Productions' commitment to depicting the Russians of the time as believable opponents, replete with a carefully-drawn spectrum of morality and motivation.[5]

Octopussy continued the theme of revenge that had begun in *For Your Eyes Only*, this time drawn between the eponymous character and Khan, whom she holds responsible for a murderous intended double-cross. Though there may appear to be similarities between this scenario and that of the Kristatos/ Havelock vendetta which ran through the previous film, any resemblance is in fact fairly superficial in nature, and the conflict is resolved in very different ways.[6] By far the more prominent subject to permeate the narrative of *Octopussy* is that of forgery and deception – a strategy played out to great effectiveness by Wilson and Maibaum. Orlov is blatantly deceiving his own government, not just through the advancement of his nuclear ruse (which, though actually designed to avoid atomic retaliation, would nonetheless kill hundreds of thousands of people at the very least) but also in his substitution of Faberge Eggs held in Soviet hands with painstakingly-crafted fakes, the originals being used as payment for the art collector Khan. Bond also manages to turn the tables on Khan by substituting a genuine Faberge Egg for one of the counterfeits, thus succeeding in deceiving the deceiver. The circus used as a cover for Orlov's planned nuclear detonation does, by its very nature, have a concealed intended purpose, while even Gogol – the head of the KGB – is only just able to unravel Orlov's plot at the last moment (even though it takes Bond's direct intervention to actually foil it). Even more than had been the case with its predecessor, *Octopussy* presented a narrative where no-one was quite what they appeared to be at face value, and where – just as in the real world of espionage – every intention had the potential to be misleading or illusory.

If *Octopussy* had manifested a concern with the cutting-edge weapons technology of the time, where one small atomic device had the capacity to lay waste to large swaths of West Germany, then *A View to a Kill* was instead to explore other applications of the fast-changing field of electronics and digital equipment in the eighties. The *Bond* films had always been successful in showcasing technical breakthroughs, most obviously in the ingenious gadgets presented to Bond by government scientific boffin Major Boothroyd (otherwise known by his Secret Service codename 'Q'), but *A View to a Kill* was to take a rather more proactive approach towards the subject by using it as the locus around which almost all of the film's action revolves. As commentators such as Barry R. Parker have sagely noted, it is in many ways a pity that the film's poor reception amongst many critics has led to it being the most overlooked of the eighties *Bond* films, as it contains many interesting scientific ideas within the course of its running time.[7]

These include electronically-operated steroid dosing, controlled seismic disruption and, perhaps most timely of all for the period of the film's production, microchips which are able to withstand damage from an electromagnetic pulse – an issue of concern at the time due to the potentially devastating effects caused by an EMP on electronic equipment in the event of nuclear conflict.

The genius behind these technological breakthroughs was French industrialist Max Zorin, played by Christopher Walken. Born in what would become East Germany, Zorin was the result of Nazi experimentation towards the end of World War II, under the auspices of scientist Dr Hans Glaub, a eugenics specialist responsible for the birth of several children who exhibited exceptional intelligence as well as psychotic tendencies.[8] Glaub continued his experiments in Soviet Russia after the conclusion of the War, along with (it is implied) the young Zorin, who was trained by the KGB and works as an operative for the Russians before eventually defecting to France and establishing himself in the booming technology business. Zorin ultimately becomes contemptuous of Soviet influence in his affairs, considering the KGB to be no more than an annoyance (and going so far as relay this sentiment explicitly to the high-ranking Gogol, cementing his rogue credentials), but likewise has no apprehension towards the West either, plotting to flood Silicon Valley using a controlled seismic disruption – and thus eliminating his only credible business rivals – with no real concern about the intervention of the American authorities.

Christopher Walken articulates well the psychological instability of Max Zorin, sketching out the character's amorality and casual viciousness with considerable efficiency. Walken was perhaps best known at the time for his role as Nick in Michael Cimino's *The Deer Hunter* (1978), which was to win him an Academy Award for Best Actor in a Supporting Role. He also later appeared in Cimino's infamous Western drama *Heaven's Gate* (1980), as well as Herbert Ross's acclaimed *Pennies from Heaven* (1981), before assuming the role of Zorin. The character is, as critic Steven Woodward shrewdly observes, an example of a Bond villain where two different compulsions – unprincipled illegality and an iniquitous disregard for human wellbeing – are combined in the course of articulating the antagonist's unusually complex motivation.[9] In the case of Zorin, however, that motivation is not global domination by military conquest, as had been the case with General Orlov, or indeed to manipulate the superpowers into their own reciprocal destruction, as was so often the force which had driven SPECTRE and their ilk. Although he does plan world supremacy of a sort, it is to be achieved solely by economic primacy through the control of market forces – albeit through the most hostile of takeover bids. Auric Goldfinger would have been proud.

Similarly, it was greed – not conquest – which would prove to be the driving force behind the two antagonists of *The Living Daylights*. Here, however, Maibaum and Wilson were to exchange the driving force of the film's villains as though to make them appear like a direct subversion of *Octopussy*'s warped adversaries: in this instance, the rogue Soviet general was to be cast as the avaricious materialist, while his Western contact was an unstable warmonger obsessed with armed conflict. Yet the similarities were largely to end there, save for the fact that the film drew on a smuggling subplot which was vaguely analogous to those of *For Your Eyes Only* and *Octopussy*. The crooked Georgi Koskov was, just like Orlov before him, a rogue factor within the Soviet forces; a general who was playing his government against the West to achieve his own ends. But Koskov has next to no concern for the balance of the Cold War, engaging in an elaborate game of mock-defection (and then mock-recapture) solely to advance his criminal agenda. His arms-dealing plan seems to be vastly less important to him than is the notion of pocketing vast profits from illegal opium smuggling (achieved surreptitiously via the Soviet occupation of Afghanistan), and although he treats both friends and allies with detached ruthlessness he has no interest whatever in achieving the spread of global communism.[10]

Although Koskov is supremely untrustworthy, and provides

The Living Daylights with an abundance of welcome intrigue due to his incessant plotting and counter-plotting, he is also a charming and charismatic individual – qualities which are advanced admirably by Dutch actor Jeroen Krabbé. Krabbé was becoming a familiar fixture in American cinema at the time, with appearances in Penny Marshall's clever comedic thriller *Jumpin' Jack Flash* (1986) and Richard Pearce's dark suspense film *No Mercy* (1986). Later to perform in films such as *Kafka* (Steven Soderbergh, 1991) and *The Fugitive* (Andrew Davis, 1993), he has more recently achieved acclaim as the director of films such as *Left Luggage* (1998) – which was to win him the Blue Angel Award (and a nomination for the coveted Golden Berlin Bear) at the Berlin International Film Festival – and also *The Discovery of Heaven* (2001). Just as Steven Berkoff had made the boggle-eyed General Orlov such a memorable villain, the very epitome of Soviet expansionist aggression perceived in the West at the time, so too does Krabbé clearly work hard to make the role of Koskov his own. In so doing, he crafts a very different kind of antagonist; warmly genial at one moment, only to become dismissively hostile the next. (This is perhaps best demonstrated in Koskov's callous betrayal of his lover Kara, whose life he has risked when playing out his various schemes only to dispose of the hapless cellist in an Afghan prison when she has outlived her usefulness.) Like Orlov, however, Koskov also functions as a contrast to a more sympathetic expression of the Soviet character, in this case personified by General Pushkin, Gogol's replacement as the head of the KGB.[11] Pushkin is an enthusiastic proponent of *détente* and international diplomacy, appalled by Koskov's disregard for protocol (to say nothing of the younger general's embezzlement of Russian government funds). Notably, Koskov is one of the very few Bond villains who actually manages to survive the film's conclusion without being killed by 007, but Pushkin heavily implies that Koskov's crimes will not go unpunished, suggesting that the USSR will on this occasion be happy to do Bond's work for him.

Balancing the internecine deceit of Koskov – who is so enterprising that he is actually operating as a kind of triple-agent, variously collaborating with the Americans, British and Russians[12] – is his similarly shady contact, Brad Whitaker. Relatively unusual in the *Bond* series given that he is an American antagonist, Whitaker is as blunt and belligerent in his dealings as Koskov is subtle and persuasive. An unhinged arms dealer sporting an obsession with the most cutting-edge military hardware, Whitaker proves to be a frustrated would-be battle commander, a bloodthirsty but largely redundant weapons fetishist who is spoiling for conflict in a world that seems intent on putting the bipolarity of the Cold War behind it. It is fair to say that Whitaker is such a psychologically pathetic figure that he may actually appear more amusing than threatening, were it not for the deadliness of his business dealings (which almost cost Bond his life). The character's balance of antagonistic bluster and genuine malice is nicely captured by veteran character actor Joe Don Baker, a fixture on American TV and cinema since the mid-sixties, who had made prominent film appearances throughout the eighties in *The Natural* (Barry Levinson, 1984) and *Fletch* (Michael Ritchie, 1985). He was also recognisable to British audiences thanks to his bravura performance as unconventional American intelligence agent Darius Jedburgh in Martin Campbell's hit BBC miniseries *Edge of Darkness* (1985), which was to see him nominated for a BAFTA Award in the Best Actor category. Baker would also later return to the *Bond* series as CIA agent Jack Wade, alongside Pierce Brosnan's incarnation of James Bond, in *GoldenEye* (Martin Campbell, 1995) and *Tomorrow Never Dies* (Roger Spottiswoode, 1997).

The drug-dealing elements of *The Living Daylights* were to give way to a far more prominent narcotics smuggling plotline in the final *Bond* film of the eighties, *Licence to Kill*. Here, the Cold War backdrop of previous entries in the series was to be eliminated completely, with the machinations of an internationally-influential drugs baron taking its place. Even more than had been the case in any of the previous films, the point was made that Franz Sanchez – the drug lord who has become so powerful that he is in virtual control of an entire South American country – had no interest in global domination, or even in currying favour with either side of the Iron Curtain.[13] Such notions were, quite simply, irrelevant to the furtherance of his business interests – his *modus operandi* was absolutely straightforward: to secure the highest profit margin possible from his operation, irrespective of the price in lives necessary to make this objective a reality.

Although Sanchez was regularly given to sanctioning acts of extreme violence, he was also a literate and cultured villain. The cultivation of his tastes seemed to accentuate his complexity as an individual (he treats his pet iguana with more affection than his partner, for instance), and there is a believability to the character's expensive tastes that somehow seems more authentic than Koskov's dalliance with the world of classical music or Whitaker's kitschy hall of heroes from the age of antiquity. Actor Robert Davi works hard to emphasise both Sanchez's quick-witted, sharp intelligence as well as the obvious menace of his character – a man whose temper always seems barely in check, with explosive consequences when his violent nature eventually gains the upper hand. Davi had been a popular fixture in eighties film, with performances in many well-received films throughout the decade including *The Goonies* (Richard Donner, 1985), *Raw Deal* (John Irvin, 1986) and perhaps most prominently *Die Hard* (John McTiernan, 1988). Although he has continued to be a prolific actor in film roles, he also achieved great success as federal agent Bailey Malone in NBC's Daytime Emmy-nominated TV drama *Profiler* (1996–2000).

What is perhaps most noteworthy about Sanchez is that, unlike many of his forerunner antagonists in the *Bond* series, his deadliness is emphasised by his unwillingness to stage intricate deaths for his victims. He is utterly pitiless in the advancement of his business dealings, exacting swift and bloody retribution on anyone who is unfortunate enough to cross him – or even get in his way. The fact that he should choose Bond's long-time CIA contact Felix Leiter as one of his targets, murdering his new bride (mirroring Bond's own loss in *On Her Majesty's Secret Service*, which the film indirectly alludes to) and horrifically maiming the American agent himself, brings the occasional theme of revenge which ran through the eighties *Bond* films to a logical conclusion. The subject of vengeance appears much more raw and uncompromising in *Licence to Kill*, however, as this time it is not a supporting character who is conflicted as they seek to settle the scores, but rather Bond himself who is seeking recompense for his old friend's suffering.[14] This brings to the film not only significant depth in terms of character development – an opportunity which Wilson and Maibaum explore to great effect – but also a heightening of suspense as Bond slowly manages to entangle himself in the affairs of Sanchez's organisation, gradually gaining the murderer's trust while the audience are left wondering exactly when Bond's anger and lust for revenge will eventually spill over.

Yet *Licence to Kill* brought the eighties films full-circle in another sense: the end of the Cold War era was to herald a new beginning both for the world and for the *Bond* franchise. While Sanchez's business operations are based in Central America, they are focused most specifically on the United States – where his primary market is located – in a manner which was entirely ideologically neutral, and which has no concern for international boundaries beyond the efficient flow of laundered cash outwith the knowledge of the authorities. There is no grand geopolitical purpose to Sanchez's operations, and – even more than Max Zorin, who at least had dealings with the Soviet Union in spite of his later contempt for them – he considers his transactions to be nonaligned with any social or cultural demarcation.[15] Sanchez was thus to herald the beginning of a new kind of Bond villain, an antagonist which would prove relevant to the rapidly-changing world order that was to emerge more fully in the following decade. The nineties, when they arrived, would see Bond facing off against post-Cold War Russian army officers, megalomaniac media barons and rogue agents of varying affiliations, as the series attempted to acclimatise to an entirely new international environment. The eighties had seen a period of transition and evolution for Bond villains, shifting gradually from the traditional to the unconventional in ways that underscored Eon Productions' commitment to maintaining their franchise's credibility and sustainability. But as box-office figures were to fluctuate over the course of that tumultuous decade, one question eventually became unavoidable: had James Bond finally discovered, in the erosion of his traditional geopolitical climate, an opponent that even his legendary skills were unable to overcome?

REFERENCES

1. Steven Jay Rubin, *The Complete James Bond Movie Encyclopaedia* (London: Contemporary Books, 2002), p.81.
2. Lee Pfeiffer and Dave Worrall, *The Essential James Bond: The Revised Authorised Guide to the World of 007* (London: Boxtree, 2003), p.126.
3. David Morefield, 'So You Want to Be an Evil Genius?', in *James Bond in the 21st Century: Why We Still Need 007*, ed. by Glenn Yeffeth (Texas: BenBella Books, 2006), 135-44, pp.140-41.
4. Ray Dempsey, 'What is the Best Bond Movie?: Bonding by the Numbers', in *James Bond in the 21st Century: Why We Still Need 007*, ed. by Glenn Yeffeth (Texas: BenBella Books, 2006), 49-72, p.56.
5. Jeremy Black, *The Politics of James Bond: From Fleming's Novels to the Big Screen* (London: Greenwood Press, 2001), p.150.
6. Maryam d'Abo and John Cork, *Bond Girls Are Forever: The Women of James Bond* (London: Boxtree, 2003), p.67.
7. Barry R. Parker, *Death Rays, Jet Packs, Stunts, and Supercars: The Fantastic Physics of Film's Most Celebrated Secret Agent* (Baltimore: John Hopkins University Press, 2005), p.20.
8. Paul Simpson, ed., *The Rough Guide to James Bond* (London: Penguin, 2002), p.185.
9. Steven Woodward, 'The Arch Archenemies of James Bond', in *Bad: Infamy, Darkness, Evil, and Slime on Screen* (Albany: State University of New York Press, 2004), 173-86, p.179.
10. Van Roberts, 'The Bond Films', in *Movies in American History: An Encyclopedia*, ed. by Philip C. DiMare (Santa Barbara: ABC-CLIO, 2011), 51-54, p.54.
11. Black, p.150-51.
12. Oliver Boyd-Barrett, David Herrera, and Jim Bauman, *Hollywood and the CIA: Cinema, Defense, and Subversion* (Abingdon: Routledge, 2011), p.81.
13. Simpson, p.181.
14. James B. South and Jacob M. Held, eds, *James Bond and Philosophy: Questions Are Forever* (Chicago: Open Court, 2006), p.98.
15. Jeremy Black, 'The Geopolitics of James Bond', in *Understanding Intelligence in the Twenty-First Century: Journeys in Shadows*, ed. by L.V. Scott and P.D. Jackson (Abingdon: Routledge, 2004), 135-46, p.143.

7

DEADLIER THAN THE MALE: THE BOND WOMEN OF THE 1980s

The term 'Bond Girl' – and, latterly, 'Bond Woman' – has become a somewhat contentious one over the years. Although even from very early in the series' history the female characters of the series had been shown to be – in the main – resourceful, intelligent and quick-witted, the 'Bond Woman' expression still conjures up deeply pejorative overtones to many. Some still associate the term with a prevailing image of young and attractive characters who perform a largely subordinate function within the film in which they appear, with their sexually suggestive, punning monikers such as 'Plenty O'Toole' and (perhaps most infamously) 'Pussy Galore' underscoring the implication of their sexual availability to the protagonist. But this view is as anachronistic as it is inaccurate, for – even at the advent of the series in the sixties – Bond's female counterparts have been resilient and independent, whether by demonstration of practical aptitudes (Ursula Andress's Honey Ryder) or highly skilled specialism (Tatiana Romanova, as played by Daniela Bianchi). The inherent sexism suggested by the 'Bond Woman' phrase is diluted still further by the fact that, quite apart from describing a *Bond* film's female supporting lead, the term has expanded to cover many other roles within any given entry in the series, referring variously to operatives within the secret service (whether allied to the UK or opposing it), adversaries who are associated with the principal antagonist, or victims who become liberated from a villain-led incarceration of one form or another, sometimes as a result of Bond's mission. Admittedly, some Bond Women are depicted as more critical to the film's narrative than others, and their physical attractiveness and often refined elegance has inevitably meant that the expression continues to divide commentators.

In the 1980s, the role of the Bond Woman was evolving in order to meet the demands of a turbulent and socially unpredictable decade. In some ways, these developments were a logical continuation of the way in which the series had been witnessing a change in the functions and expectations of the Bond Woman since Roger Moore had assumed the protagonist's role in the early seventies. In the main, Jane Seymour's Solitaire in *Live and Let Die* (1973) largely seemed to be a victim of emotional cruelty and manipulation rather than a conventional action heroine, while *The Man with the Golden Gun*'s (1974) chronically inexperienced intelligence operative Mary Goodnight was often played largely for laughs by Britt Eckland. As the seventies progressed, however, things were to change dramatically as the Moore era moved onwards. In *The Spy Who Loved Me*, Soviet agent Anya Amasova – as portrayed by Barbara Bach – proved to be the equal of Bond in every respect; in intellect, in professional competence, and in resourcefulness. Amasova was, at the time, perhaps the most overtly feminist supporting character in the series since Honor Blackman's Pussy Galore in *Goldfinger* (1964): not only does she match Bond's capabilities at every turn, but is likewise reliant upon no-one – of either gender. This theme of independence and proficiency continued into *Moonraker* (1979), where Lois Chiles's Dr Holly Goodhead was initially presented as a leading astrophysicist and then, at a crucial point in the plot, is additionally revealed to be an undercover CIA operative. As had been the case with Amasova before her, Goodhead matches Bond's guile and professionalism and also equals (indeed, in many ways exceeds) his extensive intellectual capacity. Like Pussy Galore and Diana Rigg's Tracy Di Vicenzo before them, these women were constantly so effective in their personal confidence, specialist abilities and professional skills that it was not difficult to perceive that they would have succeeded in their objectives with or without Bond's assistance.

By the time that the series had reached the 1980s, however, the role of the Bond Woman was changing once again. Commentator Robert A. Caplen has termed the period 1981-99 as the 'Post-Feminist Bond Woman Era'[1], where Bond's feminine counterparts throughout the eighties and nineties would be seen to incorporate aspects of the expertise, proficiency and independence of their predecessors along with an additional quality of thoughtfulness and occasional vulnerability. This journey began with *For Your Eyes Only*'s Dr Melina Havelock, as portrayed by Carole Bouquet. A marine archaeologist of Greek descent (though Bouquet herself was actually French), Havelock has no connection to the intelligence world and only becomes embroiled in Bond's mission when her parents are killed by Hector Gonzales, a Cuban assassin, on the orders of smuggler Aris Kristatos. Although Bond is later able to explain the reason for her parents' death (her father, Sir Timothy Havelock, had been working on behalf of MI6 to recover a missile control console from a recently-sunk British vessel), Havelock has already proven to be highly resourceful while working on her own; she tracks down Gonzales with the aid of private detectives and – in murdering her parents' assassin with a ranged weapon to cause maximum disruption – she unknowingly rescues Bond from danger when he is held captive on Gonzales's compound.

Havelock's determination to achieve revenge at any cost drives her completely, to the point that her obsession with retribution causes difficulty for Bond as his mission continues. Having eliminated Gonzales, she then becomes fixated with hunting down his paymaster, unwaveringly single-minded in her pursuit of the individual who ordered her father's death. She is, in fact, so consumed with her thirst for reprisal that – as had been the case with Anya Amasova in *The Spy Who Loved Me* – she engages in no romantic activity with Bond until the conclusion of the mission.[2] Whereas Amasova had held Bond accountable for the death of her lover in the film's pre-titles sequence, thus rendering impossible the series' usual expected romantic frisson between the protagonist and the principal supporting actress's character, it is Havelock's troubled nature and intense focus on retaliation against Kristatos which inoculates her against Bond's long-established charms. Like Dr Holly Goodhead, she uses her considerable academic prowess to aid in Bond's mission (in Havelock's case, being able to aid in the submarine recovery of the ATAC console using specialised undersea equipment), but she remains a lone, determined figure, uncompromising and completely willing to achieve her objective by any means necessary – with or without Bond's assistance.[3]

At the time of her appearance in *For Your Eyes Only*, Bouquet was perhaps best-known for her appearance as Conchita in Luis Buñuel's critically-acclaimed *That Obscure Object of Desire* (1977), though she had also appeared in films such as *The Persian Lamb Coat* (Marco Vicario, 1979) and *Blank Generation* (Ulli Lommel, 1980). She was nominated for a César Award for Best Supporting Actress in 1985 for her performance in Philippe Labro's *Right Bank, Left Bank* (*Rive droite, rive gauche*) (1984), and was later presented with the César Award for Best Actress in 1990 due to her well-received role in Bertrand Blier's *Too Beautiful for You* (*Trop belle pour toi*) (1989). Additionally, Bouquet was presented with the Best Actress Award at the Stockholm Film Festival in 2005 after headlining Juan Diego Solanas's film *Northeast* (2005). In addition to her prolific acting work, she has also directed for television in more recent years. Bouquet succeeds in creating an icily tenacious character, with Havelock's cool efficiency and intelligence providing an aloof veneer over her barely-restrained fury at the injustice of her parents' untimely demise. Though her character does have the occasional moment of comic relief (most notably her escape with Bond from Gonzales's compound, where the viewer discovers that she intends to flee from the murder scene in a rather rickety Citroen, the very antithesis of a glamorous Bondian vehicle), Havelock was very much a character who was defined by dark intentions and emotional damage, and in this sense is far removed from the film's other female characters such as Cassandra Harris's savvy Countess Lisl and Lynn Holly-Johnson's Bibi Dahl, a naive but amiable figure skater.

If Havelock had proven to be, as Maryam d'Abo and John Cork have noted, more of a traditionalist in her attitudes than many Bond Women of the previous decade,[4] she was also to advance the trend which had begun at the end of the seventies – as commentators such as Kerstin Jütting have observed – whereby the female characters' specialist aptitude and professional expertise surpass Bond's grasp of a particular key area that is vital to the mission, while they themselves prove to be entirely autonomous, operating independently from Bond and with no reliance upon his resourcefulness or assistance in order to achieve their own endeavours.[5] This theme continued in *Octopussy*, where the titular character was similarly self-reliant, though in radically different ways from the determined Melina Havelock. The leader of a smuggling ring, Maud Adams's Octopussy is a spiritual guru and circus owner (the latter providing convenient cover for her illegal activities), while her organisation is entirely staffed by highly-skilled women, providing one of the series' most potent statements on gender egalitarianism. Bond finds himself singularly unable to overawe the members of this sisterhood, being first outwitted by Octopussy's wily assistant Magda (Kristina Wayborn) and then discovering that his charisma is entirely insufficient to win over Octopussy herself. The smugglers not only prove themselves to be unassailable to Bond's famous magnetism, but also his attempts to outmanoeuvre them.

It has been noted that the producers were, at the time,

initially averse to the notion of casting Maud Adams in the title role, given that she had appeared alongside Roger Moore in an earlier entry in the *Bond* cycle – *The Man with the Golden Gun* – less than a decade beforehand.₆ In that film, Adams had portrayed Andrea Anders, the ill-fated romantic partner of Christopher Lee's assassin character Francisco Scaramanga. She would later appear in a fleeting uncredited cameo in *A View to a Kill* (as one of the crowd in the Fisherman's Wharf scene), making her technically the most prolific of all actresses to appear as a Bond Woman; to date, only two other performers have made repeat appearances in the series, Martine Beswick (*From Russia with Love* and *Thunderball*) and Nadja Regin (*From Russia with Love* and *Goldfinger*). Maud Adams had made appearances throughout the seventies in a diverse range of features including *The Christian Liquorice Store* (James Frawley, 1971) and *Mahoney's Estate* (Harvey Hart and Alexis Kanner, 1972) before making her *Bond* franchise debut in *The Man with the Golden Gun* in 1974. She was later to perform in a variety of films including Norman Jewison's science fiction thriller *Rollerball* (1975), Mario Lanfranchi's crime drama *Merciless Man* (1976) and Bob Brooks's inventive horror *Tattoo* (1981) before appearing in *Octopussy*.

The Octopussy character is the very epitome of the evolution that the Bond Woman archetype was undergoing during the eighties; a teacher and spiritual guide as much as she is a criminal, the character is sharp-witted, dignified and (largely) honourable – qualities which are lacking in her suave but disreputable smuggling associate, Louis Jourdan's Kamal Khan.₇

Not only does she prove to be impervious to Khan's treachery, teaming up with Bond to uncover the villain's double-dealing, but she also asserts a desire to avenge the lethal duplicity that comes close to destroying her organisation (along with most of West Germany) irrespective of any assistance from Bond. The character's intricate sense of morality is also useful in emphasising Bond's own principled if rather complex moral compass; it transpires that, during a previous mission, Bond had been sent by

MI6 to track down Octopussy's father, Major Dexter Smythe (who appears in Ian Fleming's original short story), to answer charges of theft and murder, but ultimately offers the man a chance to commit suicide rather than face the ignominy of a public trial. Rather than blaming Bond for her father's death, Octopussy voices gratitude that he had saved her father's reputation from widespread disgrace, allowing him to die with his reputation intact. As had been the case in *For Your Eyes Only*, Octopussy demonstrates initial resistance to Bond's romantic overtures, although their shared efforts against Khan ultimately foster an emotional connection between them before the film's conclusion.

A View to a Kill was to mark an interesting development in the series, in that it presented two entirely different female supporting characters who were to embody completely disparate attributes of what had come to typify the 'Bond Woman'. Stacey Sutton, as portrayed by Tanya Roberts, seemed – at least ostensibly – to signify a return to the conventional Bond Woman of the series' distant past, with her elegant costumes, doleful naivety and tendency towards a dated 'damsel in distress' archetype, but in fact the character was also a highly educated geologist whose detailed knowledge of seismology provides Bond with the key to ascertaining (and eventually defeating) the machinations of Christopher Walken's Max Zorin. Yet arguably more prominent throughout the narrative was May Day, Zorin's athletic, psychotic accomplice who was played by Grace Jones. A complicated character to say the least, May Day was partly a romantic interest for Bond, but mainly an antagonist. The character's attraction towards Bond is played out entirely upon her own terms, outwith the knowledge of her lover Zorin, and her sexual conquest of the British agent leaves no doubt that she is responsible for the romance's instigation, rather than (as had been traditional in the series) vice-versa.[8] Even more so than had been the case with late-seventies Bond Women such as Amasova, the film's narrative makes it abundantly clear that May Day's abilities not only equal Bond's but actually surpass them; her physical prowess is far greater than that of the average human being (of either gender), as is her exceptional intellect. Only by relying on his reserves of experience and resourcefulness is Bond able to survive May Day's fatal encounters; many of his colleagues in the international intelligence community are not as fortunate.

With her prodigious mental power and super-human strength, May Day was more than a match for Bond – a fact which was made all the more obvious by the juxtaposition of the young, agile Grace Jones and the now rather more sedate Roger Moore, whose advancing years at this point in the series' history was beginning to stretch his credibility in the central role.[9] It is ultimately the character's Damascene conversion from psychopathic disregard for human wellbeing to a heartfelt desire to assist Bond in thwarting Zorin's murderous plan – a transfer of loyalties which is triggered only by her lover's betrayal – which is responsible for saving Bond and, in the process, Silicon Valley. Though not always entirely convincing, May Day's moral complexity contrasted well with her attention-grabbing feats of physical power, and made for a memorable character. Actress and musician Grace Jones had made sporadic appearances in film since her theatrical debut in crime drama *Gordon's War* (Ossie Davis, 1973). Her later performances included roles in Gérard Pirès's satirical comedy *Attention les yeux!* (1976) and Amin Q. Chaudhri's thriller *Deadly Vengeance* (1981), though Jones's most visible motion picture appearance prior to the release of *A View to a Kill* was almost certainly as Zula in Richard Fleischer's popular fantasy sequel *Conan the Destroyer* (1984), a performance which was to earn her a Saturn Award nomination for Best Supporting Actor in 1985.

Perhaps because of the striking nature of May Day's departure from the norms of the series, the Stacey Sutton character is often overlooked as being a much more conventional, vulnerable character who harks back to earlier, less enlightened days of the franchise in not entirely edifying ways. However, this appraisal is not entirely fair. Sutton is, in her own way, as determined as Melina Havelock had been; her family and fortunes have been abused by Zorin, and she is resolute in her attempts to thwart the opportunity of his commercial ambitions coming primarily at her own expense. Admittedly, Sutton's failure to grasp just how far the mentally-disturbed Zorin's objectives truly reach aids in emphasising her victimhood at the hands of this unbalanced tormentor, making her appear a more sympathetic figure than the film's other female characters such as Fiona Fullerton's affable but cunning Soviet agent Pola Ivanova. Although her role in *A View to a Kill* has become – in the eyes of many critics – one of her most prominent film appearances, Tanya Roberts had performed in motion pictures from the mid-seventies, beginning with a starring role in Jim Sotos's *Forced Entry* (1975). Following appearances in films such as David Schmoeller's horror *Tourist Trap* (1979) and John D. Hancock's romantic comedy *California Dreaming* (1979), her profile increased with performances in a variety of cult movies including fantasy adventure *The Beastmaster* (Don Coscarelli, 1982) and in the title role of *Sheena* (John Guillermin, 1984).

The Living Daylights was to introduce a new actor in the role of Bond, and with him another take on the Bond Woman as the eighties drew nearer to their conclusion. As commentators Jeremy Packer and Sarah Sharma have noted, the casting of a new actress in the role of a Bond Woman inevitably raises considerable interest in media circles due to the fact that – whereas the Bond character himself rarely changes too much from film to film (even although the actor playing him may, of course, differ) – the main female characters are never the same in any two entries in the series, and are rarely even alluded to in any of the later films of the cycle.[10] *The Living Daylights* was already noteworthy in the way that it was to replace series veteran Lois Maxwell, who had portrayed Miss Moneypenny since the cycle's inception in 1962, with newcomer Caroline Bliss, who was to occupy the role of M's personal assistant for the two movies of Dalton's tenure as Bond.

Although Maxwell had enjoyed excellent chemistry with the

first three actors to portray Bond in the cinema (arguably reaching an apex with the playfully droll onscreen relationship between her character and Roger Moore's Bond), the casting of a much younger successor made the flirtatious verbal sparring between Bliss's Moneypenny and the comparatively-youthful Dalton more immediately plausible to new audiences. This modest alteration of the central cast (the other recurring MI6 characters, Robert Brown's M and Desmond Llewelyn's Q, remained the same for the rest of the decade) generated press interest even although the Moneypenny character is rarely – if ever – considered to be a Bond Woman herself. Thus as Timothy Dalton assumed the lead role for the first time, significant curiosity was focused upon the question of which actress would accompany this new Bond on his debut mission.

The answer would eventually present itself in the form of Maryam d'Abo, who was to portray one of the most striking Bond women of the eighties. Her character, Kara Milovy, was a professional cellist from Czechoslovakia who becomes embroiled in a deadly smuggling operation thanks to the machinations of her treacherous lover, Russian General Georgi Koskov. Persuaded to pose as a KGB assassin by Koskov in order to make his defection seem more realistic to the British agents who are involved in it, Milovy's life is spared by Bond when he goes against orders to deliberately miss hitting his target. In spite of Koskov's treachery – his intention was clearly that she should be killed to tie up any loose ends surrounding his flight from the Soviet Union – she remains loyal to him until Bond finally convinces her of the extent of the Russian officer's duplicity. In a manner similar to Melina Havelock and Stacey Sutton, Milovy has considerable specialist skills, though her profession as a classical musician is admittedly less mission-critical than her predecessors' areas of expertise had been. (Perhaps the most obvious practical application of the character's chosen career during the film is a sequence where Bond uses her Stradivarius cello case to stage an impromptu defection over the Czechoslovakian border.) Yet although she lacks Havelock's fixation on vengeance, given that her circumstances – particularly in Soviet-occupied Afghanistan – force her by necessity to concentrate more on staying alive than on seeking retribution against Koskov, she displays great self-determination, constantly drawing her own conclusions in spite of her lack of familiarity with the world of international espionage, and generally refusing to rely on Bond to provide the answers to their shared predicament.[11]

Actress Maryam d'Abo made her film debut in Harry Bromley Davenport's science fiction horror *Xtro* (1983), quickly diversifying her repertoire with roles in other films throughout the eighties which included romantic drama *Until September* (Richard Marquand, 1984) and tense political thriller *White Nights* (Taylor Hackford, 1985). d'Abo was also active on television dramas throughout the eighties, with appearances in features such as Clive Donner's *Arthur the King* (1985), Sheldon Larry's *Behind Enemy Lines* (1985) and Jerry London's *If Tomorrow Comes* (1986). She brought considerable appeal to the role of Kara Milovy, continuing the tendency of the eighties *Bond* films to present intelligent and resourceful female characters who aided and supported Bond without proving dependent on him to achieve their aims. Although it has been noted that Milovy herself was perhaps less aggressively independent than some of her immediate predecessors had been,[12] d'Abo brings such charm to the role that the character never appears to be either too reliant on Bond or too assertively autonomous; Milovy exhibits a realistic ingenuousness which allows her to demonstrate her aptitudes and character traits, even in the most extreme of circumstances, in a way that had been relatively rare within the series up until this point. The character was, in fact, one of the most realistically rendered of all Bond Women during the decade, transcending a film which has been retrospectively criticised by commentators such as Alan Barnes and Marcus Hearn for not presenting quite as forward-looking a depiction of gender equality as it may, at face value, appear to.[13]

With *Licence to Kill*, Dalton's second (and final) appearance as Bond, the agent was to be joined by a combination of female supporting characters – and a very different duo to that which had been presented in *A View to a Kill*. As Jütting has noted, although the film superficially appears to introduce a fairly standard amalgamation of Bond Women (one being an intelligence service veteran who aids Bond's mission while the other is an ally of the main villain with rather indistinct motivations), the performances of both the actresses in question elevate their respective characters beyond any straightforward categorisation that these clear-cut archetypes may initially suggest.[14] Actress Talisa Soto, who had appeared in Paul Morrissey's comedy drama *Spike of Bensonhurst* (1988) prior to her performance in *Licence to Kill*, was also a recipient of the ShoWest Award for Female Star of Tomorrow in 1989, and she mines the role of Lupe Lamora for considerable pathos and sympathy as the film progresses. Abused and dominated by the film's antagonist, drug lord Franz Sanchez, Lamora is a victim with an axe to grind; initially benefiting from her lover's romantic interest and generosity, she is soon drawn into a cycle of ill-treatment and exploitation by the possessive Sanchez until she eventually becomes receptive to the notion of assisting Bond's efforts to gain access to the narcotics baron's organisation. Bond recognises the depth of the emotional damage that has been wrought upon Lamora by Sanchez, and his compassion for her ordeal – as well as the euphoria at her liberation when her abuser is killed (at Bond's own hands) – is subtly but compellingly articulated at the film's conclusion.

Rather more prominent throughout the narrative of *Licence to Kill* is CIA agent Pam Bouvier, as portrayed by Carey Lowell. A skilled pilot and field agent, Bouvier is quickly shown to have considerable talents at infiltration, and her capacity to conceal her true identity and intent – flitting effortlessly between no-nonsense intelligence operative and a more disarming or alluring persona – is easily the equal of Bond's own.[15] Other commentators have been inclined to go even further, with some – such as Jeremy

Black – venturing the opinion that Bouvier's abilities on the ground rival or even exceed those which Bond possesses, her complex range of skills making her one of the most effectively rendered Bond Women in the history of the series.[16] Certainly the choice of an American actress to portray Bouvier was congruent with the desire of director John Glen and Eon producers Michael G. Wilson and Albert R. Broccoli to create a film that would be more immediately relevant to the audiences of the United States, and Lowell proved to be an inspired selection for the role, bringing both fiery intelligence and an intense, passionate spirit to the part. Following a successful debut in Albert Pyun's crime thriller *Dangerously Close* (1986), Lowell appeared in a variety of films throughout the eighties which included Harold Ramis's comedy *Club Paradise* (1986), Albert Pyun's action mystery *Down Twisted* (1987), and Doris Dörrie's social satire *Me and Him* (1988). In addition to winning the ShoWest Award for Female Star of Tomorrow in 1989, Lowell was in later years nominated – along with the rest of her castmates – for the Outstanding Performance by an Ensemble in a Drama Series Award at the Screen Actors Guild Awards between 1997 and 2000 for their work on the NBC television series *Law and Order*.

The feisty, capable character of Pam Bouvier marked a fitting endpoint to Eon Productions' attempts to revise and revitalise the role of the Bond Woman throughout the course of the 1980s, as part of wider efforts to enhance the *Bond* series' relevance to modern audiences. As the decade had progressed, the careful blend of specialist skill-sets, extensive intellectual capability and ardent independence had combined to redefine viewer expectations of Bond's female counterparts, and ultimately these developments would pave the way for later, even more assertive and skilful Bond Women throughout the course of the nineties. But that, of course, would involve another decade, another lead actor in the role of Bond, and another phase in the franchise's history entirely.

REFERENCES

1. Robert A. Caplen, *Shaken and Stirred: The Feminism of James Bond* (Bloomington: Xlibris, 2010), p.346.
2. Lee Pfeiffer and Dave Worrall, *The Essential James Bond: The Revised Authorised Guide to the World of 007* (London: Boxtree, 2003), p.124.
3. Kerstin Jütting, *'Grow Up, 007!': James Bond Over the Decades: Formula vs Innovation* (Norderstedt: Der Deutschen Bibliothek, 2005), p.55.
4. Maryam d'Abo and John Cork, *Bond Girls Are Forever: The Women of James Bond* (London: Boxtree, 2003), p.63.
5. Kerstin Jütting, p.63.
6. Cory Hamblin, *Serket's Movies: Commentary and Trivia on 444 Movies* (Pittsburgh: RoseDog Books, 2009), p.194.
7. Constantine Santas, *The Epic in Film: From Myth to Blockbuster* (Plymouth: Rowman and Littlefield, 2008), p.124.
8. Walter Metz, *Engaging Film Criticism: Film History and Contemporary American Cinema* (New York: Peter Lang Publishing, 2004), p.79.
9. John Rivers, 'John Glen', in *Contemporary British and Irish Film Directors: A Wallflower Critical Guide*, ed. by Yoram Allon, Del Cullen and Hannah Patterson (London: Wallflower Press, 2001), 121-122, p.121.
10. Jeremy Packer and Sarah Sharma, 'Postfeminism Galore: The Bond Girl as Weapon of Mass Consumption', in *Secret Agents: Popular Icons Beyond James Bond*, ed. by Jeremy Packer (New York: Peter Lang Publishing, 2009), 89-111, p.104.
11. Kerstin Jütting, p.63.
12. Packer and Sharma, pp.95-96.
13. Alan Barnes and Marcus Hearn, *Kiss Kiss Bang Bang: The Unofficial James Bond Film Companion* (London: B.T. Batsford, 1997), p.180.
14. Kerstin Jütting, p.63.
15. Lee Pfeiffer and Dave Worrall, p.160.
16. Jeremy Black, *The Politics of James Bond: From Fleming's Novels to the Big Screen* (London: Greenwood Press, 2001), p.153.

This page and over from For Your Eyes Only (1981)

007

FOR YOUR EYES ONLY

OPW 678W

JAMES BOND

ULTIMATE EDITION

2-DISC DVD SET

This page and over from Octopussy (1983)

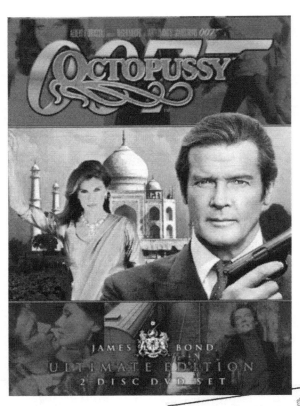

This page and over from Never Say Never Again (1983)

BLU-RAY + DVD

COLLECTOR'S EDITION

SEAN
CONNERY

NEVER
SAY NEVER
AGAIN

"SEAN CONNERY
IS BACK IN
ACTION AS
JAMES BOND!"
— VARIETY

This page and over: A View To a Kill (1985)

ALBERT R. BROCCOLI presents ROGER MOORE as IAN FLEMING'S JAMES BOND 007

007 A VIEW TO A KILL

JAMES BOND

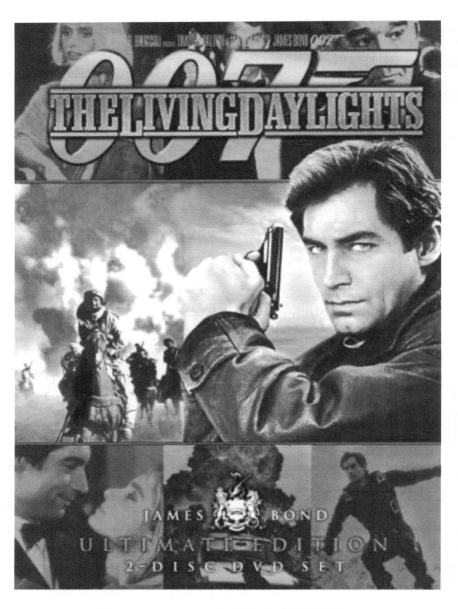

This page and over from The Living Daylights(1987)

This page and over from Licence To Kill (1989)

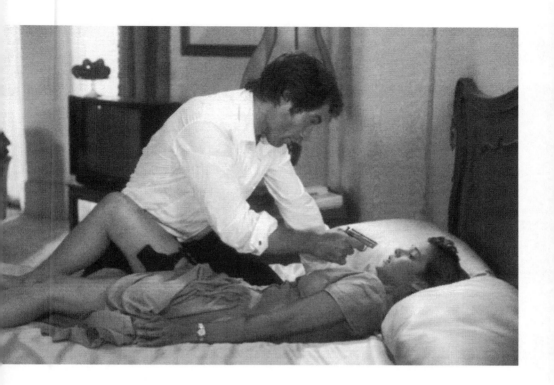

8

PAY ATTENTION, 007: AUDIENCE RECEPTION OF THE JAMES BOND FILM SERIES IN THE 1980s

If there is one factor which can be said to match the continuing cultural relevance of the *Bond* film series, it is its enduring ability to engage the interest of worldwide audiences. The *Bond* cycle has always proven to be perennially successful at the global box-office, and – as has earlier been noted – they are now recognised by a majority of commentators as the most successful British cinematic export in history.[1] However, as we will observe in this chapter, the long term economic viability of the series has not always been assured. For during the course of the 1980s the series' financial performance with audiences was to reach considerable heights as well as, ultimately, a later period of comparative stagnation as the decade progressed.

As has been the case with many highly successful films, there is a minor degree of variation between individual records of different entries in the *Bond* film canon with regard to box-office performance. For the purposes of this chapter, I have drawn statistical data from John Cork and Bruce Scivally's highly significant study *James Bond: The Legacy* (2002), which includes a detailed and very comprehensive breakdown of each *Bond* film's financial performance in cinemas not only in terms of worldwide gross, but also by assessing reception on a continental basis. It is my hope that this will provide the discussion with a more comprehensive illustration of the films' box-office dynamics over the course of the 1980s than would be afforded from a discourse based solely on figures culled from total global cinema takings alone. Sums are expressed in American dollars.

In financial terms, by the beginning of the eighties the *Bond* series found itself at a particularly lucrative period in its long history. The mid-1970s had seen a marginal dip in the series' fortunes, most notably in the comparatively disappointing performance of Guy Hamilton's *The Man with the Golden Gun* (1974) which, with a combined worldwide box-office total of $97.6 million,[2] reversed the successful trend of Hamilton's previous two entries in the series, 1971's *Diamonds Are Forever* (which grossed $116 million globally) and *Live and Let Die* in 1973 (which raised a worldwide total of $126.4 million).[3] This considerable drop in revenue was far from lost on Eon Productions, and can be seen as one of the numerous reasons for the dramatic stylistic contrast in the next film in the series, *The Spy Who Loved Me* (Lewis Gilbert, 1977). Lewis Gilbert's film was to replace the glossy, exotic travelogue of its immediate predecessor with a larger-scale action epic, and its narrative arguably introduced a greater and more tangible nuclear threat to life on the planet than had been portrayed at any prior point in the series' history, even including the heyday of SPECTRE during Sean Connery's mid-1960s occupancy of the Bond role. This redevelopment of the series' format was to quite literally pay dividends for Eon; *The Spy Who Loved Me* raised a global box-office gross of $185.4 million, almost doubling that of *The Man with the Golden Gun*.[4]

Gilbert was to maintain custodianship of the series for 1979's *Moonraker*, which built upon the epic scale of *The Spy Who Loved Me* and extended it still further, adding a more substantial science fiction/fantasy element than had been evident in any earlier entry in the series. The plot concerned an international industrialist's plan to eradicate all human life on Earth by attacking the planet from space with warheads loaded with lethal nerve gas. This served as a judicious update of the series' formula for audiences who had flocked to American science fiction blockbusters of the time such as *Star Wars* (George Lucas, 1977), *Close Encounters of the Third Kind* (Steven Spielberg, 1977), *Alien* (Ridley Scott, 1979), and *Star Trek: The Motion Picture* (Robert Wise, 1979). Although generically different in a number of ways from its predecessors in the *Bond* series, and despite many semantic similarities with the storyline of *The Spy Who Loved Me*, *Moonraker* was to prove enormously successful with audiences, grossing $202.7 million at the global box-office, $62.7 million of which was raised from the all-important American cinema audience.[5]

Thus when John Glen was offered the directorial reins of the *Bond* franchise by Albert R. Broccoli for the production of his directorial debut, *For Your Eyes Only* (1981), Eon Productions faced an unusual dilemma. Although *Moonraker* had proven to be the greatest financial success in the history of the film series to date, its atypical sci-fi setting and outlandish grandeur – even by the standard of earlier entries in the series – had garnered a generally hostile response from many critics. Broccoli also had to consider the issue of budgetary demands – at a budget of $30 million, *Moonraker* had been by far the most expensive *Bond* film to produce thus far, and had proven to be more than twice as costly as its predecessor *The Spy Who Loved Me*, which had taken a budget of $13.5 million to film.[6] In spite of *Moonraker*'s undeniable financial success, there was a definite sense that its production had bordered upon the excessive. As Karl Maskell notes:

> The film was even too big to be based only at Pinewood, with many scenes being shot in France. Nearly everyone agreed that things had gone a bit too far [...] and [Producer Albert] Broccoli decided to calm things down a bit with the next production, *For Your Eyes Only.*[7]

For Your Eyes Only's return to Bond's Cold War foundations (in the aftermath of the real-world Soviet invasion of Afghanistan) was to restore the series' relevance as a loose commentary on world affairs, with traditional East-West brinkmanship replacing the vaguely eccentric monomania of *Moonraker*'s central villain, Hugo Drax. This was to prove very much in line with the general intention of the Eon creative team that the series return to its harder, more pragmatically uncompromising roots. As Glen was later to reminisce, this drastic change from the lighter mood of the immediately preceding *Bond* films was not readily accepted by the film's star, Roger Moore, particularly when it came to shooting certain key scenes. Glen has cited the prime example of this difference of opinion being the sequence where, following a chase, Bond kicks a car carrying assassin Emile Locque (Michael Gothard) over a cliff; Moore was reluctant to depict his incarnation of Bond as being quite so ruthless or casual about murder, even in self-defence, but Glen was adamant that this direct approach was essential in returning the character and the film series to its unsentimental, hard-boiled origins.[8]

The end result of Eon's rejuvenation of the Bond formula was ultimately to prove something of a mixed blessing, even given the stalwart attempts of screenwriters Michael G. Wilson and Richard Maibaum to blend classic Bondian traditions with a stark, contemporary espionage storyline. It is difficult to deny that the merciless nature of Cold War tensions was thrown into more acute focus through the return to comparative realism and the kind of occasionally brutal heroism which had been so aptly typified by Connery's Bond. However, the frenetic action and lush location filming of *The Spy Who Loved Me* and *Moonraker* remained firmly entrenched in the public psyche, making audience expectations difficult to predict. As Maskell observes:

> Despite receiving criticism about his age for the part, Moore made 007 more human again and the film a box-office success. But the shadow of *Moonraker* still hung over the series and *For Your Eyes Only* came more as a relief than a classic Bond film, appearing more

as a formula thriller, with only the character of Bond to set it apart from other cinematic competition.[9]

As events were to transpire, Eon Productions' revised vision of the *Bond* series was to prove to be more than a modest triumph with audiences; the film was to raise $194.4 at box-offices globally,[10] and did so with a production which had cost only two-thirds the budget of *Moonraker*, $20 million.[11] This must have come as no small relief to United Artists, a company which was still reeling from the box-office failure of Michael Cimino's intriguing but expensively budgeted Western film *Heaven's Gate* the year beforehand. Even more significant was the fact that the performance of *For Your Eyes Only* at the US box-office was to raise $52.3 million;[12] although down in relation to *Moonraker*'s American takings, the film stood up admirably in the face of major competition from other productions. On general release at the time of *For Your Eyes Only*'s Stateside premiere in 1981 were action blockbusters such as Steven Spielberg's *Raiders of the Lost Ark* and Richard Lester's *Superman II*, successful comedies like Hal Needham's *The Cannonball Run* and Ivan Reitman's *Stripes*, and popular family fare including Jim Henson's *The Great Muppet Caper*.[13] The ability of *For Your Eyes Only* to perform so admirably in spite of such multifarious competition was to prove something of an affirmation of Eon's intended new direction for the *Bond* series, and would inform their approach to the next entry in the cycle, 1983's *Octopussy*.

As has been discussed in preceding chapters, *Octopussy* was to exhibit an even more resolutely ideological take on the Bond formula than had been evidenced in *For Your Eyes Only*. Given the continuing tensions between the two world superpowers, it remained to be seen whether audiences would reject the film's resolute engagement with Cold War issues in favour of more whimsical output, divorced from the grim realities of contemporary foreign policy. This escapist element was mirrored in the success of other motion pictures which were competing with

Octopussy at the time of the film's 1983 release. The conclusion to George Lucas's original *Star Wars* trilogy, Richard Marquand's *Return of the Jedi*, was performing particularly strongly, and more modest commercial success was also being enjoyed by Adrian Lyne's drama *Flashdance*, John Landis's comedy *Trading Places*, and Richard Franklin's *Psycho II*, the anticipated (but, in the main, critically unsuccessful) sequel to Alfred Hitchcock's *Psycho* (1960).[14]

Any anxieties of this nature were, however, ultimately to prove baseless – *Octopussy* performed well at the box-office, bringing in $183.7 million globally.[15] American audiences accounted for $67.9 million of this figure, not only showing a dramatic increase from *For Your Eyes Only*, but also exceeding the amount grossed from *Moonraker*.[16] It must be noted that inflation does play an important part in such an evaluation, as US cinema admissions showed 24.9 million attendees of American audiences viewing *Moonraker* in cinemas in comparison to the 21.5 million filmgoers who watched *Octopussy*.[17] However, the film's financial success did not stop with its ability to draw American audiences, as it also did better business in continental Europe than most other *Bond* films of the period. As Pierre Sorlin observes, *Octopussy* became the most successful British film to screen in France throughout the whole of the eighties, even in spite of a frosty appraisal from the French critical community.[18]

By the time of the next film in the series, *A View to a Kill*, changes were again in evidence for the *Bond* films. Albert Broccoli had only just managed to convince Roger Moore to return as Bond for a seventh appearance, and his age was – not for the first time – drawing criticism from reviewers, who now considered the actor too old to be credible as a physically dynamic protagonist even in spite of his famous suave charm.[19] Production of the film was also hampered by a catastrophic fire at Pinewood Studios, which delayed filming for some time and forced unanticipated schedule changes.[20] The film, when it did reach cinemas, was not helped by a hostile reception which was virtually unanimous amongst critics, though the intensity of analytical censure did vary. Chris

Peachment, writing in *Time Out* magazine, attacked the film's diluted action content and weak sense of peril: 'The digital countdown to Armageddon trick has worn smooth with overuse. The operatic sets of yore have shrunk, and something has gone very wrong when the climax belongs to something as serene and harmless as an airship'.[21] Other criticism was considerably harsher, as is evident in Michael Di Leo's summation of the film in *The Spy Who Thrilled Us* (2002) which lambasted *A View to a Kill* for everything from its central performances to its ill-advised chase sequences, opining that this entry in the series was about as far removed from the style and content of Fleming's original texts as it was possible to be.[22]

The wholesale critical demolition of *A View to a Kill* came to be reflected in its box-office performance, though financially the film did not suffer as badly as its reputation has come to suggest. Globally, the film grossed $152.4 million, down considerably from *Octopussy*'s worldwide total.[23] There was also a slump in the film's reception with American audiences; *A View to a Kill* raised just $50.3 million within the US.[24] It is possible that the film may have endured a far worse reception with audiences had it faced fiercer competition on release. Whereas the previous two entries in the *Bond* canon had been forced to perform against massively successful blockbusters from the Spielberg and Lucas stables, *A View to a Kill* opened in competition with a comparatively modest array of popular films including George Pan Cosmatos's action thriller *Rambo: First Blood Part Two*, Martin Brest's popular comedy *Beverly Hills Cop*, and Milos Forman's multiple Academy Award-winning historical drama *Amadeus*, which would later win the Oscar for (amongst other categories) Best Picture.[25]

A View to a Kill's performance had clearly signalled that the Bond formula once again required revision and renewal, a fact which was reiterated after its release with the retirement of Roger Moore from the *Bond* franchise. Director Glen later noted that he respected Moore's decision to leave the role that he had brought continued success to for well over a decade, adding that while a huge surge in commercial interest in *A View to a Kill* may have been a potential catalyst for an eighth Moore *Bond* film, the fact remained that everything now pointed to the need for a shift in gear and a new lead actor.[26] The very real possibility had existed since the time of *For Your Eyes Only* that Moore would not return to the role, with other actors – such as James Brolin, who came close to being cast as Bond in *Octopussy* – only narrowly being pipped to the post when Moore was persuaded by Eon Productions to return at the last minute. Moore's star power and continuing popularity with the public meant that he had not only succeeded in making the role his own following the departure of Sean Connery in the early seventies, but that he had become the established face of Bond for more official film productions than any other actor – seven *Bond* films compared to Connery's six (though if the unofficial *Never Say Never Again* is included into the equation, the two actors had achieved parity by the mid-eighties). However, times were changing, and just as Moore had presented a radically different portrayal of Bond in comparison to Connery, his own replacement would prove to be every bit as adept at redefining audience expectations.

The introduction of Timothy Dalton to the *Bond* franchise was to have immediate and profound results. Most prominent was the fact that Dalton, as a performer, quickly constructed a nuanced portrayal of Bond which was much more in tune with Broccoli and Wilson's view of the character as a seasoned and ruthless Cold Warrior than Moore's Bond had ever been. Dalton was able to convey the kind of jaded world-weariness suggested by Fleming's literary Bond in a manner that his predecessor would never likely have been inclined to engage with. As producer and screenwriter Michael G. Wilson asserted, speaking in a 1989 interview:

> When you have Roger Moore […] his personality had a certain humour and with him we went in a certain direction. With Tim Dalton we're going back to the basic Fleming character and so coming from that we create a film in the Fleming vein.[27]

The Living Daylights, Dalton's debut as Bond, returned the character to the internecine complexities of Cold War intrigue just as the Soviet Union was entering the era of *Perestroika*. Although the film broadened its scope to encompass much that had become topical in late 1980s geopolitics, including drug trafficking and arms trading, some reviewers noted that the freshness of Dalton's approach to the protagonist was counter-balanced by a lack of overt innovation in the now largely over-familiar Bond formula. However, this was generally more of a broad-spectrum analytical observation about the direction of the series than a significant criticism of the film itself, and in comparison to the glacial reception of *A View to a Kill* amongst reviewers, *The Living Daylights* was greeted reasonably favourably by commentators. Allan Hunter's review of *The Living Daylights* in *Films and Filming* is broadly representative of much criticism at the time:

> Eager worldwide audiences know what to expect from a Bond entertainment and will not be disappointed. The makers would be certifiably insane to alter such a winning formula. However, within the limitations of that well-oiled formula, *The Living Daylights* could be termed a modest departure from the recent norm. [...] Dalton's interpretation of the character seeps through to the rest of the production which displays a similar low-key, no nonsense approach.[28]

Glen's hopes for a recovery of the series' fortunes following *A View to a Kill* were to be realised at the box-office, but with qualifications. *The Living Daylights* took a global box-office gross of $191.2 million, with a particularly dramatic revival in takings within the European market.[29] The amount grossed in cinema admissions in Germany, for instance, almost doubled in comparison with *A View to a Kill*.[30] However, the effect on American audiences was considerably more muted. Although the overall US box-office takings were up marginally over *A View to a Kill*, resting at a total of $51.18 million, the number of actual cinema admissions was down from 14.1 million audience members to only 13.1 million.[31] In mitigation of this fact, however, it must be noted that *The Living Daylights* was released alongside a large number of strong box-office performers in 1987, including Joe Dante's *Innerspace*, Paul Verhoeven's *Robocop*, George Miller's *The Witches of Eastwick*, Tony Scott's *Beverly Hills Cop 2*, Brian de Palma's *The Untouchables*, and Sidney J. Furie's *Superman IV: The Quest for Peace*, amongst several others.[32]

For what was to be the final eighties film for the *Bond* franchise, Broccoli and Wilson decided to address recent criticism of the series' lack of originality, making the courageous decision to break from the long-running Bondian formula by presenting a very atypical entry in the series. Gone were the traditional, overly comfortable set-pieces that audiences had come to expect during the past 27 years of the series, and concurrently the amount of violence and gore were increased to a level far more intense than any which had been witnessed in the series before. Not only was this to be the final step in the Eon strategy to return Bond to his brutal, Fleming-conceived pedigree during the 1980s, but it was also conceived as a plan which made long-term financial sense. As actor Robert Davi, who portrayed the film's antagonist Franz Sanchez, noted in *Time Out* magazine at the time of the film's production:

> The aim, quite clearly, is that this film will be not just big, but really big in the States. That's the thinking behind bringing the film to Central America and having so many American actors in it, to make the series more relevant to audiences in the United States.[33]

Eon Productions' intention to further modernise the *Bond* franchise, bringing it closer in line with the style of mainstream American studio output and further developing the starkness and maturity that had been in evidence throughout *The Living Daylights*, was enthusiastically received by most critics. As *Variety*'s reviewer 'Coop' observed at the time:

> The James Bond production team has found its second wind with *Licence to Kill*, a cocktail of high-octane action, spectacle and drama.

It's a sure-fire click worldwide for the 16th in the United Artists 007 series and one that will rate among the best. [...] Out go the self-parodying witticisms and over-elaborate high-tech gizmos that slowed pre-Dalton pics to a walking pace. Exotic settings now serve the narrative rather than provide a glossy travelog.[34]

Regrettably, however, *Licence to Kill*'s lacklustre performance at the box-office was to prove almost catastrophic for the franchise. Despite a largely favourable reception from reviewers worldwide and the cautious approval of fans, the film's worldwide gross slumped to $156.2 million, while the American box-office takings stood at a comparatively paltry $34.67 million (only slightly higher than *Licence to Kill*'s budget), drawn from 8.7 million admissions.[35] Some would later come to blame the film's poor performance on the film's increased rating – it was the first *Bond* film to be certified '15' by the British Board of Film Classification, with the Americans also rating the film 'R' in cinemas. Others cited the underlying problem to be the marked deviation from the norms of the established Bond formula, which some considered in hindsight to be one step too manifestly removed from audience expectations of a traditional Bond adventure – in spite of initial critical enthusiasm – to be entirely palatable. However, the majority of commentators have come to consider the main contribution of *Licence to Kill*'s downfall to be the fact that it opened in cinemas directly against Tim Burton's comic-book adaptation *Batman*, which was one of the single most heavily marketed films of the entire 1980s.[36] (As James Chapman has reflected, *Batman* would achieve far higher box-office returns in its first weekend of business in American cinemas alone than *Licence to Kill* was to accomplish throughout its whole period of commercial release in United States theatres.)[37] However, the film's poor performance cannot be ascribed to *Batman*'s phenomenal commercial success on its own. *Licence to Kill* was also performing against an exceptionally strong line-up of American blockbusters at the time of its release, including Steven Spielberg's blockbuster *Indiana Jones and the Last Crusade*, and a range of popular film sequels which included Richard Donner's *Lethal Weapon 2*, Ivan Reitman's *Ghostbusters 2*, and William Shatner's *Star Trek V: The Final Frontier*.[38]

Against such a remarkably robust array of big-budget features, it is not entirely surprising that *Licence to Kill* – even with its heartfelt attempts at innovation and reinvention of the Bond format – was to fare less than favourably in competition. The film's performance was to herald the end of the screenwriting partnership of Richard Maibaum and Michael G. Wilson, the conclusion of John Glen's tenure as director of the *Bond* series and, due to the six-year hiatus that was to follow, was also to see Dalton leave the central role after only two entries in the cycle. However, Glen has been characteristically candid when looking back at the fate of what he considered to be his most accomplished work for the Bond canon, noting that although he was understandably disheartened by the film's poor box-office performance, he nonetheless considered *Licence to Kill* to be his best directorial work within the *Bond* series.[39]

The cordial retirement from the *Bond* series of a long-running director and veteran screenwriter, both of whom had played a part in the Eon Productions since the 1960s, was to mark the end of an era in the cycle's history. Whereas *For Your Eyes Only* had seen a reaffirmation of the series' Cold War roots, *Licence to Kill* had – through necessity – come to dispense with it completely. Throughout the eighties, Broccoli had vigorously attempted to maintain the *Bond* films' relevance to audiences whilst remaining faithful to what he believed were the core, Fleming-inspired values which had made the series such an overwhelming success at its inception. However, the fact that the films were ultimately to experience difficulty in their financial returns can be seen to be a failure on different fronts – some avoidable, others less so – but principal among them being a lack of effective marketing of the series at the end of the decade in the face of overwhelmingly strong competition emanating from Hollywood. This vital practicality, it seemed, had become even more of an issue than that of maintaining cultural significance with audiences both at home and abroad. While articulating the relevance of Bond to global audiences was a crucial factor in maintaining public interest in the franchise, the unpredictability of the increasingly sophisticated tastes of cinemagoers had proven itself to be an even more vexing challenge for the Eon production staff to engage with.

REFERENCES

1. James Chapman, *Licence to Thrill: A Cultural History of the James Bond Films* (London: IB Tauris, 1999), p.14.
2. John Cork and Bruce Scivally, *James Bond: The Legacy* (London: Boxtree, 2002), p.301.
3. ibid.
4. ibid.
5. ibid., pp.301-02.
6. Paul Simpson, ed., *The Rough Guide to James Bond* (London: Penguin, 2002), p.128.
7. Karl Maskell, 'No Moore Bond', in *Starburst*, 100, 1986, p.59.
8. John Glen, cited in Gareth Owen and Oliver Bayan, *Roger Moore: His Films and Career* (London: Robert Hale, 2002), p.90.
9. Maskell, p.59.
10. Cork and Scivally, p.302.
11. Simpson, p.128.
12. Cork and Scivally, p.302.
13. Steven Jay Rubin, *The Complete James Bond Movie Encyclopaedia* (London: Contemporary Books, 2002), p.146.
14. Rubin, p.317.
15. Cork and Scivally, p.302.
16. ibid.
17. ibid.
18. Pierre Sorlin, 'From *The Third Man* to *Shakespeare in Love*: Fifty Years of British Success on Continental Screens', in *British Cinema, Past and Present*, ed. by Justine Ashby and Andrew Higson (London: Routledge, 2000), 80-92, p.87.
19. Simpson, p.115.
20. Alan Barnes and Marcus Hearn, *Kiss Kiss Bang Bang: The Unofficial James Bond Film Companion* (London: B.T. Batsford, 1997), p.168.
21. Chris Peachment, '*A View to a Kill*', in *Time Out*, 773, 13 June 1985, p.37.
22. Michael Di Leo, *The Spy Who Thrilled Us: A Guide to the Best of Cinematic James Bond* (New York: Limelight Editions, 2002), p.19.
23. Cork and Scivally, p.302.
24. ibid.
25. Rubin, p.436.
26. John Glen, cited in David Giammarco, *For Your Eyes Only: Behind the Scenes of the Bond Films* (London: ECW Press, 2002), pp.192-93.
27. Michael G. Wilson, cited in Gary Russell, 'Serious Bondage', in *Starburst*, July 1989, p.43.
28. Allan Hunter, ' *The Living Daylights*', in *Films and Filming*, August 1987, p.35.
29. Cork and Scivally, p.302.
30. ibid.
31. ibid.
32. Rubin, p.247.
33. Robert Davi, cited in Simon Banner, 'Of Inhuman Bondage', in *Time Out*, 26

April 1989, p.15.

34. Coop, '*Licence to Kill*', in *Variety,* 14 June 1989, p.7.
35. Cork and Scivally, p.303.
36. Barnes and Hearn, p.186.
37. Chapman, p.246.
38. Rubin, p.237.
39. John Glen, *For My Eyes Only: My Life with James Bond* (London: Brassey's, 2001), p.208.

9

FOR OUR EYES ONLY: THE INFLUENCE OF THE JAMES BOND FRANCHISE IN 1980s POPULAR CULTURE

While the continuing cultural influence of the *Bond* films on the world of cinema has led to the series never drifting too far from the public eye over the decades, it has been matched by the reciprocal influence of cinematic trends to reshape and encourage reinvention in the cycle over time. Thus it must be said that by the time the series had reached the eighties, the cinematic Bond was being just as profoundly affected by the cultural tastes of the time as the cycle itself was proving to be influential in its own right. After all, the boom years of the spy thriller had been back in the sixties, when films such as Sidney J. Furie's excellent Len Deighton adaptation *The Ipcress File* (1965) had brought an impressive start to the Harry Palmer series and aided Michael Caine's rise to superstar status; when Cold War thrillers such as *Kiss Kiss Bang Bang* (Duccio Tessari, 1966), *The Liquidator* (Jack Cardiff, 1966) and *Ice Station Zebra* (John Sturges, 1968) were riding high in the public consciousness, and when the *Bond* series was being spoofed relentlessly in films including *Carry On Spying*

(Gerald Thomas, 1964), *Agent 8 3/4* (Ralph Thomas, 1965) and *Our Man Flint* (Daniel Mann, 1966). By the time of the 1980s, however, cinematic trends had changed profoundly, with new themes emerging as a result of the plunging temperature of the Cold War. *Bond*-style adventure thrillers were largely being supplanted by Soviet invasion scenarios or nuclear holocaust action movies set in post-apocalyptic wastelands, occasionally with the quintessential eighties theme of computer-related anxieties being thrown into the mix for good measure. This decade was, above all, the age of the action star, with muscular actors such as Sylvester Stallone in *First Blood* (Ted Kotcheff, 1982) and *Cobra* (George Pan Cosmatos, 1986), and Arnold Schwarzenegger in *Commando* (Mark L. Lester, 1986) and *Red Heat* (Walter Hill, 1988), appearing to supplant the suave urbanity of the Bondian gentleman spy.

How, then, could the *Bond* films hope to compete in a market swamped with intense, slickly-produced action thrillers such as Richard Donner's *Lethal Weapon* (1987) and John McTiernan's *Die Hard* (1988)? Certainly, there was no doubting that the complexion of Cold War cinema had changed dramatically since the turn of the decade. In the wake of the Soviet invasion of Afghanistan, films had begun to swing from a depiction of counterintelligence and containment theory to illustrations of full-scale incursions onto American soil, in films such as *Red Dawn* (John Milius, 1984) and *Invasion USA* (Joseph Zito, 1985). Post-apocalyptic scenarios were depicted either in terms of nuclear exchanges which were only narrowly averted, as in the excellent *WarGames* (John Badham, 1983), or full-blown atomic aftermath narratives such as *The Last Battle* (Luc Besson, 1983). (The post-apocalyptic film remained popular throughout the course of the eighties, though such global decimation thrillers were often expressed by means other than nuclear conflict in film such as David Gladwell's *Memoirs of a Survivor*, 1981, and Geoff Murphy's *The Quiet Earth*, 1985.) Bond, however, was considerably better known for preventing nuclear conflagration than he was for surviving it, and thus it seemed that the character would inevitably follow the former of the above trends rather than the latter. Albert R. Broccoli was a canny and highly observant media professional, whose decision to bring the first *Bond* film of the eighties back to the fundamental basics of the series re-established its spy genre credentials while also proving commercially successful enough to emphasise that the *Bond* movies had largely become a genre in and of themselves. The entries in the series which were placed under John Glen's directorial control, therefore, were pitched carefully by Eon Productions in an attempt to chime into the prevailing cultural zeitgeist, with the influences of other trends in mainstream commercial film-making – in particular, the hard action movies which had become so prevalent at the time – manifesting themselves more profoundly as the decade progressed. The eighties *Bond* films' penetration of the cultural consciousness also greatly benefited from the advent of home video, which provided new and ready access to motion pictures and revolutionised the way that individuals and families were able to watch movies: rental shops and VHS video retail now ensured that the public had far greater choice in their viewing habits, and never again would UK audiences be forced to wait until Christmas or a Bank Holiday in order to watch an entry in the *Bond* cycle.

For Your Eyes Orly was released after a relatively sparse period of development in the espionage genre. The year before had seen the production of Don Sharp's starry Alastair McLean adaptation *Bear Island* (1980), featuring Donald Sutherland, Vanessa Redgrave and Christopher Lee, while John Irvin's *The Dogs of War* (1980) had included an early starring role from Christopher Walken. That same period had also seen Roger Moore gently subverting his own Bond persona in Andrew V. McLaglen's entertaining terrorist drama *Ffolkes* (1980) (also sometimes known as *North Sea Hijack* and *Assault Force* on the international market), alongside James Mason and Anthony Perkins. But the same year as *For Your Eyes Only*'s run in cinemas, spy movies were represented by rather more traditional fare such as stylish French thriller *Birgit Haas Must Be Killed* (Laurent Heynemann, 1981) and the inventive *Blow Out* (Brian De Palma, 1981), an exploration of a murder with a definite ideological slant featuring John Travolta and John Lithgow. This early in the decade, it seemed that Bond was still very much relevant to the socio-political environment of the time, a fact borne out by the healthy box-office returns resulting from the release of *For Your Eyes Only*.

The build-up to the release of *Octopussy* was to see greater explicit emphasis placed on the threat of Soviet influence, with prominent films of this type including drama *The Solder* (James Glickenhaus, 1982), which mixed nuclear anxieties with Middle Eastern political tensions, and Anglo-French international spy thriller *Enigma* (Jeannot Szwarc, 1982), which centred on the work of elite KGB assassins and starred Martin Sheen, Sam Neill as well as one-time Bond villain Michel Lonsdale. Also screening later that year was an early directorial offering from Clint Eastwood, *Firefox* (1982), which starred Eastwood as a Cold War operative engaging in military espionage against the Soviets. The following year was to see the release of intriguingly multi-layered thriller *Exposed* (James Toback, 1983) as well as – rather more prominently – Michael Apted's wonderfully atmospheric *Gorky Park* (1983), a Soviet Russia-set thriller (filmed mostly in Finland) based on the novel by Martin Cruz Smith. Thus the cinematic battle between Bond and the expansionist General Orlov, complete with the latter's internecine nuclear plotting, remained a perfect fit for the prevailing anxieties which were surfacing in the genre at the time.

In the period prior to the release of *A View to a Kill*, the spy genre was to diversify considerably, with many different variations in tone and content emerging. Among them were defection drama *The Jigsaw Man* (Terence Young, 1984), which featured the star pairing of Michael Caine and Laurence Olivier (echoing their earlier successful collaboration on Joseph L. Mankiewicz's *Sleuth*, 1972), tightly-structured political thriller

Defence of the Realm (David Drury, 1985), and John Schlesinger's rather more traditional spy drama *The Falcon and the Snowman* (1985). There was considerable originality on display in films such as the innovative, European-situated espionage story *Gotcha!* (Jeff Kanew, 1985), tense international drama *White Nights* (Taylor Hackford, 1985), and John Frankenheimer's globe-trotting Robert Ludlum adaptation *The Holcroft Covenant* (1985). Also successful at the time, albeit much more light-hearted in nature, was John Landis's good-natured espionage comedy *Spies Like Us* (1985), a spoof which pitched stars Chevy Chase and Dan Aykroyd into a veritable sea of cameo appearances from well-known film directors of the day.

Although *A View to a Kill* had been criticised in many corners for its pedestrian pace and overly-conventional plotline, screenwriters Michael G. Wilson and Richard Maibaum had used the film to engage with the eighties electronics boom and the themes which were deriving from it; the decade was replete with explorations of this subject matter, centring on everything from anxieties about the pace of technological development and humanity's ability to control it (James Cameron's *The Terminator*, 1984) to societal unease concerning artificial intelligence (Steve Barron's *Electric Dreams*, 1984). These themes would resurface the following year in the humorous and innovative *Jumpin' Jack Flash* (Penny Marshall, 1986), which was to cast Whoopi Goldberg's unconventional American programmer into a net of intrigue involving British Intelligence and an English spy trapped behind the Iron Curtain (whose only means of communication is by computer – still a novel concept at a time before Internet access was widely available to the public).

The period prior to the release of *The Living Daylights* saw a number of well-received genre entries including *The Whistle Blower* (Simon Langton, 1986), a spy thriller adapted from the novel by John Hale, and taut drama *Hour of the Assassin* (Luis Llosa, 1987). Perhaps most prominent at the time, however, was John Mackenzie's excellent adaptation of Frederick Forsyth's novel *The Fourth Protocol* (1987), pitting Michael Caine's English intelligence operative against a KGB spy, ably portrayed by future Bond Pierce Brosnan, in a plotline which seemed not a million miles removed from the central Cold War threat that had been depicted in *Octopussy*.

By the time of *Licence to Kill*, there was – if anything – an even greater tendency towards evocations of the intercontinental and the exotic in spy films of the time, evidenced in films such as desert-based spy thriller *Laser Mission* (Beau Davis, 1989), which transplanted its Soviet antagonists to South Africa; *Black Rain* (Ridley Scott, 1989), a generally well-received international crime drama starring Michael Douglas and Andy Garcia, and the comparatively light-hearted espionage action film *Picasso Trigger* (Andy Sidaris, 1989). Philip Saville's gritty political thriller *Fellow Traveler* (1989) also saw release at this time, while the theme of South American narcotics trading – which had been so central to the narrative of *Licence to Kill* – was also to emerge strongly in Hector Olivera's *Cocaine Wars* (1989) in the same year.

It is important to remember, of course, that the influence of the *Bond* series does not end with the films themselves. The title music of the *Bond* movies has always been one of the key elements in each entry of the series, playing between the pre-title sequence and the opening of the film itself, with songs such as Matt Munro's 'From Russia with Love' (1963), Shirley Bassey's 'Goldfinger' (1964), Tom Jones's 'Thunderball' (1965), Paul McCartney and Wings's 'Live and Let Die' (1973) and Carly Simon's 'Nobody Does It Better' (1977) (from *The Spy Who Loved Me*) all proving to have lasting appeal in popular culture. The eighties saw the title songs from the five Eon Productions of the decade achieving mixed popularity with the listening public, some of them making a strong showing in the music charts while others were to demonstrate considerably less of an impact.

The decade's *Bond* music was to begin with Sheena Easton's 'For Your Eyes Only' in 1981, composed by Michael Leeson and Bill Conti. At the time Easton had recently reached the number one spot in the US music charts with her song 'Morning Train', and her rising star profile certainly did not hinder the success of *For Your Eyes Only*'s title track. The song reached the No.8 spot in the UK singles chart, but did even better in the US where it charted at No.4 on the Billboard Hot 100. (Additionally, it was to make the top ten singles charts in many European countries and across Australasia, hitting the No.1 spot in both Switzerland and Norway.)

Two years after the success of 'For Your Eyes Only', John Barry and Tim Rice were to compose 'All Time High', the title song for *Octopussy*, which was performed by Rita Coolidge in 1983. This track did not replicate the chart achievements of its predecessor in the Anglo-American music market, reaching only the No.36 position in the US Billboard Hot 100 and a relatively lowly No.75 spot in the UK singles chart. However, it did achieve greater success in Europe, reaching the Top 20 and even Top 10 charts in several countries, and the track also went on to sell copies (though often further down the charts) in various different markets across North America, Australasia and South Africa.

The next *Bond* title song to reach the charts was 1985's 'A View to a Kill', composed by John Barry and John Taylor and performed by Duran Duran. This track was the most successful song of the decade to have derived from a *Bond* film, penetrating the public consciousness with great aplomb and reaching No.2 in the UK singles chart as well as the coveted No.1 spot on the US Billboard Hot 100. The song was also to top the charts in Italy, Sweden and Canada, peaked at No.2 in Ireland and Norway, and reached the Top 10 in Austria, Switzerland, Germany and Australia. With the combination of Simon Le Bon's distinctive vocal and John Barry's orchestra, it remains – in the eyes of many – the most memorable *Bond* title song of the eighties.

Following this was 'The Living Daylights', composed by Pål Waaktaar and John Barry and performed by a-ha in 1987. In stark contrast to its predecessor, the song did not chart in the Billboard Top 100 in the US, but made a strong showing in the UK singles chart, reaching the No.5 spot. The track also performed convincingly in many other markets, hitting the No.1 position in Norway and reaching the Top 10 in the Netherlands, Ireland, Italy, Germany, Poland, Sweden and South Africa. It also charted in countries as diverse as Canada, Australia and Japan.

The final *Bond* title song of the eighties was Gladys Knight's 'Licence to Kill' in 1989, composed by Narada Michael Walden, Walter Afanasieff and Jeffrey Cohen. This track was to reach No.6 in the UK singles charts, and also charted in Germany. In spite of its failure to appear in the US Billboard Top 100, the song has achieved its own measure of longevity amongst the other *Bond* songs of the decade, largely thanks to the power of Knight's legendary vocals. One of the lengthiest songs to accompany a *Bond* film to date, this highly distinctive track formed a worthy end-point to the series' music in the eighties – ten years that had seen many different musical styles, performed both by groups and individual artists, brought together under the *Bond* banner to striking effect.

In terms of music for the *Bond* films, perhaps the most noteworthy aspect of the eighties came in the form of composer John Barry's final work for the series. Barry had been a stalwart of the *Bond* cycle since the time of its very inception in the early sixties, and his highly distinctive original scores had quickly become synonymous with the franchise. The winner of five Academy Awards (with a further two nominations) for his film compositions between 1966 and 1992, Barry had become a hugely popular figure in the world of film music thanks to his acclaimed scores for films such as *Born Free* (James Hill, 1966), *The Lion in Winter* (Anthony Harvey, 1968) and *Out of Africa* (Sydney Pollack, 1985), to name only a few. However, though his work with the *Bond* series was ultimately to win him fewer industry plaudits, his soundtracks for the cycle remain amongst the best-regarded and most immediately recognisable work of his entire career. This fact was not hindered by the sheer volume of Barry's work for the franchise: with only a small handful of exceptions, he was the credited composer on the overwhelming majority of *Bond* films between the early sixties and late eighties. He was responsible for some of the most critically esteemed scores in the series, including *From Russia with Love* (Terence Young, 1963), *Goldfinger* (Guy Hamilton, 1964) and *Diamonds Are Forever* (Guy Hamilton, 1971), and the prolificacy of his output helped to emphasise his extraordinary skill as a composer; his *Bond* soundtracks may have carried his bold stylistic imprimatur from film to film, but like the cycle itself Barry's music was constantly evolving to meet new tastes in a world of rapid change.

Barry's work on the *Bond* films throughout the eighties continued this trend of marrying versatility with familiarity, keeping pace with the changes affecting the direction of the franchise at the time. His score for *Octopussy*, for example, seems positively muted in comparison with the bombastic, overtly cinematic soundtrack that he had provided for the visual spectacular of *Moonraker* (Lewis Gilbert, 1979). Barry takes great care to slowly build a sense of atmosphere throughout the score, contrasting exotic intrigue (Octopussy's private island, and the Monsoon Palace) with the unabashedly suspenseful (the scenes set behind the Iron Curtain, and most especially during the climactic bomb defusion sequence). Yet the soundtrack also hearkens back to the heyday of the Connery period at times, its mix of understated broad-canvas grandeur and moments of surprising intimacy – especially during Bond's interactions with the eponymous anti-heroine – seeming particularly well-suited to the Eon creative team's intention to recapture some quality of the franchise's glory days.

A View to a Kill showcased an interesting stylistic melange for Barry, juxtaposing a much more action-oriented score (particularly apposite, given the film's use of modern American venues and focus on the United States' box-office) with an unmistakeable vein of quietly anticipated peril snaking from scene to scene. This is particularly well articulated by way of the antagonist's theme ('He's Dangerous'), which is used to accompany not only the psychotic Max Zorin, but also Bond's gradual discovery of the character's lunatic schemes. Music from the film's arresting theme song is also woven skilfully throughout the soundtrack, perhaps most effectively in the delineation of Bond's unfolding relationship with Stacey Sutton, while the fanfare which accompanies Bond's emergence from the burning San Francisco City Hall is suitably striking. With the film's culmination in the mine shaft and, later, during the Golden Gate Bridge sequence, Barry takes care to emphasise not only the building danger that faces Bond (and, by extension, most of the West Coast of America), but also the rather anomalous contrast with the serenity of Zorin's airship hovering over San Francisco Bay. Rather than allowing this apparent contradiction to impede the natural flow of his composition, Barry instead embraces it, intertwining themes from this apparent divergence of incident to blend a satisfyingly effective conclusion.

With *The Living Daylights*, Barry created what was to be his final contribution for the *Bond* series, and indeed the score arguably contains his strongest work on the franchise for the entire decade. Indeed, the soundtrack is comfortably the equal of many of his earlier entries in the cycle, and is suffused with much energy and dynamism to accompany the debut appearance of Timothy Dalton's younger, more relentless incarnation of Bond. Standout pieces include the Rock of Gibraltar scenes during the pre-titles sequence, where the instantly-familiar *James Bond* theme is thrown into unusual but highly compelling configurations, and the high-octane Soviet Airbase sequence, which makes particularly trenchant use of the film's title theme to excellent effect. Also well employed are the themes from The Pretenders' songs 'Where Has Everybody Gone?' (to accompany the professional assassin Necros) and 'If There Was a Man' (which complements Bond's burgeoning relationship with Kara Milovy). There is much to enjoy, too, in the skilful contrast between the tension which Barry carefully builds during Bond's flight from Czechoslovakia with the defecting Kara, and the up-tempo evocation of the couple's affection when they spend time together in romantic Vienna directly afterwards. Of all Barry's eighties *Bond* scores, *The Living Daylights* perhaps best emphasises the sophisticated equilibrium that his compositions struck between the traditional and the unconventional, keeping the soundtracks of the cycle in step with the changing musical tastes of cinematic audiences whilst never losing sight of the recognisable thematic styles of the franchise which had proven to be so perennially recognisable.

John Barry was not the only composer to work on the *Bond* films during the eighties. Bill Conti, the celebrated American composer who had won much acclaim for his work on films such as *Rocky* (Sylvester Stallone, 1976) and *Escape to Victory* (John Huston, 1981), was to follow in the footsteps of others such as Marvin Hamlisch in providing a score for the series, recruited by Eon Productions when Barry proved to be unavailable. Himself a multiple award-winning composer of no small repute, his work in film winning him an Academy Award alongside two other Oscar nominations, Conti was quick to stamp his mark on the series with the score he provided for the first *Bond* film of the decade, *For Your Eyes Only*. His soundtrack captured well the scenic Mediterranean setting of the film, incorporating a distinctive Greek flavour throughout which blended agreeably with the edgy claustrophobia of the underwater action scenes and the taut suspense of the film's nail-biting climax at St Cyril's Monastery. Conti takes care to retain a suitably Bondian zest as his score plays out, and his approach brought a general sense of freshness to the franchise which marked it out as being just as divergent from Barry's towering contribution to the series as had been the case, for instance, with George Martin's vibrantly contemporary soundtrack for *Live and Let Die* (Guy Hamilton, 1973).

Rounding off the music of the *Bond* films in the eighties was music legend Michael Kamen, who was appointed composer by Eon Productions when Barry became unexpectedly unavailable to create the score for *Licence to Kill*. The selection of Kamen proved to be a timely one; given the prominence of his work in writing scores for hugely popular action films in the eighties – most especially *Die Hard* (John McTiernan, 1987) and *Lethal Weapon* (Richard Donner, 1988) – he seemed an eminently logical choice for the role given the stated objective of producers Broccoli and Wilson to introduce a greater emphasis on mainstream action-thriller elements into the *Bond* franchise at the time. Indeed, right from his commanding arrangement of the opening gun-barrel sequence, it is clear that Kamen was determined to take the music of this *Bond* film in a very particular direction. There is a sense of unrelenting momentum throughout the soundtrack, most especially surrounding Franz Sanchez and his brutal misdeeds, and the sophisticated urban bustle of Isthmus City which Kamen evokes is soon energetically swept away by a score which never misses a beat in punctuating the film's unusually brutal (for the franchise at the time) panoply of action sequences. Though Barry's replacement as composer had not been anticipated, Kamen's uncompromising approach to the film's soundtrack helped to mark out the sea-change in production attitudes which had been typified with *Licence to Kill*: the score, like the narrative of the film itself, emphasised the effort at every level of production to inject an unyielding aspect of both present-day cultural relevance and the ruthlessness of the contemporary cinematic thriller back into the *Bond* franchise.

Beyond the impact of the films themselves, the eighties were important for the *Bond* franchise due to the fact that the decade saw the release of several official novels featuring the James Bond character, all of which were written by author John Gardner. Although several *Bond*-related texts had been released following the death of Ian Fleming in 1964, including Fleming's own posthumously-published *The Man with the Golden Gun* (1965), Kingsley Amis's *Colonel Sun* (1968) (which Amis published under the literary pseudonym Robert Markham), and a variety of movie novelisations and non-fiction reference works, Gardner's novels were the first to present entirely original fiction – employing

James Bond as the protagonist – since the 1960s. An experienced critic with a considerable journalistic body of work, Gardner was already a well-established author of several spy and crime novels – perhaps most notably including his *Boysie Oakes* series (1964-76) and the *Professor Moriarty* cycle (1974-75) – before he assumed the daunting mantle of Fleming's literary successor.

Gardner's first *Bond* novel was *Licence Renewed* (1981), which brought many of Fleming's recurring characters into a contemporary setting (including M, Miss Moneypenny and Intelligence Chief of Staff Bill Tanner), complete with modern technological developments. The story, a fast-paced tale of nuclear intrigue and terrorism, laid the groundwork for a further eight novels by Gardner throughout the decade. *For Special Services* (1982) was to see Felix Leiter's daughter Cedar facing off with Bond against the newly-active SPECTRE organisation, who plan to seize control of the United States' critical NORAD military installation, while *Icebreaker* (1983) pitched Bond and rival agents from Mossad, the CIA and the KGB against a fascist terror leader who, in years past, had been allied to Nazi Germany. In *Role of Honour* (1984), Bond finds himself on a perilous undercover mission within the revived SPECTRE; as a result, the following novel – *Nobody Lives For Ever* (1986) – saw him fighting to avoid capture and assassination by operatives who were in the employ of the organisation's vengeful leader. *No Deals, Mr Bond* (1987) was a more traditional Cold War tale of double-dealing behind the Iron Curtain; *Scorpius* (1988) dealt with an international arms broker with decidedly lethal intent, and *Win, Lose or Die* (1989) was a naval-themed novel centring around the preparations for an international summit between Margaret Thatcher, George H.W. Bush and Mikhail Gorbachev which saw Bond promoted from his long-held rank of Commander in the British Navy to that of Captain. Gardner's contribution to *Bond*-related writing in the eighties concluded with the novelisation of *Licence to Kill* (1989), a rich adaptation of Richard Maibaum and Michael G. Wilson's screenplay, which expanded upon the events of the film in a number of key areas.

Gardner's work was always very much in the spirit of Fleming's novels, energetically synchronising the world of Bond with real-world events and re-establishing the literary character's cultural relevance for a contemporary readership. Gardner would pen a further seven *Bond* novels in the nineties – *Brokenclaw* (1990), *The Man From Barbarossa* (1991), *Death is Forever* (1992), *Never Send Flowers* (1993), *SeaFire* (1994), *C.O.L.D.* (1996) and a novelisation of *GoldenEye* (1995), before passing his literary baton to American author Raymond Benson, who was to produce many new works of fiction featuring the Bond character between 1997 and 2002.

The eighties were also a very significant period for the *Bond* cycle in that it was the first decade to see the release of video-games which were adapted from the films for the burgeoning home computer market. Today the *Bond* franchise has been responsible for the release of many games which have achieved huge commercial success, not least during the creatively-fruitful Pierce Brosnan years (almost certainly the most critically acclaimed being Rare's unforgettable *GoldenEye 007* for the Nintendo 64 in 1997). In the eighties, however, home computer games technology was still in its relative infancy, and early in the decade film licences remained something of a new development for the industry. The first *Bond* licence to be produced for the commercial home market was the Parker Brothers' *James Bond 007* (1983), a platform-based driving game where an all-terrain vehicle (supposedly manoeuvred by Bond himself) is controlled by the player on a number of missions based around various *Bond* films including *Diamonds Are Forever*, *The Spy Who Loved Me*, *Moonraker*, and *For Your Eyes Only*. Although the limitations of the hardware meant that the gameplay was, by necessity, rather basic in nature, *James Bond 007* made an impact on gamers of the time and is best remembered from its appearance on the early Atari consoles such as the Atari 2600 and Atari 5200, although it also made a showing on some 8-bit platforms such as the Commodore 64 and Atari 8-bit. A few years later in 1985, *A View to a Kill* became the first *Bond* film to receive a videogame adaptation which was based upon one particular entry in the series alone – rather appropriate, given the movie's focus on computers and technology. The first, and lesser known, of these adaptations was a text-based adventure by Angelsoft, published under the Mindscape label. Text adventure games were very popular in the eighties; given their descriptive nature (graphics were later introduced to illustrate scenes on the more powerful 8-bit systems), they allowed for immersive gameplay which was controlled via verb-noun textual commands rather than by joystick or controller input. The Mindscape version of *A View to a Kill* was released for the Apple II and Apple Macintosh, as well as IBM PCs. However, today the game's stature amongst retro gamers has been largely obscured by Domark's much more widely-circulated adaptation of *A View to a Kill*, an arcade-style adventure which was available for the most popular 8-bit formats including the ZX Spectrum, Commodore 64 and Amstrad CPC. Domark's game was split into three separate mini-games, each based on a different sequence from the film. The first was an overhead driving game where Bond must manoeuvre his way through the streets of Paris in an attempt to apprehend Max Zorin's henchwoman May Day as she parachutes from the top of the Eiffel Tower. The second section centres on Bond and Stacey Sutton as they escape from the burning San Francisco City Hall in a sideways flip-screen game. The third and final part of the game is set in the Californian mineshaft where Zorin's bomb is counting down to detonation. Bond must make his way past numerous obstacles in order to find all of the parts of the combination that he needs to defuse the bomb before it explodes, flooding Silicon Valley in the process.

In 1987, *The Living Daylights* was also to receive the videogame adaptation treatment from Domark. Like their version of *A View to a Kill*, this game was released on the popular Amstrad CPC, ZX Spectrum and Commodore 64 platforms, as well as the BBC Micro. *The Living Daylights* was a rather more conventional game than its predecessor, though it featured greatly-improved graphics. A horizontally-scrolling shooter, the game focused on Bond as he made his way through various scenes from the film – including the Gibraltar training mission, the Bratislava Conservatoire and the Wiener Prater in Vienna – switching between a variety of weapons depending on their suitability for each level. Throughout the game, Bond encounters characters from the film including Koskov's henchman Necros and the heavily-armed Brad Whitaker.

Dalton's second outing as Bond was adapted into a videogame in 1989, when *Licence to Kill* was released for a wide variety of platforms. These included not just 8-bit systems such as the BBC Micro, MSX, ZX Spectrum, Amstrad CPC and Commodore 64, but also a growing range of 16-bit computers including the IBM PC, Atari ST, and the increasingly popular Commodore Amiga. Developed by Quixel and published by Domark, the game was a highly polished, vertically-scrolling shoot-'em-up which featured a number of sections based on elements of the film, with Bond sometimes being in control of a vehicle and, at other points, fighting his way through Franz Sanchez's minions on foot. Standout sections included the opening sequence, where Bond and Felix Leiter must disable Sanchez's private jet to prevent him from leaving United States airspace, and the tense finale where an exploding petrol tanker spells doom for the murderous drug lord (provided that the player's efforts are successful). As well as slick graphics for the time, especially on the more powerful 16-bit systems, the game benefited enormously from an atmospheric score which was composed by talented British digital musician David Whittaker, whose prolific work became something of a legend in the computer circles of the time.

In addition to the above games which were released to tie in with the cinematic screenings of the late eighties *Bond* films, other videogames also made an appearance in the decade with connections to the series. These included the now rather obscure *James Bond 007: Goldfinger* (1986), another text adventure developed by Angelsoft for Mindscape, which was released for the IBM PC, Apple Macintosh and the Apple II. More popular was Domark's *Live and Let Die* in 1988, a third-person speedboat racing game which was based around the memorable Louisiana Bayou chase sequence from Guy Hamilton's 1971 film of the same name. Comprising of a number of varied levels, each featuring a different terrain, the game was available on the more popular 8-bit platforms including the Commodore 64, Amstrad CPC and ZX Spectrum.

The *Bond* computer games, like the films that spawned them, were very much a product of their time, and like the *Bond* title songs of the period they provide testament to a period of rapid development in the franchise's history. With the dawning of a new decade, and one which was to bear witness to a very different geopolitical environment, the *Bond* series would undergo yet more changes: another new leading actor, new challenges in maintaining cultural relevance, and a new necessity to meet audience expectations. But Eon producers Albert R. Broccoli and Michael G. Wilson had ensured that the series had not only survived the eighties, but had emerged from it as an adaptive brand which had proven its versatility. The flexibility of the *Bond* format, which had been demonstrated many times in the cycle's long history, had allowed the films to keep pace with the tastes and fashions of their time of production. The obligation to sustain this relevance had been observed even when, as had been the case nearer the end of the decade, the franchise had struggled to match the tempo of contemporary film-making trends; it may have strained to achieve this goal, but there was no questioning that it had made a valiant attempt to do so. But perhaps the most significant achievement that Broccoli, Wilson, Maibaum and Glen could claim was that even in spite of all the efforts that were made to maintain the series' credibility with the cinema-going public, the franchise had retained its own distinctive identity even as cultural attitudes changed and the old certainties of geopolitical bipolarity were being shattered. The *Bond* film was, and remained, unmistakeably unique amongst cinematic franchises.

10

BOND THE HERO:
FITTING JAMES BOND
INTO 1980s FILM CULTURE

To consider the portrayal of James Bond in the eighties, and how the character can be placed into the film culture of the time, is naturally to play a game of two halves: Roger Moore's familiar, genially charming depiction of Bond on one hand, and Timothy Dalton's darker, more intense interpretation on the other. Yet even given the perennial commercial popularity of the series around the world, the producers were to face an uphill struggle to keep Bond relevant to audiences and preserve the character's immense recognition amongst audiences; the 1980s brought about some of the most enduring cultural icons in modern cinema, with some truly memorable – and vastly profitable – films being released by studios right throughout the course of the decade.

Roger Moore started the decade with a definite advantage, in that his incarnation of Bond had already been well established from the early seventies as a charming, capable and often quite warmly affable character, arguably making him a rather more likeable (if less dangerously ruthless or charismatic) manifestation of Fleming's protagonist than the original Connery portrayal had been. Though, as has been widely documented, Moore was to find himself thinking long and hard before agreeing to reprise the Bond role for a fifth outing, there is a considerable contrast to be made between the suave globetrotter of *Moonraker* and the case-hardened, no-nonsense Cold War spy of *For Your Eyes Only*. Although Moore retained some vestige of his earlier light-heartedness in places (particularly in Bond's awkward rebuffing of the amorous Bibi Dahl's affections), the film was to strike a more serious tone from the get-go, relying on a performance from Moore that was more in keeping with his other big screen dramatic roles of the time, such as *The Wild Geese* (Andrew V. McLaglen, 1978) and *Escape to Athena* (George Pan Cosmatos, 1979), as opposed to the amiable *The Saint*-like approach which had typified some of his earlier appearances in the *Bond* series.

It is perhaps interesting to note how Moore's Bond was to fit into the wider pantheon of cinematic heroes at the time of *For Your Eyes Only*'s production. The previous year had seen the American box-office dominated by Luke Skywalker in Irvin Kershner's monumentally successful science fiction sequel *The Empire Strikes Back*, followed closely by the return of Superman in Richard Lester's similarly well-received *Superman II*. For a British Intelligence agent who lacked both Jedi powers and Kryptonian strength, however, it was probably fortuitous that *For Your Eyes Only* was instead released in a year where cinemas were presiding over the runaway success of another kind of hero entirely. The emergence of Harrison Ford as archaeology lecturer turned global adventurer Indiana Jones, in Steven Spielberg's massively popular *Raiders of the Lost Ark*, was to present moviegoers with an audacious protagonist who possessed not only youth, vitality and good looks, but also abundant intelligence and ingenuity. Though the capacious mental power of Bond would be most heavily suggested during Pierce Brosnan's tenure in the role, Eon Productions seemed keen for Moore's performance to subtly emphasise this aspect of the character's repertoire of distinguishing attributes during the eighties, a fact made all the more timely given the obvious academic qualities of the widely-admired Dr Jones. And just as *For Your Eyes Only* seemed like a conscious attempt to hearken back to the Cold War scenarios of the early Connery years, so too was *Raiders of the Lost Ark* a nostalgic recreation of the atmosphere and exhilaration of 1930s adventure serials – a wistful evocation which Spielberg succeeded brilliantly in creating.

The following year brought the arrival of the Falklands War, which lasted from the April to the June of 1982. The conflict brought about a wave of patriotism throughout the United Kingdom which augured well for the reputation of fictional British characters such as Bond, whose Naval training and long-running defence of the realm made him appear more culturally relevant to audiences than had seemed to be the case for many years. Perhaps as a partial result of this arguable elevation of the character's status in the public consciousness, *Octopussy* performed strongly upon its release in 1983, beating off competition even from the return of the ever-popular Sean Connery in Irvin Kershner's unofficial, non-Eon produced *Bond* movie *Never Say Never Again* the same year. Moore's portrayal continued in a similar vein to the practical, slightly more hard-nosed approach that he had taken throughout *For Your Eyes Only*, while the film's narrative afforded him similar dramatic depth (exchanging the theme of revenge for that of betrayal) as well as allowing him additional latitude to develop Bond's traditional romantic conquest in a manner which was quite different than had been the case throughout the previous movie.

Film heroes had varied wildly in the intervening year between *For Your Eyes Only* and *Octopussy*. While another Spielberg-helmed film – *E.T.: The Extra-Terrestrial* – had achieved a position of pre-eminence at the box-office, 1982 was also to see the emergence of a wide range of memorable protagonists, among them Jeff Bridges's Kevin Flynn in Steven Lisberger's *Tron*, Harrison Ford as detective Rick Deckard in Ridley Scott's *Blade Runner*, and the effective double-act of Eddie Murphy and Nick

Nolte in Walter Hill's *48 Hours*. But also significant in terms of commercial success were sequels such as Sylvester Stallone's *Rocky III* and Nicholas Meyer's *Star Trek II: The Wrath of Khan*, both films which contained a subtext concerning their protagonists – Rocky Balboa and James Tiberius Kirk, respectively – coming to terms with their advancing years and questioning how to remain relevant in a changing world. This theme was arguably more germane to Moore's Bond than any of the following year's top box-office successes, which were led by the conclusion to George Lucas's original *Star Wars* trilogy, Richard Marquand's *Return of the Jedi*. Alongside the final bow of Han Solo and Princess Leia Organa in 1983 were a host of youthful leading actors which included Matthew Broderick as teenaged computer hacker David Lightman in John Badham's *WarGames* and William Hurt as Soviet agent Arkady Renko in Michael Apted's Martin Cruz Smith adaptation *Gorky Park*, alongside returning stars such as Christopher Reeve in Richard Lester's *Superman III* and Clint Eastwood's 'Dirty Harry' Callaghan in Edward Carfagno's *Sudden Impact*.

Eon Productions and Roger Moore had both done well to maintain Bond's popularity against this rising tide of American talent, but with *A View to a Kill* it seemed that Moore's collaboration with Albert R. Broccoli had finally reached its conclusion. Although he retained the dry wit and warm charm of his earlier appearances, and in spite of the fact that the film allowed him to engage with moments of light-heartedness that had otherwise been absent from his tenure throughout the early eighties, the fact remained that Moore had aged visibly since the production of *Octopussy*, something which seemed painfully apparent in the juxtaposition of his rather seasoned Bond with the comparatively youthful Grace Jones and Christopher Walken as genetically-enhanced antagonists with vastly increased physical strength and intelligence. Quite in spite of this fact, Moore clearly gives the role his all, compensating for the reduced credibility of the character's physical dynamism with both drollness and enthusiasm.

The year prior to *A View to a Kill*'s release had been witness to a virtual roll-call of eighties popular culture, with 1984 producing some of the decade's most enduring feature films including Ivan Reitman's *Ghostbusters*, Martin Brest's *Beverly Hills Cop*, Steven Spielberg's *Indiana Jones and the Temple of Doom*, John G. Avildsen's *The Karate Kid* and Robert Zemeckis's *Romancing the Stone*, to name but a few. While Hollywood movies, particularly of this period, were most often to be found featuring fit, good-looking leads of either gender, the increased emphasis on youthfulness at this point in the mid-eighties did not augur well for Moore's Bond. And although *A View to a Kill* did perform respectably enough at the box-office, there was a noticeable slump in comparison to the strong performance of *Octopussy* two years earlier, while cinemas were dominated by dynamic protagonists such as Michael J. Fox's time-travelling teenager Marty McFly in Robert Zemeckis's *Back to the Future,* Harrison Ford's troubled city detective John Book in Peter Weir's *Witness*, and Michael Douglas and Kathleen Turner's memorable adventuring double-act in Lewis Teague's *Jewel of the Nile.*

The time had come for a new incarnation of James Bond; an actor who could harmonise the character with changing cultural tastes and once again make this ever-resourceful product of the Cold War relevant to modern audiences. This responsibility would eventually lie with Broccoli's choice for Moore's successor, respected stage and screen actor Timothy Dalton. Although Dalton's name had been linked to the role in years past, his eventual assumption of the Bond mantle came at a particularly apposite time for the franchise; he would bring the character a renewed drive and sense of mercilessness, while his saturnine features and agile physique marked a clean break from the Moore era. In spite of the fact that Dalton's Bond was less quick with a tongue-in-cheek pun, and significantly less inclined towards casual romantic liaisons throughout his missions, the actor's renowned Shakespearean background and the air of dark melancholy that he brought to the role signified a definite departure from Moore's lightness of touch, and certainly upped the ante in terms of Eon's determination to bring a renewed sense of gritty realism and cultural relevance to the franchise.

Dalton's arrival as Bond seemed particularly timely given the raft of box-office action heroes who had held the gridlock over cinemas during 1986; Tom Cruise in Tony Scott's *Top Gun*, Paul Hogan as Peter Faiman's eponymous *Crocodile Dundee*, Sigourney Weaver in James Cameron's high octane sci-fi sequel *Aliens* and Eddie Murphy in Michael Ritchie's *The Golden Child* had all performed impressively as remarkable (if sometimes unconventional) protagonists, and thus the *Bond* franchise would need to raise the bar if it was to compete effectively in what was to be its 25th anniversary year. Although the well-judged production values and slightly moodier tone of *The Living Daylights* marked it out as a change of pace in comparison to its immediate predecessor, the film also performed strongly against other popular films of 1987 including Paul Verhoeven's *RoboCop* and Sidney J. Furie's *Superman IV: The Quest for Peace*, although it struggled to compete with the likes of John Badham's *Stakeout*, Tony Scott's *Beverly Hills Cop 2* and Richard Donner's *Lethal Weapon*.

Arguably, it was the stylistic approach of films such as *Lethal Weapon* which was to influence the direction of the eighties' final entry in the *Bond* franchise, and Dalton rose to the challenge with considerable gusto. Whereas much of *The Living Daylights* had seemed pitched specifically to underscore the differences between Dalton's Bond and Roger Moore's more mannerly portrayal, with *Licence to Kill* the Eon production team were to ramp up the momentum still further, reinventing the character as a modern action hero in ways that would demonstrate his flexibility beyond the Cold War scenarios of his origins. The audience appetite for this kind of hardened approach seemed to be amply confirmed by the commercial success of films such as Peter MacDonald's uncompromising *Rambo III*, Roger Spottiswoode's *Shoot to Kill*,

Peter Hyams's *The Presidio* and most especially John McTiernan's gleefully high-octane *Die Hard*, all features which had screened throughout the course of 1988.

Licence to Kill was to boast the darkest screenplay of Michael G. Wilson and Richard Maibaum's screenwriting collaboration, and John Glen's most energetic direction for the series. Dalton was to pull out all the stops in presenting a newly-unleashed Bond who is willing to bend or break every rule in the furtherance of his errand of vengeance. But in spite of the best of creative intentions, the film even today struggles to evade its reputation as a major box-office disappointment. The film suffered badly due to its release on a year which saw it faced with an incredibly strong cinematic line-up; 1989 was to bear witness to Harrison Ford and Sean Connery's well-received father-and-son pairing in Steven Spielberg's *Indiana Jones and the Last Crusade*, some hotly-anticipated sequels which included Richard Donner's *Lethal Weapon 2*, Robert Zemeckis's *Back to the Future: Part II* and Ivan Reitman's *Ghostbusters 2*, and – most significant of all – Tim Burton's smash hit comic adaptation *Batman*. It seemed supremely ironic that the one *Bond* movie of the eighties which was most keenly influenced by the style of action film-making common to the period was ultimately to be the most adversely affected due to the commercial performance of those same films. Thus although Dalton had amply delivered in the dramatic stakes, portraying a damaged and angry Bond consumed by retribution, this new, hard-boiled take on the secret agent proved unable to win over audiences at the time of films like *Cobra* and *Red Heat*, to say nothing of landmark cultural icons like Martin Riggs and John McClane. Despite Eon's most valiant efforts, nothing could ensure that this most experimental of *Bond* films was to carve itself a comfortable niche, to the point that its radical deviation from the recognisable Bond formula is unlikely to be repeated again at any point in the near future. (Even the complete reboot of the *Bond* mythos brought into effect by Martin Campbell's *Casino Royale*, 2006, for instance, arguably appears more faithful to the key mission-based tropes of the series by comparison.)

Although Dalton's tenure in the role was only to last for two films, he was to firmly put his stamp on Bond nonetheless; his keen awareness of Fleming's literary aims and self-conscious attempts to reconstruct the ruthlessness and immediacy of the early years of the franchise were certainly in concert with Broccoli, Wilson, Maibaum and Glen's ongoing attempts to reconnect with audiences and emphasise the series' developing relevance in a changing geopolitical environment. That his efforts did not translate directly into commercial success, particularly given general critical enthusiasm for his performance, is particularly unfortunate when the lengthy hiatus period following *Licence to Kill* ultimately meant that the actor chose to move on from the series and embrace other roles instead. Although Moore had undoubtedly been a crowd-pleasing Bond, his witty banter and genial manner winning him many admirers, Dalton instead played the character as though aiming for a much closer interpretation of the protagonist of the Fleming novels. Though his portrayal was not entirely without wit and charm, he was able to evoke the psychological damage and world-weariness of the literary Bond in ways that would not be seen again until the arrival of Daniel Craig's tenure many years later.

Ultimately, Eon Productions' efforts to reinvigorate the *Bond* franchise's significance to mainstream audiences throughout the eighties can be seen as a qualified success. Although the commercial fortunes of the series were to wax and wane as the decade progressed, Broccoli had remained true to his stated decision to draw the *Bond* films back to the cultural relevance that they had enjoyed in their sixties heyday and – although he was unable to recapture the iconicity of the golden age of the franchise – he and his creative team had nonetheless succeeded in diverting the course of the series away from the excesses of the films of the late seventies back towards a greater reliance on socio-political pertinence. Aided by Timothy Dalton's intense performance style in particular, writers Wilson and Maibaum had also begun to explore the depths of James Bond's character in ways that had rarely, if ever, been witnessed at any point in the series' history thus far. Finally, Bond was no longer simply a cipher, the key player at work in a rigid formula. Instead, as the seemingly-invincible spy's veneer of indomitability was pierced by a motivated production team and accomplished stage actor, audiences began to see – albeit fleetingly – a discontented and sometimes melancholic human being, a jaded widower with unmet emotional needs. This turning point would bear fruit throughout the nineties and, more obviously, from the beginning of the new millennium. However, those days would form another chapter in the long-running saga of *Bond* film production, with a different teaming at the head of Eon Productions in the form of Barbara Broccoli and Michael G. Wilson, and a new era which would be quite different from those which had come before it.

11

CONCLUSION

Earlier in this book, I noted an observation by James Chapman – as pertinent today as it was when he originally made it a decade ago – that placing the *Bond* films within the wider context of film history is a complicated task when the cycle has not yet been concluded.[1] At time of writing, the *Bond* series has undergone another recent overhaul – arguably the most radical in its long history. At the hands of director Martin Campbell and, later, Marc Forster, Eon Productions has subjected 007 to a kind of stylistic 'reboot' with the introduction of actor Daniel Craig in the leading role; a harder-edged Bond who seems perfectly suited to the rigours of the twenty-first century intelligence community (a cycle of creative revitalisation which arguably reached its culmination with Sam Mendes's *Skyfall*, 2012). But as we have seen, reinvention is just as much an intrinsic part of the *Bond* cycle as its now-familiar tropes and recognisable structural formula. By the opening years of the 1980s, the *Bond* series had nearly two decades of financially successful and almost-exclusively illustrious history behind it. Following John Glen's departure as the official *Bond* film director in the wake of *Licence to Kill*'s unfortunate box-office performance (the film's strong showing with most critics notwithstanding), the series was to undergo an almost phoenix-like resurrection in the mid-nineties, rising from the ashes of the Cold War era to reinvent Bond as a Vodka Martini-sipping hero of the New World Order. Chapman observes that the *Bond* series can only be evaluated in terms of its significance to film culture – and, indeed, popular culture generally – when the cycle has finally reached a state of narrative completion,[2] and there is little doubt that if and when such an analysis comes to be compiled, the eighties' slice of the *Bond* canon will be an integral and culturally significant part of the enquiry.

It is difficult to overstate the cultural impact of the *Bond* phenomenon; as we have seen, the perennial popularity of the film series over the decades has been attributed to a number of factors, and the eighties were no exception. It is also important to note that in the past few decades, especially since the 1980s, the influence of the films has also extended well beyond cinemas. With the advent of home entertainment, the films have sold strongly to new audiences on video cassette, laser disc and, most recently, DVD and Blu-Ray. Moreover, a loyal audience has been built up around the ITV network's regular screenings of the films, including Bank Holiday and Christmas Day showings which have become something of a national tradition in their own right. As Jeremy Black remarks, the films' popularity over the festive season since the mid-seventies was so pronounced that they were actually responsible for electrical surges on the National Grid at the time of their screenings.[3] There is little doubt, then, that Bond's overwhelming domestic and international success has assured the character a prominent and distinctive position in popular culture – and not only British popular culture. In spite of Eon Productions' scrupulous maintenance of the character's distinguishing credentials as a British national (even when an actor of non-British origin – George Lazenby – was cast in the role), the palpable internationalism of many plotlines within the series has blurred the distinction somewhat between Bond the British agent and Bond the jet-setting action hero. This certainly appeared to be the case in *Licence to Kill*, where the traditional

Bond formula is all but entirely abrogated in favour of an increasingly Americanised approach towards the broader action genre in order to appease contemporary international audience expectation. However, this trend has highlighted a further analytical tendency which has surfaced in the latter years of the franchise; as Chapman has noted, by embodying the function traditionally associated with the square-jawed American action hero, the Bond character has now come to be appropriated by some critical observers as an American cultural figure as well as his traditional function as a British one.[4]

Clearly, then, it is important to ask what it is about the *Bond* series in the 1980s that made the films' Cold War credentials relevant not only to British audiences, but to the wider international audience. The filmic Bond, after all, had always been a globe-trotting hero, never grounded in British affairs in the manner that his literary precursor had often been. Furthermore, the 1980s – a period of sharp contrasts and significant cultural change in recent British history – was defined, at least in part, by the expectations of the country's geopolitical role in the international conflict between superpowers. As Tony Bennett and Janet Woollacott were to observe in 1987, there was an inherent paradox in the way that Bond – a character who had, in his sixties heyday, been the very epitome of progressiveness – was being lionised anachronistically within a British cultural environment which had become, in a sense, reflective and backward-looking, due to a combination of recent historical events which had included the Falklands Conflict and the Royal Wedding between the Prince of Wales and Lady Diana Spencer.[5]

This distinction between the 'traditional' Bond (suggested by the familiar plot formulation and anticipated set-pieces which have been constructed over the series' history) and the 'modernising' Bond, inventive and resourceful, is a particularly fascinating one. It is, however, relevant to note that Bond's innovation is reflected as a matter of attitude as much as it is in the character's increasing reliance on new gadgetry or developing cinematic trends. As Pierre Sorlin has stated, later entries in the *Bond* series have been increasingly reliant on effects work, but the earliest days of the franchise – which are often held up as among the most successful and enduring in popularity – were largely free from such pyrotechnics and flamboyant visual spectacle.[6] Therefore, it seems especially germane to observe that it may well be this juxtaposition of modernisation and traditionalism that has been constructive in the formation of the distinctive Bond phenomenon that audiences, not least in the 1980s, would have come to expect. As Chapman has argued, the series' ability to adapt and evolve has become key to its continuing success with audiences, with the *Bond* cycle proving to be adaptable in response to cultural tastes as well as sensitive to variations in the political temperature and ideological environment (both internationally and at home).[7]

The series' ability to remain creatively flexible whilst maintaining a discrete 'brand identity' has led commentators such as Dennis W. Allen to observe that the durability of the Bond character is at least partially due to his robust ability to adjust in order to suit changing socio-cultural mores, and subsequently to indicate such changes through a subtle adjustment in his actions and attitude.[8] In the context of the 1980s, this was most clearly exemplified by Albert R. Broccoli's recruitment of Timothy Dalton to the Bond role, which was perhaps the clearest signal of the thematic course to which he had been committed since the beginning of the decade. For screenwriters Richard Maibaum and Michael G. Wilson, realism and cultural relevance – particularly in a Cold War context, at least until *Licence to Kill* – were paramount, an artistic intention which was enthusiastically shared by director John Glen. This is most notably observed in Eon Productions' replacement of Moore's essentially genial, gentlemanly protagonist with Dalton's ruthless, world-weary operative, which was central to Broccoli's drive to regain the film series' underlying Flemingite identity. Discussing Dalton's appointment by Eon in 1987, Glen asserted that 'Timothy Dalton was very different, much more sinister in the sense he's very real – you can believe he's going to kill someone. He's very much nearer Fleming's Bond. He's the hardest Bond we've ever had'.[9] This statement is particularly relevant in the face of latter-day criticism originating from commentators such as Sarah Street, who observed in *British National Cinema* (1997) that the conclusion of Cold War hostilities need not necessarily reduce *Bond* films to mere shadows of their former selves, where Bond becomes a reassuringly recognisable English hero even when such a figure – no matter how hearteningly familiar he may seem – appears incongruous in a globalised intelligence arena assailed by vague, faceless but eminently threatening antagonists.[10]

Yet in the wider context of the series' history, Eon's selection of Dalton for the central role can be seen as an exemplification of the *Bond* cycle's propensity to successfully reinvent itself for changing times. As Bennett stipulates:

> Bond is a mythic figure who transcends his variable incarnations. He is always identical with himself but never the same; he is an ever mobile signifier, fleshed out in different ways and subject to different ideological inscriptions and material incarnations at different moments in the history of the Bond phenomenon.[11]

Bennett's evocation of Bond's mythic qualities mirrors Black's assertion that the Bond character is essentially an enduring one, who effectively belongs to no specific time but instead reveals the cultural, social and political conditions of any distinct age that he is placed in.[12] Furthermore, this vaguely Levi-Straussian theme has been explored by other cultural commentators in recent times, including Lee Drummond, who has asserted that the *Bond* films have achieved unparalleled audience interest and cultural resilience due to their ability to offer up a persuasive but simultaneously overstated account of their fictional incidents in order to present the viewing public with an attractively appealing fantasy, replete with knowingly off-kilter verisimilitude, which transcends mere escapist entertainment (given the undeniable fact that, when all is said and done, not even the most enthusiastic commentator would be inclined to confuse a *Bond* movie with cinematic realism).[13]

Despite these assertions as to the continued and long-lasting cultural relevance of the *Bond* series, there can be little doubt that the series did undergo one of its weakest periods of financial, if not critical, performance towards the end of the 1980s. As has been discussed, the retrospective burden of blame has been placed more upon incredibly strong box-office competition than on the creative efforts of the production team – not least when the largely-enthusiastic critical appraisals of the time are considered. However, the issue of the viability of the films' social pertinence was not entirely ignored by critics. Writing in the mid-1990s, Tom Hodgkinson offered the opinion that it was not the production team's creative intentions that were at fault so much as the Bond phenomenon in general:

> *Licence to Kill* was all wrong for its time. In 1989, with many of us feeling alienated from yuppie Britain. [sic] We felt superior to such an escapist cinema genre, particularly one which seemed to promote anachronistic attitudes. It was silly. It was vulgar. Bond's central pursuits – gambling, drinking, promiscuity – were off the agenda. We were trying to improve ourselves.[14]

It is thus a vindication of the *Bond* films' resilience in the face of such criticism that the series has, in latter times, amply regained its blockbuster reputation. Martin Campbell's *GoldenEye*, released in 1995 and starring Pierce Brosnan as Bond, grossed $350.7 million worldwide, more than doubling the global takings of *Licence to Kill* six years beforehand.[15] The film also rekindled the interest of American audiences, with the US box-office providing $106.4 million of *GoldenEye*'s total revenue thanks to 24.45 million cinema admissions – both figures almost trebling the equivalent statistics recorded for *Licence to Kill*.[16]

On the subject of the timeless appeal of the *Bond* series, I have considered above only a small sampling of the many numerous competing theories as to the manner in which the films have come to maintain their lasting hold on audiences. From Bond's mythic status as a changing hero, constantly adapting in order to correspond to the modern age, to the series' reputation as a cultural and geopolitical barometer, there have come to be almost as many notions as to the reason for the films' unwavering allure as there are dedicated fans of the series. However, on the subject of what factor is responsible for making the series so enduringly popular with audiences, it seems appropriate to conclude with Glen's retrospective view that the Bond films are not simply spy movies or action adventure films, but a cinematic banquet, the kind of feature that assails the senses in a way that few others can match.[17] And this, more than any other reason, may be the reason why – in the eighties as much as in the present day – the Eon films have proven that when it comes to iconic figures in popular culture, there remains nobody who does it better than James Bond.

REFERENCES

1.　James Chapman, 'A Licence to Thrill', in *The James Bond Phenomenon: A Critical Reader*, ed. by Christoph Lindner (Manchester: Manchester University Press, 2003), 91-98, p.91.
2.　ibid.
3.　Jeremy Black, *The Politics of James Bond: From Fleming's Novels to the Big Screen* (London: Greenwood Press, 2001), p.xiii.
4.　James Chapman, 'Bond and Britishness', in *Ian Fleming and James Bond: The Cultural Politics of 007*, ed. by Edward P. Comentale, Stephen Watt, and Skip Willman (Bloomington: Indiana University Press, 2005), 129-43, p.140.
5.　Tony Bennett, and Janet Woollacott, *Bond and Beyond: The Political Career of a Popular Hero* (London: Palgrave McMillan, 1987), pp.20-21.
6.　Pierre Sorlin, 'From *The Third Man* to *Shakespeare in Love*: Fifty Years of British Success on Continental Screens', in *British Cinema, Past and Present*, ed. by Justine Ashby and Andrew Higson (London: Routledge, 2000), 80-92, p.90.
7.　James Chapman, *Licence to Thrill: A Cultural History of the James Bond Films* (London: I.B. Tauris, 1999), p.272.
8.　Dennis W. Allen, 'Alimentary, Dr Leiter', in Comentale, Watt, and Willman, 24-41, p.24.
9.　John Glen, cited in Stephen Payne and Gary Russell, 'James Bond Returns', in *Starburst*, July 1987, p.12.
10.　Sarah Street, *British National Cinema* (London: Routledge, 1997), p.87.
11.　Tony Bennett, 'The Bond Phenomenon: Theorising a Popular Hero', in *The Southern Review*, July 1983, p.205.
12.　Black, p.93.
13.　Lee Drummond, *American Dreamtime: A Cultural Analysis of Popular Movies and their Implications for a Science of Humanity* (London: Rowman and Littlefield, 1996), p.13.
14.　Tom Hodgkinson, 'Bonding Experiences', *The Guardian*, 16 November 1995, p.10.
15.　John Cork and Bruce Scivally, *James Bond: The Legacy* (London: Boxtree, 2002), p.303.
16.　ibid.
17.　Glen, cited in Cork and Scivally, p.312.

Some of the people behind the scenes in the James Bond productions of the 1980s. Clockwise from top left: Michael G. Wilson. Barbara Broccoli. Cubby Broccoli. John Glen. Kevin Mclory. John Barry. Irvin Kershner. Richard Maibaum.

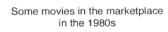

Some movies in the marketplace
in the 1980s

James Bond movies of the 1960s

James Bond movies of the 1970s

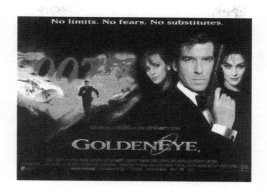

James Bond movies of the 1990s to the present day

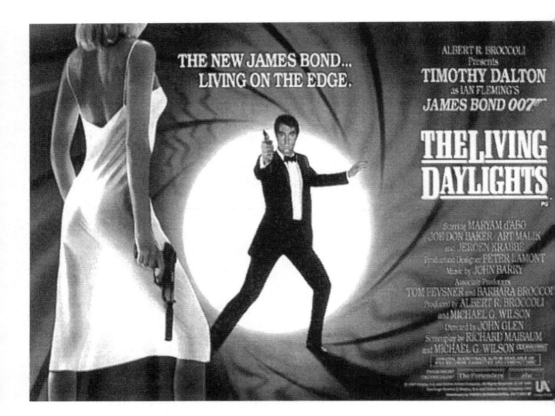

12

SCENE BY SCENE:
THE LIVING DAYLIGHTS (1987)

The Living Daylights *was a significant film for the* James Bond *series in a number of ways. The twenty-fifth anniversary entry in the cycle, it was to present a new lead actor in the form of Timothy Dalton, and a new drive by screenwriters Richard Maibaum and Michael G. Wilson and director John Glen to take the series back to its uncompromising roots as espionage-based thrillers situated within the shadowy world of the international intelligence community. With heightened public interest in the series on its anniversary year, this film was to prove crucial in Albert R. Broccoli's attempts to maintain the relevance of the* Bond *cycle to audiences across the world. The following analysis examines the manner in which Eon Productions were to achieve this goal.*

The Living Daylights opens, as had been the case for so many of its illustrious predecessors, with Maurice Binder's famous Eon Productions gun barrel logo. This was to be the cinema audience's first glimpse of Timothy Dalton as the new, fourth Eon incarnation of James Bond – in customary black bow-tie and dinner suit, he immediately makes a visual impact by switching from his predecessor Roger Moore's usual two-handed grip on the character's trademark Walther PPK in order to fire the pistol with one hand, whilst he crouches slightly while shooting in a manner loosely similar (though the motion is not as pronounced) to Sean Connery's Bond.

The gun-barrel aperture fades in to a rather bleak image of the Gibraltar shoreline. A military aircraft is in the foreground, while the camera pans over to reveal the famous Rock of Gibraltar in the distance. We then cut to what appears to be an office, complete with an orderly desk upon which rests a braided peaked cap. Rising from behind this desk is M (Robert Brown), the head of MI6, in a military jumpsuit bearing Admiral's epaulettes. Addressing three unseen operatives, only the back of their heads visible to the viewer, M explains that the Double-O section are to engage in a training exercise with the aim of infiltrating Gibraltar's radar installations. The SAS have been notified in advance of the agents' arrival, and will attempt to seize them on sight during the course of the mission. As M issues his briefing, a secret service operative clips a safety harness to the belt of his jumpsuit. Wishing the agents good luck, it soon becomes apparent that M's office is, in fact, situated aboard a military plane. The three agents pull goggles over their eyes, and – although still only visible in reverse – we can now see that they are dressed for stealth combat. As the plane's cargo ramp opens up, allowing the three agents to jump off, the subsequent inrush of air causes an annoyed M to scramble over to his desk in a vain attempt to stop the papers on its surface being disturbed.

The three agents silently cruise down through the air from the plane (an RAF Hercules C-130) as their transit is intercut with shots of the heavily-guarded military installation on the ground. As the trio's descent continues, each of their parachutes open up, but their approach is being closely observed through binoculars by a mysterious man in dark clothing (Carl Rigg). The first agent lands on a narrow stretch of beach, hurriedly racing into the undergrowth as he gathers up his trailing parachute. Further away, the second operative lands on a length of winding road, quickly obscuring himself behind a wall as he swiftly hides away his own parachute. The third and final agent finds that his parachute has become entangled in the branches of a tree, costing him vital time. Although it only takes him a few moments to disengage himself, by the time he falls to the ground Agent 002 (Glyn Baker) is discovered by an SAS soldier and promptly shot by a paintball; much to his frustration, his involvement in the exercise is over before it had even begun.

Back on the beach, Agent 004 (Frederick Warder) is throwing a grappling hook up onto an outcropping above his position. He is unaware that his other colleague, already on the Rock, is reasonably close to his position. Checking that the hook has made good contact, 004 begins his treacherous ascent. Far above, however, the mysterious black-clad operative is watching him climbing towards his location. He is so intent on his prey, in fact, that the man is unaware that an SAS trooper has spotted him. The soldier fires at the mysterious figure with a paintball and cheerfully informs him that the game is up, but without compunction the unknown operative produces a silenced handgun and shoots the interloper in the chest, killing him instantly. Now midway through his ascent, 004 becomes suspicious when he spots the distant figure watching him from far above. His expression impassive, the operative attaches what looks like a luggage tag on a metal clip to the rope that 004 is using to climb the rock. Then, to the agent's horror, the unidentified operative produces a knife and begins to hack at the rope. 004 cries out to his assailant in desperation, but his plea is ignored; his life-line severed, the agent plummets towards his death.

The mystery operative seems oblivious to the fact that 004's screams have been heard by his nearby colleague, a certain Agent 007. For the first time in the film, Timothy Dalton appears in medium close-up as he reacts to the distant cries of Bond's fellow agent as the man plunges to the ground below. The training mission now seemingly abandoned, Bond tears down a steep flight of steps towards his fallen comrade. First he discovers the rope, sliced clean through, and realises that 004's death was no accident. Spotting that the agent's body has landed in a nearby ditch, Bond scrambles down to investigate and discovers another corpse; this one belongs to an SAS soldier who had also fallen victim to the unidentified operative. Bond is momentarily startled when he is pushed aside by one of Gibraltar's resident monkeys, scurrying past him on its way up the Rock. But he barely has time to register this disturbance when he hears a silenced gunshot nearby and the sound of yet another deceased SAS trooper hitting the ground heavily.

Realising that the operative is attempting to make a getaway in one of the SAS's Land Rovers, Bond races along a dirt track which runs parallel to – and above – the length of road that the mysterious man is driving along. He soon reaches an SAS checkpoint, where a soldier orders him to halt and – his command unheeded – proceeds to hit him with a paintball. But the training exercise now little more than a distant consideration, Bond elbows the trooper aside and continues his pursuit, diving off the path to land on top of the Land Rover. Baffled, the SAS soldier calls after Bond to remind him that he is – under the regulations of the training mission, at least – now technically dead. But his warning falls on deaf ears; Bond is now clinging to the roof of the Land Rover for dear life. Hearing his pursuer's approach, the operative instigates a series of hard turns in the hope of thwarting Bond's attempts to maintain his grip on the speeding vehicle. But 007 is able to maintain his balance, and gradually climbs closer to the driver's side door of the Land Rover. Frustrated, the operative begins firing indiscriminately through the roof of the vehicle with his silenced handgun. Bond, alarmed, pitches himself onto the side of the Land Rover's roof to avoid being shot. The vehicle's velocity seems to be increasing as it speeds along the road. Another SAS soldier, manning a checkpoint further down the Rock, seems confused at the Land Rover's trajectory – it's heading away from the radar installation rather than towards it. As the operative continues to pick up the pace, the trooper signals him to halt at the checkpoint and – when he is ignored – fires paintballs at the windscreen in an attempt to slow the vehicle down. But the Land Rover ploughs straight into the hapless soldier and continues to race down the road, causing one of his alarmed SAS colleagues to barrel out of a nearby guard station with a machine gun and fire live ammunition at the fast-retreating vehicle. His desperate efforts to reduce its speed are fruitless, however.

Only just avoiding the hail of SAS bullets, Bond is startled to discover that the gunfire has ignited several wooden crates containing explosives which have been stored at the rear of the Land Rover. He frantically attempts to extinguish the flames, but succeeds only in briefly setting one of his boots on fire. Realising that time is now running out, Bond produces a field knife and cuts through the tough fabric hood of the Land Rover. The operative is startled at this new development, and struggles to maintain control of the vehicle while simultaneously fighting with Bond, who is trying hard to wrestle his way into the interior of the Land Rover. Eventually the operative is able to break Bond's grip on his knife, but at the cost of losing his grasp of the steering wheel. This forces Bond to make a desperate grab for the wheel so as to avoid hitting an oncoming car containing an oblivious family, though this in turn leads to the Land Rover tearing through a nearby kiosk full of postcards and tourist trinkets instead. Unable to believe their eyes, the family in the car watch slack-jawed as the out-of-control military vehicle rams its way though picnic tables; even some nearby Gibraltar monkeys seem stunned by the unexpected disturbance.

The fight in the Land Rover becomes ever more frenzied as a burning crate of explosives falls off the back of the vehicle and, seconds later, detonates on the road behind. Bond finally succeeds in forcing his way onto the passenger seat, and eventually manages to gain the upper hand in the struggle by head-butting his opponent. He is again forced to fight with the steering wheel as the Land Rover races past another collection of tourists, cars and monkeys, eventually careening off the edge of the Rock and plummeting towards the sea. The fire from the explosive crates is now glowing visibly from the rear of the vehicle. The operative continues to brawl with Bond, but 007 now has other ideas. Breaking one of the Land Rover's windows in the last throes of their clash, Bond releases his secondary parachute which pulls him clear of the burning vehicle. Gaining distance just in time, the operative yells in panic as the Land Rover finally explodes as a result of its incendiary cargo. Although Bond is unharmed by the resulting blast, fiery debris rains down on his parachute, damaging it upon impact. Fortunately for him, however, a private yacht (a Moonmaiden II model) is sailing close to his position. Seeming relieved, Bond aims to make his landing there, unaware that the yacht's owner, Linda (Kell Tyler) is speaking to a friend on the phone, complaining at how quiet Gibraltar has proven to be and bemoaning her inability to find an interesting man there. (She seems oblivious to the exploding Land Rover which, logically speaking, can only have blown up a short distance from her location.) Linda looks on, stunned, as Bond thumps down onto the yacht's canopy, swings down to join her, and then commandeers her phone. Briefly introducing himself to the ship's owner and telling her unseen friend that Linda will call her back, Bond rings Exercise Control and tells them that he will report in within an hour. When Linda offers him a drink, however, Bond changes his mind and suggests that maybe two hours would be a better estimate of his arrival. With that, we cut to the opening title sequence and a rendition of a-ha's song *The Living Daylights*.

Like many (but by no means all) Bondian pre-title sequences, the above scenes do eventually tie in to the main film – the label which was placed on the hapless 004's body by the mysterious operative will later signify the supposed threat (actually a red herring) which Bond and his allies are facing, and in turn forms part of the main antagonist's convoluted plot. But the sequence is significant in other ways beyond the excellent use of atmospheric location filming in Gibraltar. Glen shows both skill and dramatic playfulness in revealing the identity of the new Bond very gradually, not showing his profile during M's briefing and then introducing two separate diversions (Agents 002 and 004) before Dalton's features are eventually shown to the audience. Additionally, Glyn Baker's 002 appears deliberately chosen to have a passing resemblance to a young Roger Moore, while Frederick Warder bears an even more striking similarity to George Lazenby as 004. But, of course, their appearances are little more than fleeting, and they mark a kind of subtle passing of the baton to this latest incarnation of Bond. Glen also seems keen to establish Dalton as quickly and effectively as possible; the high-octane chase sequence between Bond and the murderous operative is rather more brutal and no-nonsense than the tongue-in-cheek approach that many of the Roger Moore films had displayed, and even the iconic 'Bond, James Bond' line is dispensed with during the first five minutes of the film.

Following the opening titles, we fade in on an orderly Eastern European city street. As a tram passes by, a superimposed caption informs the audience that they are currently viewing 'Bratislava, Czechoslovakia'. The camera pans across to the austere exterior of the Bratislava Conservatoire as classical music begins to become audible. Cutting to inside the building, an orchestra is playing the first movement of Mozart's 40th Symphony in G-minor. The recital is well-attended by many well-dressed patrons. Some of the auditorium's audience boxes bear Soviet Union and Czechoslovakian flags. Sitting rather anxiously in one of these boxes is Saunders (Thomas Wheatley), a British Intelligence agent, who is glancing impatiently at his watch. A few moments later, Bond emerges into the box – in black tie and dinner suit, his mode of dress is rather more formal than Saunders's own lounge suit. Saunders introduces himself as head of Section V: Vienna, and upbraids Bond for his lateness. Bond is unconcerned by the prim Saunders's censure, however, and asks where their target is located. Saunders indicates a middle-aged man sitting in a ground-floor box, dressed in an expensive-looking three-piece suit and flanked by two burly KGB minders. Using a pair of opera glasses, Bond peers across to get a better look at his objective, Russian General Georgi Koskov (Jeroen Krabbé), who is watching the orchestra intently. Bond traces Koskov's line of sight and realises that the General is looking at a beautiful cellist, Kara Milovy (Maryam d'Abo). He remarks on this to Saunders but, assuming that Bond is merely indulging his well-known eye for the ladies, he urges his colleague to keep his mind on the mission. Koskov is due to leave the building during the interval, meaning that Saunders and Bond will need to be prepared for the operation which is to come. Saunders is hushed by an irritable woman in the adjacent audience box, and decides to choose that particular moment to withdraw from the auditorium.

A large sickle-and-hammer Soviet emblem is in evidence on the exterior of an apparently-abandoned shop across the road from the Conservatoire. Saunders unlocks its door and ushers Bond inside before securing it again. The shop's interior seems to have been derelict for some time; various papers and other fragmentary ephemera are strewn around the main customer area, and the walls are plastered with old, weathered Marxist-Leninist propaganda posters. Not a word passes between the two agents until they have ascended a spiral staircase into an upstairs apartment. This area seems somewhat better appointed than the shop below. Saunders turns on the room's electric lighting, but Bond quickly asks him to switch them back off again. 007 closes the lapels of his suit jacket over his shirt and secures them with a velcro strip, greatly reducing his visibility to the casual eye. Opening a door onto a balcony area, he emerges from behind the huge metal sickle-and-hammer sign, providing him with a clear view of the Conservatoire directly opposite. Saunders pulls back the cover of a nearby double bed, revealing a sniper rifle, scope, and ammunition. As Bond readies the gun for firing (a Walther WA2000 rifle), Saunders informs him sternly that this operation has been set up by his department following a secret communication from Koskov himself: he will tolerate no failure at this stage in proceedings. The General, one of the top strategists in the KGB, intends to defect to the West, and Saunders is determined that everything will go according to plan. He asks Bond if he will prefer soft-nosed ammunition for the rifle, but Bond instead requests steel-tipped bullets in order to overcome any contact with KGB body-armour. Bond asks Saunders for the details of his escape route, but the other agent refuses to disclose the information, asserting that it is on a need-to-know basis only. Bond seems unimpressed by his pretensions. Saunders does warn Bond, however, that the KGB have assigned a sniper of their own to murder Koskov if he attempts to flee Czechoslovakia, and that this assassin will need to be neutralised in order to ensure the success of the General's defection. Bond becomes curious when Saunders tells him that Koskov specifically requested 007's presence on the mission; when he asks why, Saunders witheringly replies that Koskov seems to be under the impression that Bond is the best that MI6 has to offer. His tone clearly implies that this is not an assessment that Saunders agrees with, to say the least. Stopping only to ask where the escape car is located – Saunders informs him that it's at the rear of the building – Bond asks his colleague to bring a chair over to the balcony. He sits down with the scoped rifle at the ready while Saunders dons a night-vision headset. As Saunders struggles with his goggles, which seem unfamiliar to him (Bond tersely disengages the safety shutters for his fellow agent), 007 grimly remarks that it'll take about ten seconds for Koskov to run from the Conservatoire to the shop – more than ample time for a KGB sniper to gun him down.

Back in the auditorium, Koskov gives the orchestra a standing ovation as their recital comes to an end. Grinning, he is particularly intent on Kara, but although the graceful cellist appears to notice him she also seems to be trying to avoid his gaze. Carefully laying down her cello, she heads off the stage. Koskov, on the other hand, has gone to the gents' toilets. Moving for a W.C. that is closest to the exterior wall, he locks the door of the stall behind him just as his trailing KGB minder enters the room seconds later. Flushing the toilet to mask the sound of his escape, he struggles with the window and escapes out onto the street outside. Across the street, Saunders reacts instantly as he spots the General racing to a hiding spot behind a parked van. The agent is confused by the way that Koskov appears to be waiting for something, rather than racing across the road to safety as expected. Bond spots movement on the second floor of the Conservatoire and mentions it to Saunders, who recognises a figure emerging at a window there – Kara, the cellist from the orchestra. Koskov now starts his run across the road at last, though he keeps glancing up in the direction of the sniper as though somehow waiting for her to fire instead of trying to evade her line of sight. This unusual behaviour piques Bond's interest. Saunders orders him to kill Kara, but 007 instead decides to target her rifle, causing her to lose her grip. Realising that her cover is blown, she quickly retreats from the window. Angered, Saunders accuses Bond of deliberately missing his target, sparing Kara's life unnecessarily.

In this Bratislavan sequence, chilly in more ways than one, Glen and screenwriters Maibaum and Wilson establish much about Bond's complex code of honour; he will show no compunction in killing a professional, but in detecting that the visibly inexperienced Kara was merely masquerading as a KGB operative he is unwilling to take her life, instead giving her an opportunity to withdraw with a superficial injury. Saunders is used as an interesting counterpoint to Bond; a rather pompous, by-the-book agent, he never seems completely out of his depth, but his field experience appears less than sufficient compared to Bond's, almost as though he is following a defection textbook (much to his colleague's regular irritation). Bond is apathetic to the other man's posturing, and has little time for his self-important reprimands; although clearly unimpressed by Saunders, Bond remains too professional – and jaded – to bother saying so explicitly.

Downstairs, Koskov is desperately knocking on the shop door. Saunders quickly lets him in and ushers him through the building to another entrance at the back of the shop. Bond watches from the balcony as members of the public, alarmed by the gunshot, are looking around in alarm for the source of the disturbance. Just before the police arrive on the scene, Bond spots Kara as she rushes from the Conservatoire, cradling her arm as though injured. But there is no more time to waste. Heading down to the rear of the shop, Bond demands to know where Koskov is being hidden. When Saunders replies that he is being concealed in the boot of the car, an Audi 200 Quattro, Bond derisively informs him that this would inevitably be the first and most likely hiding place that the police would check. Instead, he informs him that he is dispensing with Saunders's intended route of escape and plans to improvise instead. Moving Koskov (who is ecstatic to be in the presence of the legendary 007) into the front passenger seat, where he will hide in plain sight of the authorities, Bond tells Saunders to keep the police off their tail and then to regroup at 23:00 at the border with Austria. Puzzled as Bond dumps the sniper rifle into his arms, leaving him mere seconds away from a seemingly inevitable investigation by the Soviet authorities, Saunders asks him what his new plan will be. But Bond, responding to the self-important Saunders's earlier briskness, informs him that this information is on a need-to-know basis only. He then races off into the night, leaving an apprehensive-looking Saunders in his wake.

As more police cars tear off towards the Conservatoire, Bond and Koskov are heading in the opposite direction. Koskov mentions to Bond that the KGB sniper had been a woman – but then, many of the Soviets' best shots are female. The General seems particularly eager to know if Bond had killed his intended assassin, but believing the question to be distasteful 007 refuses to answer. As the police presence grows, Koskov becomes increasingly distressed; as the KGB now know that he intends to defect, they will close the border, making his escape virtually impossible. But Bond's composure is unruffled; telling the General not to concern himself overduly, he informs him that his organisation has a 'pipeline to the West'. His knowing glance suggests that this is more than just a figure of speech, however – and sure enough, the car soon speeds past a sign for the Trans-Siberian Pipeline, with a large section of metal piping visible behind it.

A pipeline operative, Rosika Miklos (Julie T. Wallace) is watching the approach of Bond's car, and opens a metal gate to admit the agent and his Russian guest. Bond introduces Miklos as a British Intelligence contact within the organisation; she recognises Bond and appears to be on good terms with him, having worked with the agent before. Warning Bond and Koskov to remain quiet, she sneaks them both past the exterior of the plant's control room and into a secluded maintenance area where a scouring plug awaits entry into the pipeline. Bond explains that this particular unit has been designed to carry a human being through the pipeline; this will be the method by which Koskov will be transported out of Soviet jurisdiction, as the pipeline was designed to pipe natural gas into Western Europe. Koskov, who seems somewhat claustrophobic, is less than thrilled at this suggestion, but time is of the essence and Bond quickly persuades him that this is the only way to assure his safe delivery from the KGB. Growing concerned as time passes, Miklos instructs Bond on the correct procedure to dispatch the plug when the pressure reaches a particular point; misjudging this moment will most almost certainly prove fatal for the increasingly anxious Koskov.

Telling him to breathe into an oxygen mask, Koskov is

particularly alarmed when he discovers that he will be the first to test this method of escape, but is unable to protest further before Bond slams the hatch closed and injects the plug into the pipeline, readying it for its journey.

Sealing the pipe closed, Miklos informs Bond that he will need to wait until the pressure gauge gives the correct reading before he can pull the lever and release the plug. By necessity, this involves her distracting the plant's supervisor (Peter Porteous) so that he is not alerted by the abundance of warning lights that will illuminate when the plug begins its journey. She returns to the control room and enters it, startling the supervisor who is dividing his attention between his regular duties and a football match which is being displayed on a tiny monochrome television set. Seductively, Miklos releases her utility belt, lets down her hair, and begins to unzip her boiler suit. Stunned, the supervisor has no time to react before Miklos embraces him, pushing his face into her chest just as the pressure warning lights begin to flash. Right on time, Bond releases the plug at the exact moment that the gauge indicates the optimum pressure, speeding Koskov on his way. The supervisor, otherwise occupied, is completely oblivious to what is going on. 007 then sneaks past the control room again, stopping only to indicate his success to Miklos. Realising that the threat of discovery has now passed, she roughly casts the bewildered supervisor back into his chair, angrily rebuffing his advances and leaving him baffled as to the vacillations of her behaviour.

This early introduction to Koskov is interesting in the way that the character is initially set up as a rather bumbling, cowardly figure, warmly embracing Bond as the means of his deliverance but seeming oddly out of touch with the world of espionage for someone who is a senior ranking officer in the KGB. His apparent uncertainty with regard to his high-risk mode of escape, while eminently understandable, nonetheless sits awkwardly with someone who is desperate to flee the Eastern Bloc by any means necessary, and thus Maibaum and Wilson skilfully foreshadow the character's later chicanery and tendency towards subterfuge. That the circumstances surrounding the defection have actually been carefully orchestrated by this seemingly-genial spymaster is, at this stage, concealed by the immediacy of his apparent knife-edge getaway. Likewise, the General's seemingly-casual enquiry as to the fate of the sniper is later significant; clearly he had intended for Bond to kill Kara outright, thus robbing her of the potential to inform anyone that Koskov himself had asked her to pose as a Soviet assassin and ultimately concealing his deception in the wake of any later investigation. (Indeed, Bond's renowned status in the intelligence community as a flawless shot may actually have been the reason why Koskov had requested his presence in the first place.) Contrasting Koskov's deceptively ingenuous manner is the genuine comic relief provided by Rosika Miklos, the efficient but drolly-depicted gasworks operative. Judged brilliantly by Julie T. Wallace, the character clearly saves Bond's (and particularly Koskov's) bacon at short notice, and her proficiency in the field – even though sometimes reflected through a rather light-hearted lens – emphasises the fact that Bond's alternative route of escape is all that has saved the defection after the apparent ineffectiveness of Saunders's strictly by-the-numbers approach. (The later presence of Q and the Harrier technical crew in Austria suggests that this is indeed the method of escape that Bond has had planned all along.)

Standing at a roadside border control post, waiting to meet his rendezvous with Bond, Saunders is stunned when a deafening roar screeches past him from the gas pipeline nearby. The unexpected commotion likewise alarms customs officials and members of the public alike. A dog-walker similarly looks stunned by the tumult as the plug races through a sharp bend in the pipeline. Eventually, this particular length of piping terminates in a gasworks installation just over the Austrian border. The plug, now looking somewhat grimier than when it started its journey, is opened by a pair of MI6 technicians as well as Q (Desmond Llewelyn), British Intelligence's foremost technical expert. Q welcomes a rather disoriented Koskov to Austria, helping the disoriented Russian out of the plug. But before the General even has time to catch his breath, he is urged to climb a very long flight of stairs by yet more Secret Service staff, keen for him to pick up his pace.

Back at the border crossing, Bond arrives with the Audi and picks up Saunders, who has been waiting impatiently nearby. As they head off, Koskov is being fitted with a safety jacket and led into a British Aerospace Harrier T10 jet which is parked at the top of the Austrian gasworks building. Struggling up the stairs behind him, Q (who, unlike Bond, is clearly not as young as he used to be) stops to swallow a couple of pills as the technical crew quickly prepare the plane for departure. With Koskov and the pilot suitably equipped, the Harrier makes a vertical takeoff as Q and the ground crew watch nearby. Bond, who is now at a passport checkpoint, watches with satisfaction as the jet flies off in the distance. While the customs officials watch with detached interest, Saunders is stunned and stares at Bond with an awestruck expression. But Bond's slick, wordless facial response suggests that he does this kind of thing every day.

Now safely in Western territory, Bond is back behind the wheel of the Audi. 007 tells Saunders that there is no need for his glum demeanour; the defection was a complete success, and on paper the mission was carried out under Saunders's jurisdiction. But the livid Saunders will not be mollified. He tells Bond that he intends to report 007 to M for deliberately disobeying the order to kill the KGB sniper on sight, knowing that Bond's missed aim had been entirely intentional. But Bond is neither chastened nor concerned; he knew that Kara had not been a trained assassin by the amateurish way that she had been holding her rifle, and was unwilling to murder someone who clearly wasn't a professional. Informing Saunders that he is free to complain to M as much as he likes, Bond wearily observes that if he is dismissed from the service, he would be more inclined to thank his superior than protest his judgement. Still curious as to the beautiful sniper's identity, however, Bond quietly reflects that she must have been totally out of her depth: 'Whoever she was, I must have scared the living daylights out of her'.

Bond's disagreement with Saunders reaches its apex here, and emphasises the character's sense of relative autonomy in comparison to his peers. Saunders seems unable to accept that only Bond's quick thinking and adaptability have salvaged the mission, even when he is theoretically still able to take the credit for its success. Bond's utter indifference at Saunders's threat of disciplinary action underscores rather neatly Eon Productions' desire to highlight the growing world-weariness of 007, showing that – in a manner similar to the character's literary forebear – the endless cycle of intrigue and murder has begun to weigh down on his cynical worldview even although it hasn't yet eroded his ironclad professionalism. Saunders's retrospective of the sniper incident also foregrounds Bond's later affections for Kara; though his moral choice to spare her life is clearly stated, the enigmatic woman's unexplained actions during the defection are clearly foremost on his mind, presaging his later attraction to her. Bond's throwaway mention of the film's title also alludes to the 1962 Ian Fleming short story of the same name (originally entitled 'Berlin Escape' when it first appeared in *The Sunday Times*), which concerned Bond's part in the flight of a British Intelligence agent from East Berlin over to the safety of West Germany. Amongst many similarities between the prose story and the Bratislava defection sequence of the film, in the literary tale Bond also reflects after the event that he had 'scared the living daylights' out of his target.

Next we see a London street scene, near Trafalgar Square, complete with a passing red bus and nearby Underground station. As a newspaper seller calls out the breaking news of Koskov's recent defection, the camera pans up to a sign marked 'Universal Exports' hanging from a building's exterior. (This is a well-established cover name for British Intelligence throughout the *Bond* series.) Cutting inside, Q is busy in his lab, currently going through a computer database detailing information that MI6 has gathered regarding female KGB assassins. Bond is watching over his shoulder, but is dissatisfied with Q's findings – none of the potential snipers on the database match Kara's features, leaving him no closer to discovering the mysterious woman's identity. M's personal assistant, Miss Moneypenny (Caroline Bliss), arrives and quickly enters into her customary brand of flirtatious banter with Bond. Q, barely seeming to register Moneypenny's arrival, tells Bond that they have now reached the end of the database – no further female KGB operatives are listed on record. He suggests going through information on non-Soviet freelance assassins instead, but Moneypenny tells them that the search must be temporarily curtailed; M has ordered Bond to report to an MI6 safe-house at the Blayden Estate. Bond seems less than enthused by this command, but his continued presence at Q's offices would be pointless in any regard – the search has come up empty, frustrating his efforts to pinpoint Kara. They are interrupted by a blast of loud music from elsewhere in the lab. Q becomes more animated than usual when he hears the sound, scurrying off to a toughened glass partition to look over into another part of the workshop. Bond and Moneypenny follow him. In this adjacent area, a white-haired scientist in a lab coat and safety goggles (Alan Harris) is pointing what looks like an ordinary eighties ghetto blaster at a mannequin at the far end of the lab. Seeing him take aim, two other technicians race to get out of his line of sight. Sure enough, moments later a hatch opens at the end of the ghetto blaster, revealing a small rocket which is fired directly towards the mannequin, blowing it to pieces. Behind the safety glass, Q seems delighted by the success of the experiment, proudly telling Bond that the gadget is being trialled for use by the Americans. Eagerly pacing away through a sliding door to take a closer look at the fruits of his labours, Q departs. Moneypenny advises that Bond should head off to his arranged rendezvous at Blayden, and hands him a folded piece of paper –

he must also pick up an ordered package from the Harrods department store on his way to the secluded country house. Before he goes, Bond asks Moneypenny to check in with the MI6 records department and request that they monitor Czechoslovakian news sources for any incidence of a female cellist at the Bratislava Conservatoire. Seeming impressed by his interest in fine music, Moneypenny invites Bond to join her sometime so that he can enjoy her collection of Barry Manilow records at his leisure. Bond, in his time-honoured tradition, gently declines her offer, causing her to sigh longingly in his wake as he heads off.

This was the debut appearance of Caroline Bliss in the long-running role of Miss Moneypenny; Bliss would be the first actress to replace series stalwart Lois Maxwell as the character (in the Eon series, at least), who had so memorably occupied Moneypenny's desk from *Dr No* in 1962 all the way through to 1985's *A View to a Kill*. Maxwell's excellent comic timing had established the character in the public consciousness even although the character's screen time in each film was invariably brief, and Moneypenny's playful verbal jousting with Bond – as well as her reputation for efficiency and professional excellence – had become one of the cycle's running conventions. Although *Octopussy* had toyed with the concept of a younger replacement for Moneypenny in the form of assistant Penelope Smallbone, it wasn't until *The Living Daylights* that Eon Productions were to recast the part altogether; although Maxwell had enjoyed excellent on-screen chemistry with Roger Moore's Bond, a more youthful successor seemed logical to provide a more plausible sense of attraction – and unrealised romantic frisson – between the character and Timothy Dalton's Bond. Like Dalton himself, Bliss was only to appear in two films of the *Bond* series, but she quickly established an appealing interplay between the proficient personal assistant and 007. Her screen time was greatly reduced in *Licence to Kill*, but Bliss did succeed in putting her stamp on the character before she herself was succeeded in the role by Samantha Bond throughout the nineties. That said, the character herself nonetheless proved contentious in some quarters, with Bond's casual chauvinism towards this intelligent and capable professional – even if apparently in jest – seeming rather awkward and misplaced in the ostensibly more enlightened 1980s.

On a country road, a man in white exercise clothing – Necros (Andreas Wisniewski) – is jogging past some picturesque cottages. A farm hand is guiding some cows across the quiet road into a field. Affecting an American accent, Necros apologises when he briefly collides with a milkman, causing the man to drop a bottle from his float as he moves to make a delivery. The music from Necros's personal stereo is so loud that it drowns out the milkman's barbed comment at the runner's clumsiness. A white horse watches curiously from a stable as the milkman makes his delivery to a cottage nearby, collecting empty bottles as he does so. Returning to his float, the man can hear music – 'Where Has Everybody Gone' by the Pretenders – and seems momentarily confused as to where it is coming from. Shrugging, he remains intent on stacking milk crates on the back of his float, unaware that Necros is silently emerging from the top of a wall which is directly behind the milkman. Using the unusually durable flex of his headphones, he strangles the hapless milkman and lifts his corpse over the wall, obscuring it from the view of passers-by.

Bond is arriving at the grandiose metal gates of the Blayden safe house in an Aston Martin V8 Volante. He stops to identify himself to a security operative at the gatehouse checkpoint (Marc Boyle) before driving up to the estate itself. Based in expansive grounds, Blayden is a large country house which – superficially, at least – betrays nothing of its secret service function to the outside world. Necros, meanwhile, is now wearing the deceased milkman's clothing, and is heading back to the float with a basket of milk-bottles. Bond emerges from his Aston Martin carrying the aforementioned Harrods package, but is stopped by another security agent who has detected his Walther PPK pistol with a radar device planted in a garden rake. Bond complies with the regulations, handing over his handgun to the operative who removes its cartridge and temporarily confiscates it. A butler (Bill Weston) then emerges from the building, offers to carry Bond's parcel (though his offer is politely refused), and informs 007 that he is expected in the drawing room.

The butler guides Bond through a beautifully-appointed entrance hallway before knocking on the drawing room door. At M's acknowledgement, the butler opens the door to admit Bond… who is immediately embraced by a jubilant Koskov, his iron projection of geniality maintained to a fault. As the butler withdraws, closing the door behind him, M enquiringly watches the Russian's overly enthusiastic hug with Bond, as does the Minister of Defence, Sir Frederick Gray (Geoffrey Keen), and a government secretary (Antony Carrick), both of whom are seated near the MI6 chief. In the customary Eastern European convention, Koskov kisses Bond on both cheeks in greeting and assures him that he will never forget the agent's part in his defection. Spotting Bond's parcel from Harrods, Koskov swings open the lid to reveal a food hamper and is overjoyed – the food at Blayden, he assures Bond with mock-confidentiality, is awful. Bond quietly tells the General that the *foie gras* in the package is to be particularly commended. As Koskov rifles through the contents of the hamper with some degree of snobbery, superciliously dismissing the caviar as 'peasant food' but reacting with delight at the presence of Bollinger champagne, Bond is passing the receipt to M, whose eyes widen at the unseen cost of the order. 007 softly informs his superior that the choice of champagne in the original order was not to be recommended, and that he had made a substitution of his own choosing. The overall package certainly seems to have gone down well with Koskov, whose approval is tangible. Seeming on the verge of losing patience, M suggests that the assembled group now resume the debriefing session. Outside, however, Necros is arriving at the main gate in the stolen milk float. Suspicious, the security operative at the gatehouse asks where the usual milkman is, but Necros – now sporting a rather generic English accent – replies that he's gone down with a case of the flu. Seeming suspicious, the security man orders Necros out of the float and frisks him for concealed weaponry. Finding nothing on his person, the operative tells Necros to head for the kitchen entrance, directing him to the rear of the building.

Back in the drawing room, Koskov is telling the small assembly that the reason for his defection was due to the actions of his superior – the head of the KGB, General Leonid Pushkin. His words are being diligently recorded by the secretary on his typewriter. Gray seems rather nonplussed at this confession, but Koskov tells them that although he and Pushkin were once close friends, the power of high office has clouded Pushkin's viewpoint, leading him to despise the Soviet government's recent *détente* with the West. As he continues to speak, there is a brief cut to Necros as the milk float approaches the building's back entranceway. Koskov removes his right shoe and produces a piece of paper from inside it, attesting that it holds the key to a secret directive from Pushkin codenamed *smiert spionam* – literally, 'death to spies'. This note contains a list of British and American agents who are to be flagged for assassination by the KGB; Koskov notes that as Russian spies will inevitably be killed in retaliation, the whole situation has the potential to end in catastrophe or even – as a worst case scenario – thermonuclear warfare. However, he suggests, if Pushkin were to be liquidated before his plans are put into action, it may be enough to defuse the situation before it begins. Gray asks if Pushkin is currently in Moscow, and Koskov replies that although that is indeed the case for now, in three days' time he is due to leave for Tangiers in order to address the North African Trade Convention. This visit, Koskov asserts, is merely a cover to enable Pushkin to start putting his murderous plans into operation. Bond looks deeply unconvinced of the Soviet's honesty. M, knowing that Koskov's news has potentially grim implications for the balance of power between East and West, suggests to Gray that they return to London and consult with their superiors in government. Gray readily agrees. As they leave, Bond gives Koskov a profoundly suspicious glance.

The scenes in the drawing room are, of course, intended primarily to allow Koskov to weave his web of deceit around the British Government and its Secret Service operatives. But they also succeed in foregrounding Bond's misgivings over the General's true motives. After the Herculean efforts required in extracting Koskov from the Eastern Bloc, it may seem oddly anticlimactic to accept that the entire reason for his mock-defection (and later 'recapture' by the Soviets) was just to deliver a note that was small enough to be hidden in his shoe. A KGB mastermind such as Koskov would surely have had other means at his disposal to communicate this information without compromising himself: his defection would no doubt have informed Pushkin that his *smiert spionam* operation had been leaked to the West, spurring him to put his plans into action earlier than expected. Yet the plausibility of Koskov's tale is paramount in planting the seed of distrust in the minds of the Western intelligence agencies regarding Pushkin; they must be absolutely convinced of the KGB chief's mental instability if they are to be manipulated into assassinating him. The key question at this point in the film is the reason why – if Koskov is lying, as Bond suspects – this peculiar General really wants his superior killed.

Blayden's chef (Michael Percival) is feeding his pet parrot in the house's well-stocked kitchen as Bond leaves the estate. 007's Aston Martin is followed closely by two other cars bearing M and Gray. Necros enters the kitchen and, under the cover of a daily milk delivery, puts his bottles on the floor near the chef. In reality, this is simply a ruse to enable him to strangle the hapless cook (again, with the headphones of his personal stereo) while he is momentarily distracted. Passing a rather incongruous bank of computer surveillance equipment, the butler lets himself into the kitchen only to interrupt Necros's attack. He barely has time to radio in a distress call, which is picked up by the security operative at the gatehouse, before Necros springs into action. The butler is clearly well-trained, however, and enters into a fist-fight with Necros. The gatehouse security man radios back for confirmation, but the butler is only narrowly fending off an attack from an electric carving knife and is unable to respond. Necros forces the butler against a heated grill and struggles with the carving knife, sending catering instruments cascading in every direction. With an act of supreme effort the butler is able to hook his leg around the power cord connecting the electric knife to a wall socket, eventually cutting off its source of electricity. Infuriated, Necros forces the butler's face onto the grill, badly singeing him. Desperately, the butler kicks out in retaliation, sending Necros springing back into some shelves and flinging their contents onto the ground. The butler attempts to attack again, but Necros pitches him over a trolley facing the sink and tries to stab him in the back with a sharp knife. Kicking out again, the butler forces his assailant to drop the knife, but Necros is only momentarily disoriented and flings a pan of boiling water at the butler. The pan and hot liquid only narrowly miss their target. Getting the better of him in combat one more time, Necros subjects the butler to a series of rapid kicks, sending him flying backwards into a shelving unit full of towels. As they fall around him, the dazed butler has no time to react before Necros hits him over the head with a frying pan, finally knocking him unconscious. As the butler's walkie-talkie is still broadcasting the gatehouse security agent's request for confirmation, Necros answers it – with a very close approximation of the butler's voice. He tells the gatehouse operative that he has discovered that the building is currently affected by a gas leak, and that an urgent evacuation of the estate is necessary. Necros then picks up the butler's dropped pistol, putting his fallen adversary's walkie-talkie into his own jacket's inside pocket. He pauses only to collect his wire basket of milk bottles before moving on.

The gatehouse security operative puts out a signal to all personnel that the building must be evacuated immediately. Agents scramble to put the relevant procedures into place. Necros steps into an ornate dining area and, confronted by two agents, throws one of his milk bottles at them. The bottle contains an explosive cocktail, it soon transpires, and on impact with the floor it throws the men clear across the room with the resulting blast. From outside the building, the detonation seems – if anything – even more severe, adding weight to Necros's faked warnings of a gas leak. Sure enough, he radios the gatehouse again and warns of imminent danger from gas explosions, urging all staff to keep clear of the main building. Koskov and the government secretary, disturbed by all the commotion, turn a corner and spot Necros in the building. Alarmed, Koskov believes that the KGB is trying to recapture him and hurriedly retreats again, the secretary following close behind. Stopping to send another agent hurtling out of the way by flinging an explosive milk-bottle onto the house's stairs, Necros pursues Koskov into the drawing room. The General desperately pleads for his life. Unmoved, Necros finds the list that Koskov gave M and throws it onto the room's fire, then removes the cassette from the tape recorder that was used to detail the contents of Koskov's debriefing with M and Gray. Wasting no time, Necros ushers the two men out of the room at gunpoint. Heading back towards the kitchen, he throws a further milk-bottle towards the main entranceway of the building, causing another violent explosion and forcing personnel in the grounds to retreat further. A public announcement system warns all staff to stay clear of the building due to the string of violent disturbances.

The chef's parrot watches as a Red Cross helicopter suddenly arrives outside (in reality a Bell UH-1H Huey with the relevant decals), manoeuvring to land near the main building. When Koskov enquires as to its purpose, Necros knocks him unconscious. The secretary catches the Russian's prone form, and Necros warns the speechless government employee that if he doesn't carry the General where he orders then he will waste no time in murdering them both. Operatives on horseback watch from a distance as the helicopter circles the estate's grounds on its approach to land. In the kitchen, the secretary watches carefully as Necros removes his striped milkman's apron, revealing a white doctor's coat beneath. He then puts a stethoscope around his neck, completing the disguise. With greater urgency, he demands that the secretary moves out of the building with Koskov immediately. The parrot watches quizzically, toying with Necros's discarded apron as the men depart. The Red Cross helicopter now reaches the ground, a couple of stretcher-bearing paramedics jumping out as police vehicles and an Armed Forces Land Rover arrive at speed. Necros and the secretary, supporting the semi-conscious Koskov between them, place the Soviet onto the stretcher, where Necros secures him with a safely harness. The secretary looks on questioningly at these developments, but Necros signals for him to stay alongside. Koskov, now starting to regain some degree of consciousness, is alarmed at his predicament and tries to disentangle himself from the harness, but lacks the co-ordination to do so. Necros and the paramedics load the stretcher onto the helicopter and, closing the door behind them, waste no time in leaving the scene. Appearing slightly amazed that he is still alive, the secretary races away as the helicopter takes to the air again; it only just manages to retreat from the area as the emergency services – a fire engine and two ambulances – arrive by road.

The fast action and explosive nature of these sequences at the Blayden estate help to balance the expository nature of Koskov's revelations, and also aid in making his apparent detention by the KGB seem eminently more convincing to the British government. For a henchman in the Bondian tradition, the chameleonic Necros is marked out from the beginning as an oddly economical and often strangely bloodless villain: during the extraction mission he is only seen to make two clear kills (the milkman and the Blayden chef), and although given to the casual use of high explosives he ultimately spares the lives of the vast majority of the operatives that he comes across – even when an ample opportunity for murder had presented itself. Interestingly, he knocks out the butler when he had an abundant chance to kill him, and allows the government secretary to go free when common sense may otherwise have dictated that it may have been more prudent to bring the man aboard the Red Cross helicopter and then dispose of him later to avoid detection. The answer, perhaps, lies not in any particular altruism on Necros's part, but rather that it better suits his purpose (and Koskov's) to leave as many living witnesses as possible to attest that the apparent kidnapping was indeed a genuine one.

In M's office at MI6 headquarters in London, the head of the secret service is far from happy. During Necros's attack, he grimly advises, two people have been killed, a further two have had to be hospitalised, and Koskov's whereabouts are unknown: if the Russian is not back in Soviet territory, he may well have been executed as a traitor already. Gray, who is seated in one of M's guest chairs, is also infuriated; the reputation of Britain's intelligence services has been badly diminished by Koskov's capture by Soviet forces, particularly when it took place on British soil. MI6 were only able to hold the General for a matter of hours before he was taken back into KGB hands, and – of course – this leaves his lurid accusations of Pushkin's alleged megalomania unresolved. Gray is then forced to withdraw on account of an imminent meeting with the Prime Minister. Now that the two of them are alone in the office, M informs Bond that the government have ordered Pushkin to be assassinated as per Koskov's suggestion. As he confirms that Pushkin is set to arrive in Tangiers within two days' time, M hands Bond a dossier detailing the mission. But Bond has deep misgivings about the situation. He tells M that the *smiert spionam* plan seems implausible at best, and that its implementation feels very out of character for Pushkin, whom Bond has encountered in the past. A frustrated M replies that he arguably knows Pushkin even better than Bond does, having had professional contact with him more than once. But orders are orders nonetheless. Carefully, Bond suggests that though Pushkin is a robust and inventive spymaster, he cannot believe that the KGB director is given to psychopathic behaviour. M responds that until recently he would have been inclined to agree, but he has now discovered that Pushkin's complicity in the plot appears better grounded than they had realised. Reaching into his desk, he produces the clip and luggage tag that was found on the rope bound to 004 during the training mission in Gibraltar. While M explains its origin, Bond turns the label over and discovers the words 'smiert spionam' handwritten in marker pen. Grimly, M also reminds 007 that Bond's own name was on Koskov's list of targeted British spies. Bond informs M that he also intends to investigate Kara's identity, as the presence of the cellist on the night of Koskov's defection remains unexplained. Somewhat reproachfully, M tells Bond that he has read Saunders's report on the matter and is not impressed by Bond's deviation from his orders. Bond replies that the decision not to kill Kara was made on the spur of the moment; it would have felt wrong to murder an apparent innocent, even under the circumstances. M advises Bond that he will order 008 to report from Hong Kong to Tangiers instead; the other agent has had no prior contact with Pushkin and will thus act on his instructions rather than his gut instincts. Perhaps more forcefully than he had intended, Bond refuses M's interpretation of his position on the matter and assures him that he is more than capable of carrying out his orders. Opening the dossier, he reveals a glossy monochrome photograph of his intended assassination target: Leonid Pushkin (John Rhys-Davies).

Bond's relationship with M is sometimes a problematic one. M is not only Bond's superior, but had also formed something of a vaguely father-son relationship with the resourceful agent throughout the years. Although he usually seems reproving of Bond's unorthodox methods, occasionally (as in this case) threatening to replace Bond with another agent when he gets too emotionally entangled with a case or seems to have difficulty following orders, M also has high regard for Bond's competence in the field and respects his professional ability to get the job done at any cost. This film marked the third of Robert Brown's four appearances as the character, who had previously been portrayed by Bernard Lee. *The Living Daylights* also marked the final appearance in the series of Geoffrey Keen, who had played Sir Frederick Gray – the often-harried Minister of Defence – since the mid-seventies. Gray had been a recurring character in the *Bond* cycle since Lewis Gilbert's *The Spy Who Loved Me* in 1977.

Over at Q Branch, Q is in the process of winterising Bond's Aston Martin with a hard top (substituting the convertible soft top version seen earlier). He is supervising the installation from inside the car while a group of technicians slowly lower the new hard top into position. Bond enters the lab and greets Q, causing the eccentric technical expert to momentarily forget what he's doing and strike his head off the still-lowering car roof. But dedicated to his work as ever, the impact doesn't even slow Q down. Instead, he ushers Bond over to another part of his workshop and signals for a metal shield to be lowered into position over a section of the far wall. Q hands Bond a remote control keyring – the type that bleeps in response to a whistle, making it easy to find if mislaid. Bond tries it out and, seeming surprised by the device's apparent simplicity, hands it back to Q. But as always, nothing is quite as it seems at Q Branch. Q taps a button on top of the keyring to arm it and, explaining the function to Bond, lays the device on a table near the now-fully-extended metal shield. He throws Bond a gas-mask, tells him to wear it, and then does the same himself. Q then asks Bond to whistle the first few bars of 'Rule Britannia' – a task which necessitates Bond removing the gas mask that he has just put on. In response, the keyring emits a small cloud of gaseous vapour; Q informs him that it is a stun gas with a range of approximately five feet, which will affect anyone who comes in contact with it for around thirty seconds. Bond jokingly asks if it will explode if he whistles 'God Save the Queen', but Q doesn't see the humour in his observation – the keyring actually does contain a highly concentrated plastic explosive which, if detonated, will promptly deal with any safe door that it is attached to. It is also magnetic, a fact which Bond puts to the test by attaching it to the base of Q's gas-mask. Bemused, Q tells Bond that the explosive can only be set off by an activation signal – which, in the case of 007, is a wolf-whistle. To Q's alarm, Bond teasingly begins to purse his lips, as though to whistle, but is interrupted both by a shocked cry from Q and Miss Moneypenny knocking on a nearby safety glass partition to attract his attention. She signals to Bond that she wants to talk to him. Seeming relieved at the interruption, Q tells Bond that the keyring itself is not the only useful instrument to hand; the device also has a variety of masterkeys within it which are capable of opening 90% of the planet's locks. He extends the keys from the keyring to demonstrate. Handing the multi-purpose tool over to Bond, Q seems as exasperated as ever at the agent's glibness in response to this cutting-edge gadgetry. Removing his gas-mask as Bond moves to depart the lab through a sliding door, Q asks one of his technicians to take a seat on a nearby couch. Once the lab-coated man has done so, however, the seat and back of the couch roll around at a 180° angle, causing him to disappear beneath it with a startled exclamation. Seeming amused at the results of his new invention, Q then sits down on the couch himself – quite safely.

Bond's visits to Q Branch to collect mission-critical materials are another of the series' long-established staples, and most entries in the cycle involve at least one interaction between Bond and the unconventional technological expert. Desmond Llewelyn had played the character of Q, alias Major Boothroyd, since Terence Young's *From Russia with Love* in 1963 (the role had been briefly occupied by Peter Burton in 1962's *Dr No*), and developed a witty rapport with each actor to play Bond until the late nineties. If M was Bond's stern surrogate father, Q became more of an affable but eccentric uncle, and the two enjoyed sharp but good-natured banter throughout the cycle. Llewelyn's warmth and charm became just as instantly recognisable as his outlandish gadgets, though *The Living Daylights* – in line with the film's intention to return the series back to some semblance of realism – featured a rather modest range of contraptions in comparison to some of the more outlandish efforts on display throughout the Roger Moore years.

In the information area next to Q's workshop, Bond is ecstatic; the records section has sent over a newspaper cutting of a Czechoslovakian cellist who Bond instantly identifies from the night of the defection. Moneypenny explains that from the translated text of the article, the musician's name is Kara Milovy and, in spite of an unexplained arm injury that she sustained during an intermission at a recent recital (actually caused by her sniper rifle striking her forearm at speed when Bond shot it from her hands), she will soon be returning to the Bratislavan orchestra for a performance of Borodin's String Quartet No.2 in D. Realising that this will be taking place the following day, Bond quickly asks Moneypenny to book him passage to Tangier, via Czechoslovakia… and not to inform anyone of his travel plans. Realising that Bond clearly wants M to remain unaware of his activities (not for the first time in his career), Moneypenny teasingly notes that Bond must have a keen interest in this mysterious cellist given that he is willing to alter his mission plans to find out more about her. But Bond, never one to give away his intentions, only replies to the effect that his curiosity has more to do with work than play. Heading out of the room just as Q enters it, Bond tells the genial expert that he will be taking the Aston Martin out for a ride. Fearing for the car, given Bond's well-deserved reputation for pursuing missions that don't quite turn out as planned, Q tells him to drive cautiously for once – the bodywork has just been repainted. But his warnings, as ever, fall on deaf ears.

The next time that we see the Aston Martin (now actually a Vantage model, complete with the recently-fitted hard top), it is parked on a familiar street in Bratislava, directly across from the Conservatoire. Inside, Kara Milovy and another three musicians are rehearsing the same Borodin String Quartet that Moneypenny had mentioned from the newspaper article. Bond is among a scattering of other audience members present for the practice session. He notes how intent Kara remains on the music, always giving a totally professional performance. Some time later, she is emerging from the Conservatoire with a cello case in her hand. A member of the public holds open the door for her to exit more easily. Bond, who is pretending to read a nearby information board, immediately notices her departure and follows her. We then cut to a street tram, which – we soon discover – bears Kara as a passenger. She is situated at the rear of the vehicle, whereas Bond is midway along; both are standing due to a lack of available seating. The tram reaches an intersection, where a variety of police cars are clustered around an apartment block on a street corner. The carriage then reaches a standstill, and a plain-clothes operative wearing a black leather jacket gets on board. He wastes no time in heading towards Kara and, flashing the contents of an identification wallet at her, roughly bundles her off the tram. Bond, realising that she has left her cello behind, watches as the operative and some colleagues march Kara over to a parked car. Its door opens to reveal General Pushkin, who steps out onto the street beyond. By now the tram has started moving again, but Bond continues to look on as Pushkin guides Kara into his car, which then drives off.

Bond disembarks when the tram comes to a halt at a nearby station, carrying Kara's cello case with him as he does so. Spotting a nearby public toilet, he heads inside with the case, briefly startling the building's attendant (Leslie French). Bond locks himself into one of the lavatory stalls and opens up the cello's container, but is surprised to discover not the string instrument that he had expected but rather the sniper rifle that Kara had used on the night of Koskov's defection. He is further confused when he finds that the weapon has been loaded with blanks, which he briskly pockets. The toilet attendant looks on, confused at the strange noises coming from the stall, but is forced to disguise his curiosity when another member of the public enters the area. Searching the case further, Bond discovers an address card which bears the details of Kara's home as well as her telephone number.

Looking drained and exhausted, Kara is returning to her apartment. The street around her seems relatively quiet. Still seeming a bit shaken after her earlier ordeal, Kara reaches into her coat pocket and produces the keys to her apartment door. But as she lets herself in, an unmarked secret police car slowly coasts around the corner, parking directly across the street. Now inside her apartment, Kara reacts with shock when she discovers that it has been ransacked. Her possessions lie strewn around the room; clearly the KGB have been looking for something. Before she has had time to allow this information to sink in, Bond appears at the doorway. The cello case is in his hand. Surprised at the stranger's presence in her home, Kara looks at him enquiringly; in response, Bond simply tells her that he discovered the sniper rifle inside the case and has safely disposed of it in the river. Closing the door behind him, Bond remarks that whatever the KGB may have been looking for, they obviously had little respect for Kara's property. Confused by Bond's appearance out of the blue, Kara asks who he is – and what business an Englishman would have in her Bratislava apartment. Deliberately evasive, Bond replies that he heard her play at the Conservatoire and was impressed by her skill. He gathers up some sheet music which has been scattered across the floor and places it carefully on a music stand. Bond then tells Kara that he saw her being removed from the tram and taken into Soviet custody the previous day. He asks if they had taken her to KGB headquarters, to which Kara replies only that she had been released by the secret police that morning. Bond invites her to look out of her apartment window. Gently parting the net curtains, Kara sees the unmarked car across the street. Bond tells her that the KGB only released her in order to watch her actions. Taking a seat at Kara's table, which is strewn with various household items, Bond watches as the cellist eyes him suspiciously. Clearly apprehensive, Kara asks Bond why he should want to help her, but 007 remains guarded and answers with a question of his own: what was Pushkin's interest in her?

Bond ventures the possibility that her questioning had to do with Koskov's defection, placing a shattered frame containing a photo of the errant General onto the table (and thus precluding any denial from Kara that she is acquainted with him). Kara responds that Pushkin wanted to know of Koskov's current whereabouts but, when Bond enquires further, she denies that she gave Pushkin any information regarding the Russian's location. Producing the blank bullets from the rifle, Bond tells her that Koskov was very judicious to have used fake ammunition during the defection; British Intelligence had been convinced that he really was in danger of death from a sniper, and believed that the operation at the Conservatoire had indeed been genuine. Kara is puzzled at Bond's in-depth knowledge of the situation, and Bond emphasises that he is only aware of these details because Koskov had told him of the deception. Kara brightens when Bond mentions the General's name, and asks when he last saw him. Bond responds truthfully that he had last seen Koskov just two days previously, and adds that the Russian is safe and well. He is also honest when Kara asks if Bond and Koskov are friends, as he only replies that the two of them had 'been through a lot together'. Kara is overjoyed to hear of Koskov's survival, and tells Bond that the General had vowed to her that he would send for her after his defection. She asks Bond if he is there to take her to London, but he replies that Koskov is still being moved from place to place in an effort to maintain the security of his location. Instead, he says that it may be more prudent to see the General in Vienna instead – news which visibly delights Kara. Bond urges haste though; they must depart before the KGB decide to call her in again. Kara is confused as to Bond's chosen plan of action, but the agent remains tight-lipped, telling her only to pack some belongings and stressing that she should bring some warm clothing along. As she moves further into the apartment, Bond looks out of the window and notes that the unmarked KGB car has never moved from its stakeout position across the road.

Although this scene is largely expository, it is significant in a number of key ways. Perhaps most importantly, it begins to lay the foundations for a mutual attraction between Bond and Kara; their chemistry is subtle, but it is believable. Kara obviously believes that Bond presents her means of escape from the Eastern Bloc, much as Koskov had viewed him earlier but in a radically different way, and is more trusting of his intentions than may otherwise have been the case if his credentials as an intelligence insider – and Koskov's friend – were not so apparent. Yet there is also much pathos in Kara's obvious romantic affection for Koskov when his name is mentioned; although the scheming General had promised that he would have her taken care of, the reality of these words have an evident double meaning: it is becoming increasingly plain that Koskov had intended for an unwitting Bond to assassinate Kara during the defection to tie up any unfinished business, while the blank bullets ensured that she had no way of injuring Koskov himself if she had fired at him as planned.

The KGB driver, still in the car, is watching Kara's apartment block vigilantly. He notices Bond emerging from the front doorway with a black holdall, closing the door behind him as he goes. The driver keeps an eye on 007, who walks down the street towards his Aston Martin – which is parked further along the street – and lets himself in. Shortly after, Kara leaves her apartment in a red hat and overcoat, carrying her cello case. She moves towards a telephone kiosk which lies midway along the road between her apartment door and Bond's parked car. The driver watches carefully as she enters the kiosk with the case, closing the door behind her. A tram then rolls by, momentarily obscuring his line of sight. When it passes a few seconds later, Kara appears to still be in the kiosk, while Bond drives off in the Aston Martin. Believing that there is nothing strange about the situation, the driver seems satisfied that nothing untoward is going on.

Bond is now speeding through the streets of Bratislava, putting as much distance between himself and the KGB car as possible. Kara, who has been hiding in the footwell of the passenger side of the car, eases herself into the seat next to Bond. Relieved, Bond tells her they seem to have managed to get away from the Soviets while evading detection. But Kara is not so sanguine about the situation; she has just remembered that she has left her cello at the Conservatoire. Bond, intent on making a clean getaway, promises her that he will buy her a substitute when they arrive in Austria, but Kara is insistent – the instrument must be recovered. Bond is equally persistent, however; the ruse will only keep the KGB occupied for a short while, and then they will be pursued relentlessly. But his warnings, no matter how adamant, are disregarded by Kara.

Looking pensive and perturbed in equal measure, Bond waits in the driver's seat while his Aston Martin is parked outside the Conservatoire once again. Moments later, Kara arrives with her cello (in an alternative black case, as opposed to the white one that had been used to transport the sniper rifle). Hurriedly, Bond flips forward the passenger seat to allow Kara to store the case across the car's back seats. Now with an air of increasing urgency, Bond asks her why she couldn't have played a more conveniently-stored string instrument like the violin instead. He performs a fast U-turn and tears off along the streets of Bratislava. Meanwhile, back at Kara's flat, the suspicious KGB driver is heading for the telephone kiosk, where he soon discovers that Kara has placed her hat and coat around the white cello case to make it look, from a distance, as though she herself had been standing there.

The Aston Martin is now being driven along a snowy mountain road. Bond activates the automatic scan function on the car's radio, and the unit immediately begins to skim through various different frequencies before it settles on the channel used by the Czechoslovakian police services. When Kara remarks about it in surprise, Bond feigns innocence and smoothly tells her that it must simply be an atmospheric glitch of some kind. He turns the volume up, and Kara tells Bond by way of translation that the police have issued an alert for a man and a woman driving in a foreign car. Bond wryly points out that they forgot to mention the cello in the back seat. Just after he points this out, a police car on the other side of the road spots the Aston Martin and executes a brisk handbrake turn. Looking over his shoulder through the rear window, Bond tells Kara that it looks as though the police search is over already. Through the rear view mirror, we can see the police car accelerating towards the Aston Martin. Bond flips open a retractable lid which has been covering a multi-function control panel next to the car's gear stick. As he does so, the police car pulls alongside and its driver signals to Bond to slow to a halt. Bond gestures back pleasantly, but as he does so the wheel hub of the front passenger-side wheel suddenly stops in mid-motion (while the wheel itself continues to turn). As the Czechoslovakian policeman calls out to Bond, in heavily-accented English, to pull over to the side of the road, a laser emits from the Aston Martin's wheel hub and slices into the underside of the police car. As Bond begins to decelerate (albeit only slightly), the laser cuts across the entire length of the police vehicle. Inside their car, the two policemen react with alarm as acrid smoke rises from beneath their feet. The driver then slams on the brakes, only for the main body of the car to fly off into the road ahead, independent of its chassis. Kara's eyes widen at the strange display. Frustrated, the two policemen – their severed car now completely immobile – watch as the Aston Martin speeds away from them. Amazed, Kara asks Bond what had happened to the other car, to which the agent replies dryly that it must have been the result of salt corrosion on the vehicle's bodywork.

Continuing to accelerate along the wintry road, the car's radio continues to broadcast the police frequency. Kara tells Bond that the police are now in the process of setting up road blocks. Sure enough, we then cut to an (apparently commandeered) heavy goods lorry being reversed into position across a further stretch of road with the intention of making it impassable to traffic in any direction. The area is full of frantic police activity, and numerous police cars are also nearby. The Aston Martin is heading right towards their position, and Bond takes a deep breath. As he nears the road block, a group of policemen (some armed) flag down the car to halt its progress. Bond, however, clearly has no intention of doing so. He hits another button on his control panel, and an onscreen digital display appears on the windscreen. Kara is again astonished at the car's technical sophistication, but Bond offhandedly tells her that he has had the vehicle fitted with some discretionary customised additions here and there. A crosshair begins to centre upon the lorry parked across the road ahead, and two of the Aston Martin's indicator lights – just beneath the main headlights – flip open to reveal a small rocket launcher on either side of the car. Seeing that Bond clearly has no intention of stopping, the policemen break ranks and scatter to either side of the road in order to avoid being run over. The crosshair now fully lined up, Bond fires the rockets, which tear into the lorry and explode violently. He then drives straight through the fiery debris, revealing – as the car emerges on the other side – that the rockets have effectively torn the lorry clean in half.

As his colleagues regain their bearings, a policeman begins firing a machine gun at the rapidly-disappearing Aston Martin, but to no avail. Bond's car heads into a road tunnel, the policemen scrambling into their own surviving vehicles to give chase. The Aston Martin soon emerges from the other end of the tunnel, where another (more modest) police roadblock has been set up. Bond dodges around other parked police vehicles to evade the blockade, and again a police officer fires a machine gun at the retreating car. This officer has a significantly better aim than his colleague, and bullets from his gun impact violently on the rear window of the Aston Martin. But they prove unable to penetrate it, due to bulletproof glass having been installed. Once more, Kara observes the car's exceptional durability in awe, but Bond ascribes the window's resilience to new safely glass. As he makes his quip, he only narrowly manages to avoid a collision with a Soviet tank which – much to his shock – has just appeared on the road ahead. He desperately steers the Aston Martin off-road, though he is pursued by the tank as well as a snowmobile which is occupied by a group of heavily-armed soldiers. The tank's main turret fires, blasting a rocket at the Aston Martin but narrowly missing its intended target. Bond and Kara look shaken at their close call. The snowmobile gives chase as the Aston Martin hurtles past a wooden lodge. Bond hurriedly hands a map to Kara and asks where their current trajectory will take them. Kara anxiously responds that the trail leads to only one destination – a frozen lake. Bond looks uncertain about his next course of action, but determined to improvise. As the car approaches the lake, a fisherman is unloading an outboard motor next to a wooden fishing shack. But rather than slowing down, Bond just keeps going. Kara screams as the Aston Martin slams straight into the shack, leaving the hapless fisherman watching in astonishment as the entire building – resting on top of the car – flies out onto the frozen lake at high speed. Fortunately for Bond and Kara, the ice seems solid enough to support their speeding vehicle. The snowmobile arrives at the edge of the lake, and the soldiers on board seem similarly nonplussed at the mysteriously mobile fishing hut out on the lake. They begin to fire machine guns and explosives at the moving shack, but are unable to score a clean hit. Inside the Aston Martin, Bond decides that their luck will soon run out and accelerates sharply, leaving the rickety shed behind them... mere moments before it explodes on contact with a Soviet rocket.

As the soldiers continue to fire indiscriminately towards Bond's fleeing car, a police vehicle ventures out onto the ice to give chase. One explosion from a Soviet projectile weapon tears off the Aston Martin's front passenger-side tyre, causing the metal rim of the wheel to cut into the ice. His vehicle now unbalanced, Bond sweeps around the pursuing police car, cutting through the ice with the sharp metal wheel rim. When his work is done, a large frozen circle of ice has been cut around the police car's position, leaving both it and its inhabitants stranded. As the police officers desperately climb onto the roof of their car to avoid being plunged into the freezing waters, Bond hits a button marked 'outrigger' on his control pad, causing two motorised skis to extract themselves from either side of the Aston Martin. He then pushes another switch, which produces metal spikes on the car's remaining tyres. Kara cries out as another police car accelerates towards them; the officer on the passenger side of the pursuing vehicle fires intently at Bond's car with a handgun. Bond then accelerates again, the Aston Martin now handling with greater proficiency on the ice.

Soviet troop transports are arriving on the far edge of the lake, where a considerable array of military hardware – including armoured tanks – is rapidly assembling. With nowhere else left to go, Bond continues to head in their direction. He deftly hits a 'rocket motor' button on his control panel which causes a large exhaust port to open up behind the car's rear licence plate. Telling Kara to hang on for dear life, he hits the motor's ignition, which causes the car to accelerate sharply as it hits a concrete ramp. The ramp's gradient, combined with the sudden increase in speed, allows the Aston Martin to fly straight over the Soviet blockade. Even in spite of frenzied firing from the soldiers' automatic weapons, the car still manages to land on the far side of the assembled troopers and their vehicles. The pursuing police car attempts to follow Bond's lead, but as it has only a fraction of the Aston Martin's velocity it ends up crashing into a wooden guard hut instead.

Buffeted by foliage and unable to slow down safely, Bond is unable to steer the Aston Martin down the hill, eventually leading to the car becoming hopelessly stuck in a snow drift. The Soviets, however, are giving chase – and they are not far behind. Bond rapidly gets out of the car, assisting Kara to do likewise. He pauses only to retrieve the cello from the back seat and then, urging Kara to head off, hits the car's self-destruct switch. Armed troopers on skis are in hot pursuit, firing at the absconding Bond at point-blank range. He is only just able to stumble over the heavy bank of snow to join Kara in a race to safety. The troopers, on spotting the deserted car, slow down momentarily... but are then disoriented when the self-destruct mechanism kicks in, causing the car to explode into a fireball. Hearing the explosion, Bond dryly tells Kara that he has decided that he is now actually quite pleased that they brought along her cello after all. She seems puzzled by the comment.

The troop carrier continues to trail Bond and Kara, though its driver is struggling to steer it through the wintry terrain. The soldiers on board are vigilantly searching for any sign of their two targets. Kara and Bond, however, are currently seated inside the cello case, which has been converted into a kind of makeshift two-person sledge. Bond uses the cello itself to manoeuvre a path through the snow. As they pick up speed, the Soviets spot them and begin to fire. However, due to the case's velocity the pursuers are unable to pinpoint the escapees accurately with their weapons. Shortly after, the troop carrier is joined by more armed ski troopers, who emerge from a wooded area in chase of Bond and Kara. Bond waves the cello in an attempt to distract their firing, leading to a bullet raking through the wooden instrument. Meekly, he apologises to Kara, but points out that a customs checkpoint is nearby – they have almost succeeded in crossing the border into Austria. Sure enough, further down the hill two Austrian passport officials are watching in surprise as the rapidly-approaching cello case is being pursued by an increasing number of Soviet personnel and military vehicles. Bond briskly passes his passport to Kara and asks her to wave it at the checkpoint operatives as they pass. Then telling her to duck – as he does so himself – beneath the checkpoint barrier (throwing the cello over it and catching the instrument as it falls), Bond knows that they have only just made it: the Soviets, with no jurisdiction in Austria, cannot proceed beyond the checkpoint. Hugely relieved, as the cello case continues to skid along the snow Bond tells the customs officials that he and Kara have nothing to declare – except, as Kara adds archly, her cello. They then slide off into the sunset, passing a large, colourful 'Welcome to Austria' sign as they do so.

No *Bond* film would be complete without a high-octane chase sequence, and after the abundance of explanatory dialogue at Kara's apartment this series of ostentatious set-pieces – drawing the film's first act to a close – increases the narrative's sense of momentum once more. As *The Living Daylights* boasts fewer flamboyant gadgets than the average entry in the series, this sequence also allows for a showcase of Bond's heavily armed (and armoured) Aston Martin, which is by far the most visually prominent of Q's contraptions to feature throughout the film. (Its later destruction by Bond was, of course, knowingly foreshadowed by Q's warning to handle the car gently on account of its new coat of paint.) The sequence's wintry ambience is also highly effective as a counterpoint to much of the film's later action scenes, which would largely take place on desert terrain and in arid environments. The dialogic interplay between Kara and 007 during their race through the frozen Czechoslovakian countryside is additionally interesting, not least in the way that the knowing banter emphasises just how much less comfortable Timothy Dalton seems with Bond's customary one-liners than he is with the film's grittier dramatic elements.

We next move to a panoramic establishment shot of the Moroccan city of Tangier. A superimposed caption alerts the audience as to the new location. A call to prayer can be heard from a minaret as the camera pans across the sprawling vista. Some unobtrusive-looking black cars are being driven along a road, coming to a stop outside a large guarded residence. High up on another building nearby, hidden inside a pigeon loft, a concealed camera is taking shots of the car's passengers as they emerge. Several pigeons are milling around nearby. One of the passengers to step from of the car is none other than General Leonid Pushkin. A security operative in a dark suit opens one of the vehicle's rear doors to let Pushkin out onto the street. Cutting back to the hidden camera, the sound of a data transmission stream can be heard as the shot slowly zooms in on a yacht which is cruising in the distance, just off the coast.

Pushkin is being shown into a hallway which is lavishly decorated in a North African style. A trim young man dressed in a U.S. Army uniform bearing sergeant's stripes (Derek Hoxby) asks Pushkin to wait for a moment while he informs his employer of the General's arrival. (We are later to discover, however, that this 'sergeant' is not a real non-commissioned officer, nor indeed does he belong to any country's armed service – he is simply Mr Stagg, Whitaker's private employee.) As the man strides off along the hallway, Pushkin is bemused to discover that the room has been lined with life-sized mannequins dressed in various different military regalia. The costumes span several centuries, from classical antiquity up to recent history, and feature generals and dictators from societies from all over the globe. Yet the face of each model is exactly the same. As Pushkin studies, with some distaste, an Adolf Hitler model featuring an identical countenance to all the others, one of the figures in the historical line-up suddenly steps forward – but unlike the mannequins, this is the genuine article. Wearing a U.S. Army Major's uniform, the man introduces himself as Brad Whitaker (Joe Don Baker), and pumps Pushkin's hand vigorously. The Soviet General looks deeply unimpressed by his host. Whitaker asks whether Koskov is accompanying Pushkin, to which the latter replies somewhat aloofly in the negative. The fast-talking American then invites Pushkin further into his hall of fame, boasting proudly that armed conflict has always been humanity's principal preoccupation. He asks Pushkin for his opinion on the military leaders which surround him (all of whom, from Napoleon Bonaparte to Genghis Khan, look exactly like Whitaker himself), to which the General – with obvious disdain – responds that each of the tyrants are 'butchers'. But Whitaker disagrees, describing them admiringly as 'surgeons' due to their role in excising the dead meat of society. Pushkin's contempt for the remark is palpable.

Stopping only to order his 'sergeant' to stand at ease, Whitaker ushers Pushkin into his museum of warfare. An exquisitely detailed scale model of the Battle of Waterloo is one of the room's centrepieces, but the entire area is replete with rare curiosities. Whitaker proudly points out items such as the first automatic machine gun, and a model of a battle during the British Empire's occupation of Afghanistan in the late nineteenth century. Noting that the Soviets are now the occupiers of that same country, Whitaker suggests that Pushkin and his allies require the same kind of quantum leap in weapons technology as the early machine gun had once represented. (Here, the overbearing arms dealer sets a precedent for giving slightly inaccurate information, subtly undermining his pretentions towards being a military historian. He stipulates that the British had first deployed a machine gun in 1895 when, in actual fact, the Maxim had been used in the field some time before then and was in Army hands since 1888.) Using a remote control, Whitaker opens a series of motorised drawers around his Waterloo model, revealing sample models of highly advanced machine pistols with laser-sighting scopes and long-range miniature missiles with the capability of penetrating all known forms of armour. The order, he states, can be ready for dispatch in next to no time, but – much to his apparent surprise – Pushkin coldly tells him that he is cancelling it, and expects the deposit payment of $50 million U.S. Dollars to be refunded to the Soviet authorities within two days. Whitaker blusters that he has had to pull out all the stops to illegally obtain such sophisticated weapons technology, and has had to bribe top people in both Europe and the United States, but Pushkin knows that he is lying: he tells Whitaker that the KGB have been monitoring his Swiss bank account, and the money from the deposit has been resting untouched for two months. Therefore, no such illegal payments have actually been made to anyone. Unabashed at the transparency of his deceit, Whitaker nonetheless asserts that he can't cancel such a large order at such short notice. Whitaker assures Pushkin that they share a military code of honour, but the KGB director is utterly apathetic towards the American's protests – he derisively points out that Whitaker has never been a serving officer in any army, having been given a dishonourable discharge from West Point due to cheating and then working briefly as a mercenary in the Belgian Congo. Whitaker seems to be getting hot under the collar at Pushkin's withering – but presumably accurate – assessment. The General then tells Whitaker that it was only by working for the criminal underground that he was able to raise enough funds to begin financing arms deals of his own, leading the humiliated con-man to state (wholly unconvincingly) that these are merely malicious untruths that have been circulated by his rivals. Whitaker affirms that he has already supplied many weapons to the U.S.S.R. via previous deals with Koskov, thus proving his reliability in this capacity, but Pushkin is rapidly losing his patience. The General demands repayment within 48 hours, as previously stated, or else the KGB will deal with Whitaker and his business interests harshly. Pushkin adds that this is also true for Koskov; he is certain that the two of them are involved in some kind of nefarious conspiracy, and thus he is determined to end their plans before they even have a chance to begin.

The introduction of Whitaker, the second of the film's joint antagonists, establishes much about the character: his blustering martial pretensions, obsession with military hardware, and an unvarnished bloodlust in spite of having never experienced real field combat. Situating Whitaker's residence in Tangier – necessitating Pushkin's interaction with him there – throws further doubt on Koskov's far-fetched story that Pushkin is in Morocco to kick-start his *smiert spionam* operation, making it seem ever clearer that both the KGB and British Intelligence are being drawn into Koskov's elaborate network of misinformation. The scenes also emphasise Pushkin's disparagement towards the kind of sadistic brutality that Whitaker so obviously lionises, encouraging the audience to side with Bond's assessment of Pushkin's character rather than Koskov's depiction of his superior as a power-mad despot who is ready and willing to trigger a bloodbath within the intelligence community even at the risk of starting a nuclear conflict.

Back in Austria, a goods truck pulls over to the side of the road, allowing Bond to jump out. Clearly the ever-resourceful agent has been engaging in some hitch-hiking since his snow-bound escape from Czechoslovakia. He helps Kara down from amongst several wooden crates of vegetables, though only after she has handed him her cello first. As Bond waves in thanks to the truck's driver, the camera pans around to reveal the famous Wiener Prater, establishing that they are now in Vienna. Bond calls for a taxi, and we next see him and Kara when they are seated in the back of a horse-drawn carriage, looking at the sights of the city. Several men in ceremonial uniforms pass by on horseback, heading in the opposite direction. As the carriage turns down an autumnal avenue, Kara remarks that Vienna is just as picturesque as Koskov had always told her. Bond enquiringly mentions that the Russian must mean a lot to her, to which she responds that Koskov has given her so much – not only was he responsible for arranging her scholarship at the Bratislava Conservatoire, but he also bought her notorious cello, a famous Stradivarius called the 'Lady Rose'. Bond looks stunned when he realises the rarity of the instrument, especially when she tells him that Koskov had acquired it in New York. 007 tells her that such an obviously costly purchase must have been some gift indeed. Kara says that her ambition is to one day play at Carnegie Hall, to which Bond replies that he has absolutely no doubt that she has the talent and aptitude to do so. Keen to see Koskov again, Kara asks if they are heading to meet with him now. Bond responds that this will depend on whether Koskov has had to be moved on by MI6 for his safety, adding shrewdly that he hopes the General will have left a message if this is the case.

High on a balcony, a group of musicians are playing a Strauss piece while down on a plaza several well-dressed couples are dancing a waltz. The horse-drawn carriage passes by, and Kara looks enraptured by this archetypal Viennese scene. Shortly after, the carriage pulls up at a hotel, the Palais Schwarzenberg, where a uniformed concierge opens the vehicle's door to allow Bond to step down on the street. Kara grabs hold of her cello from the driver, passing it to Bond before she disembarks to join him. Bond thanks the driver, tipping him, before urging the concierge to handle the cello carefully as he hands it over. The concierge makes the same plea to a hotel assistant as he passes the instrument on. Bond then walks into a splendidly-appointed hotel lobby – which Kara eyes with ill-disguised awe – and heads to the check-in desk. A receptionist (Heinz Winter) recognises Bond from previous visits and welcomes him back, asking if he will require his usual accommodation. Bond says that on this occasion, two separate rooms will be necessary, but does agree to his customary Vodka Martini being prepared by room service – provided, of course, that it is delivered 'shaken, not stirred'. Satisfied by the arrangements, Bond heads for the reception's courtesy telephone and dials an unseen number. The voice on the other end of the line crisply responds 'Universal Exports'. Bond asks for two tickets to be reserved for the Vienna Opera House, and to be made available for collection at the box-office. The voice on the phone confirms Bond's request, and then promptly hangs up. During his call, Kara has gravitated over to a small boutique, where she is eyeing up a beautiful but expensive-looking dress. Bond asks her if she likes it, to which she responds enthusiastically in the affirmative; at first Kara thinks that he is joking about purchasing it, but when she realises that he is being serious she asks him who would be paying for such an exorbitant item. The answer, Bond believes, is simple: who else but her lover, Georgi Koskov.

Dalton and d'Abo both make good use of these scenes to further establish the developing attraction between their two characters. Kara's wide-eyed enthusiasm for scenic Vienna is a delight to behold, while Bond's consideration for her feelings – never giving away his suspicions surrounding Koskov's apparent treachery, for instance – is underscored by his gentlemanly insistence that they have separate rooms at the Palais Schwarz-enberg. Clearly this is not the callous, philandering playboy spy of urban legend, and he clearly views Kara with a respect not usually afforded to Bond's traditional 'conquests'. This change in Bond's social attitudes does suggest that while Glen's intention was to return the character to his Fleming-inspired roots, he and screenwriters Wilson and Maibaum were also aware of a need to update 007's awareness of changing cultural mores so as to make him appear a more rounded and believable individual within a 1980s setting. Yet not for the first time, Bond also seems puzzled by Koskov's behaviour when he learns that the Russian was willing to go to some length – and expense – to win Kara's affections, only to have now inexplicably cast her aside. This further deepens the mystery of the inscrutable General and his internecine scheming.

At Whitaker's compound in Tangier, a reclining Koskov is enjoying the attentions of several beautiful women as he lounges at the end of an expansive swimming pool. The athletic Necros, having dived into the pool, is dipping through the water close by. Unlike the General, he seems unmoved by the wide array of stunning females sunbathing nearby. Koskov's pleasures are interrupted by the arrival of Whitaker's 'sergeant', who tells him that his presence has been requested. Koskov grudgingly gets up and dons a bath-robe and slippers, pausing only to embrace one of the bikini-clad women... and then jokingly pitching her into the swimming pool by surprise. Fortunately, she seems to see the humorous intent of his actions, as do her companions. Seeing Koskov moving to leave, Necros swims to the side of the pool and is informed that Whitaker has asked them to report.

The arms dealer, meanwhile, is tucking into a lobster at an extremely well-stocked table covered with food, situated not far from the pool area. Unlike Koskov and Necros, who are in beachwear, the stiff-necked Whitaker remains in his officer's uniform. The 'sergeant' snaps to attention, announcing the arrival of Whitaker's associates, and is then briskly dismissed. Wearily, Whitaker tells Koskov that the Russians want their arms deposit returned, but Koskov unctuously replies that there is no need for him to be concerned. He is confident that he has hoodwinked MI6 into believing that Pushkin is a threat to world peace, and that they will send an assassin – most likely Bond himself – to eliminate him. But Whitaker's fears are not remotely alleviated. He suggests that Necros should make the kill instead, thus avoiding any difficulties that may otherwise arise if the British did not believe Koskov's version of events. Necros is reluctant to comply, pointing out that he has worked with the Soviets before and is unwilling to risk being identified in case it should endanger his efforts – and those of his unnamed terrorist associates – in bringing about global revolution. (His accent, ever changeable, now seems to have turned vaguely East European.) But Whitaker reminds the assassin that it is he who has been supplying arms to Necros's comrades; if their professional relationship should end, they will inevitably have difficulty in sourcing a new reserve of weapons. Keen to pour oil on troubled waters, the wily Koskov again assures Whitaker that everything will go according to plan. Whitaker is still deeply sceptical, pointing out that Bond has had an opportunity to murder Pushkin ever since the KGB chief arrived in Tangier and, as yet, has not done so. Koskov notes that British Intelligence tends to approach such situations cautiously, but that they may be encouraged to act more urgently if further persuasion is applied. He suggests murdering another British agent in the same manner as 004 was eliminated at Gibraltar, thus spurring retaliatory action. By no means convinced, Whitaker says that he will only go ahead with Koskov's plan to a point – if Pushkin is still alive at the end of the conference, Necros must take action to avoid any possibility of the Russian spymaster returning home alive.

Here, Koskov's collusion with Whitaker finally becomes explicit, and their business dealings start to come into focus. Koskov's urging of the British authorities to remove Pushkin from the intelligence world can now be seen for what it is – not motivated by a need to maintain the balance of power, but to ensure that he does not interfere with Whitaker's vastly expensive weapons deal to arm the Soviets who are occupying Afghanistan.

The reason for Koskov's desire to ensure that Whitaker's arms dealing is a success is not yet clear, but his treachery does of course vindicate the suspicions of both Bond and Pushkin. Necros, who masterminded Koskov's extraction from Blayden, is naturally also revealed to be in league with both Koskov and Whitaker, though his allegiance to a rather nebulous-sounding anarchist organisation – which is reliant on Whitaker to provide their cause with arms – seems to be what is really underpinning his loyalty. The scene also emphasises that while Kara remains longingly committed to her lover, Koskov is clearly spending little time reciprocating her affections as he cavorts with beautiful women at Whitaker's poolside.

At the Opera House in Vienna, Bond and Kara are watching a scene from Mozart's *Cosi Fan Tutti*. The auditorium is packed with impeccably-dressed patrons. Kara is clearly enthralled by the lavish performance, and Bond momentarily leans over to share a whispered joke with her. As she laughs, the camera pans over to the balcony, where Saunders is seated. The fellow agent is watching Bond silently, his expression pensive. He raises his programme, signalling to Bond, and 007 responds wordlessly. Shortly after, the operatic scene comes to an end and the stage curtain drops, triggering a standing ovation from many of the audience members – including Kara – as the intermission begins. She tells Bond that she has always dreamt of attending a performance here, to which the agent responds that perhaps she may one day play there herself. Believing that such an ambition is too grand to ever realise, Kara excuses herself and heads out of the auditorium just as Saunders arrives, heading straight for Bond's position. Deeply confused by Kara's presence, recognising her from the defection mission in Bratislava, Saunders asks Bond exactly why he has brought a KGB sniper to Vienna. Bond replies that she is Koskov's romantic partner, not an assassin, and that he hopes to learn more about the wayward Russian General by posing as a friend of Koskov. Saunders is incredulous at the news that Kara had been instructed to fire blanks at Koskov: if his defection had been staged then why did the KGB go to such effort to apprehend him in England so soon afterwards? Bond is resolute in his belief that Koskov has deceived MI6, but Saunders is more concerned at the indiscretion of his colleague's course of action. However, Bond's suspicions will not be appeased; he tells Saunders about Koskov's purchase of the rare cello that he later gifted to Kara, and is keen to know where he had sourced sufficient funds to buy such an exorbitantly expensive item. Time is of the essence, though – Bond impresses on Saunders the need to have this information before the night is over, as he will need to move Kara on from Vienna the following day. He also passes on a strip of passport-sized photos of Kara to aid in Saunders's search (and, as we later find out, to have a passport produced to allow her to travel internationally). Saunders is reluctant to assist, telling Bond that there is no way that he will be able to receive confirmation from London to make these enquiries in time, but Bond presses the point, insisting that Kara is the only lead they have in the search for Koskov – and, more importantly, unravelling the Russian's murky schemes. As a bell rings to signal the end of the intermission, Saunders finally relents, sensing that Bond's urgency is genuine. Admitting (albeit with heavy irony) that he has comparatively little to lose as a result of his assistance, he tells Bond that he will gather the required information and rendezvous with 007 at the Prater Cafe, near Vienna's famous Ferris wheel, at midnight. Saunders then makes a swift getaway to avoid any chance of raising Kara's suspicions, leaving the auditorium just as she returns.

We cut to a wide-angle shot of the famous Wiener Prater amusement park at night, taken from a rollercoaster carriage. We then see that Bond and Kara are on the rollercoaster as it speeds along its track. Kara seems exhilarated at the experience; Bond puts his arm around her supportively as the carriage continues along its trajectory. We then see the couple on a waltzer ride, and then in a dodgem car, before joining Bond as he takes aim through an air-rifle at a fairground shooting game. The attendant gently pleads with Bond to stop with his current target, suggesting that Bond's legendary aim has won him some prizes already, and Kara chooses a large stuffed elephant toy as the reward for this particular round. The attendant passes the toy to Bond, who then hands it to Kara with an amused glance. Next, they walk past the exterior of a ghost train, where a model of a ghoulish figure suddenly illuminates, momentarily scaring Kara. She throws her arms around Bond, who seems far from uncomfortable at her proximity. Suddenly aware of her closeness to Bond, Kara seems vaguely awkward, but not embarrassed. Smiling, she asks him to take her onto the Ferris wheel, and they move away together.

Next, there is an establishment shot of the famous Viennese Ferris wheel. Loud fairground music can be heard all around. Looking agitated as ever, Saunders arrives just to see Bond and Kara inside one of the wheel's carriages as it ascends into the air. Bond turns off the light, telling Kara that this will allow her to enjoy the view more effectively. Back on the ground, Saunders looks exasperated, knowing only too well Bond's reputation for womanising. Bond looks down and sees Saunders waiting impatiently. A helium balloon seller passes Saunders and, in German, offers to sell him one of his wares. Brusquely, Saunders refuses, but as he brushes past we see that the seller is in fact Necros – once again in disguise. Bond watches the exchange from the carriage, but – having had no personal contact with Necros, whose features are obscured by the balloons in any case – he finds nothing unusual in it. Enchanted, Kara asks Bond if the whole experience is really just a dream. They move closer. Meanwhile, Saunders is striding indignantly towards the Prater Cafe, and is admitted through a sliding door. As he heads for the service counter, the Pretender's song 'Where Has Everybody Gone' can be heard for the first time since the Blayden sequence, signifying the fact that Necros can't be too far away.

The Ferris wheel suddenly stops with Bond and Kara's carriage at the very apex of its journey. Kara is startled and, fearing a mechanical breakdown, asks Bond what is going on. Slickly, Bond replies that this temporary standstill had been organised by him – perhaps they will be there for some time. Bond gently casts aside the stuffed toy that rests between them and puts his arms around Kara, inviting an embrace. But Kara, though clearly attracted to Bond, is forced to reject his advances. She tells him that no relationship can be achievable between the two of them... but also admits that ever since she met Bond, her mind has been racing with possibilities questioning what kind of couple they would make. Gently convincing her that sometimes it's better not too think too much about a situation, Bond guides her to sit with him on one of the carriage's seats, and they share a kiss. She offers no protest as they rest back against the toy elephant, which seems never to be too far away.

Down at the Prater Cafe, Necros is waiting outside as he quietly keeps watch on Saunders. The nervy section chief is sitting alone at the service bar with a hot beverage. Still in black tie, the British agent seems rather overdressed in comparison to the other diners there. Wearily, he takes a sip from his cup as he waits for Bond. He is unaware that the Ferris wheel carriage has now returned to the ground; the surrounding queue who are awaiting their own tour on the wheel react with amusement at Bond and Kara, who are so engrossed in their passionate embrace that they seem oblivious to the fact that their fairground journey is over. Not unkindly, the Ferris wheel operator (Hanno Pöschl) asks Bond if he intends to wait for the carriage to make another revolution. Bond and Kara take his comment in good spirit as they retrieve the ever-present stuffed elephant and leave the carriage. Back at the cafe, however, Saunders is starting to look agitated, looking over his shoulder as soon as anyone enters through the main door. Bond and Kara saunter past a tourist goods stall, where Kara stops to admire a wire frame full of colourful postcards. Bond tells her that he must go for a few moments, just to check if there are any messages for him to collect.

Still clutching her cuddly toy, Kara watches his departure

with a little trepidation, as though feeling less safe when he has gone. Bond finally heads into the Prater Cafe, unaware that Necros is watching his every move from close by. As Bond enters through the automatic door, Necros activates a remote control device built into his personal stereo. Bond moves to sit beside Saunders at the service bar, and Necros flicks a switch on his control which puts an electronic mechanism into action within a gear-box near the cafe's doorway. Saunders is telling Bond that according to his investigations, Kara's Stradivarius cello was bought recently at a New York auction house; it had cost $150,000, but had not been purchased by Koskov – the successful bidder was a man named Brad Whitaker. Bond instantly recognises the name: Whitaker's reputation as an arms dealer goes before him. He wonders aloud what kind of business relationship could exist between Koskov and Whitaker, and asks Saunders where Whitaker is currently located. When Saunders answers that he is based in Tangier, Bond seems to make an immediate mental connection – after all, that is where he has been ordered to assassinate Pushkin. Thoughtful, 007 thanks his colleague for his support. Reaching inside a folded newspaper next to Saunders, Bond retrieves a passport – presumably brought with Kara in mind – and quickly pockets it. Shaking his colleague's hand with sincerity, Saunders wishes Bond good luck on his mission. As he heads for the exit, however, Necros is ready with his remote control and activates it just as Saunders steps through the automatic doorway. A wider shot makes it apparent that Necros's device is linked to modifications that he has made to the sliding door's control mechanism. Instantly, the door smashes into Saunders at high speed, killing him instantly. This causes a major commotion in the area, with people rushing around to ascertain what has happened. The cafe owner (Gertan Klauber) is so shocked that he drops the plate that he is carrying and rushes, with Bond, to the door. Kara watches with concern as a crowd pushes past her, running towards the cafe. Next to the shattered glass of the door, Bond grimly inspects the corpse of his fallen comrade. As he does so, he notices a blue balloon floating nearby, which comes to rest near Saunders's leg. Grabbing hold of it, Bond sees that the balloon has the words '*smiert spionam*' written on it in black marker pen. Outraged, Bond bursts the balloon in anger. He spots two balloons floating just above the top of a nearby hedge, and immediately springs into action. Racing away from the cafe, he runs alongside the balloons, almost knocking over Kara as she heads towards him in the opposite direction. Confused, she asks Bond where he's going, but Bond is too intent on his target to answer. Hoping to intercept the assassin, Bond jumps over an iron gate, his Walther PPK instantly in his hand. But he is faced with a little boy holding some balloons (Gregor Grubhofer) and his frightened mother (Suzy Herman) who, at the sight of the gun-wielding agent, hurries off with her son in tow. Bond sheepishly returns the pistol to its holster without delay. He looks around his position, but realises that Necros must already have fled the area. Kara finally catches up with Bond and again asks him what is happening. Bond, still shaken at Saunders's fate, tells her that he has just witnessed a nasty accident at the cafe. Remembering that Bond had told her that he was there to check for a message, Kara asks if he had heard any news of Koskov. Bitterly, Bond replies that he had no difficulty discovering what the Russian had to say to him. Kara enquires as to her lover's current whereabouts, and Bond replies that the General is currently in Tangier – with Brad Whitaker. When Kara recognises Whitaker's name, Bond is surprised and asks how she knows of him. Kara replies that Koskov had always spoken highly of Whitaker, who she describes as a 'patron of the arts'. Bond's scorn at her belief in the arms dealer's benign intentions could not be more blatant. When she questions at what point they should rejoin Koskov, Bond responds that they must leave without any further delay. Kara seems disappointed, clearly enjoying her time in Vienna, and asks if it wouldn't be possible for the two of them to spend a few more days together. But Bond coldly tells her that this is out of the question, pulling her away into the night. Kara is bewildered at Bond's sudden aloofness towards her.

These final scenes in Vienna are effective in charting Bond's growing fondness for Kara, and her explicit reciprocation of his feelings. Although she remains loyal to Koskov, she also cannot deny an attraction to Bond, and the conflict in her affections is made explicit during her interactions with 007 on the Ferris wheel – both verbal and physical. But the sequence also develops Saunders's character, somewhat rehabilitating his earlier appearance as a priggish, hidebound pedant: his eventual willingness to help Bond in his investigations signifies that he has begun to recognise that sometimes just following orders is an insufficient method of getting the job done. By realising that Bond is actually on to something, Saunders is willing to forgo his usual reliance on the rule-book, putting his own neck on the line in order to circumvent his own superiors and source the relevant facts for Bond, thus aiding in 007's unorthodox mission. By agreeing to assist Bond at the Opera House, the irony of Saunders's off-the-cuff comment that he has 'nothing to lose but his pension' ultimately presages his death, but the genial camaraderie between the two agents at the Prater Cafe seems far removed from their earlier bickering during the defection in Bratislava. Necros's assassination of Saunders is also interesting; again, he has more than sufficient opportunity to bring about mass carnage, and yet is satisfied to claim the life of his single intended victim. Though it could be argued that the isolated murder had been deliberately planned to further deceive British Intelligence (the *smiert spionam* angle having less of an impact if multiple casualties had been claimed), Bond is clearly furious at the death of his fellow agent, especially given that Koskov's deception – and outright malignity – are becoming ever more apparent. Realising that Saunders's demise may never have come about if Bond had not specifically asked him for help, thus making him a target, the mission suddenly appears to have become more personal for 007.

We then cut to a busy street scene in Tangier, complete with bustling crowds and even some camels in transit. Bond is hiding behind a newspaper in the driver's seat of a car. He lowers it to get a better look at his surroundings. Attached to the windscreen is a green sticker which bears the words 'Trade Conference Press'. The undercover Bond is surreptitiously keeping an eye on dignitaries leaving a conference centre across the road from his current position as they depart in a range of expensive cars. His viewpoint is obscured by the sudden arrival of a traditional Moroccan dance troupe; unable to persuade them to move on, he quickly gives them a monetary donation which succeeds in dispersing them. As they do so, he spots Pushkin and some associates getting into a chauffeur-driven Mercedes-Benz Pullmann outside the building. Bond quickly starts the engine of his own car – an Audi 100 Avant – and gives chase at a safe distance. Although the road is lined with Moroccan soldiers, his press pass appears to give him sufficient clearance to manoeuvre through the area at will. The streets beyond are narrow and packed with people, but Bond is still able to pursue Pushkin's vehicle without attracting undue attention. Eventually, the Russian's car disappears through the grand gates of the Hotel Ile De France, an impressive building. Bond stops outside a restaurant on the other side of the street and dons a pair of sophisticated-looking spectacles. Although they superficially look like a set of optician's lens testers, these glasses are actually miniature binoculars; switching to Bond's point of view, we can see the distant Pushkin warmly embracing his personal assistant, the glamorous Rubavitch (Virginia Hey), as the car drops her off at the hotel. Bond smiles to himself as Pushkin gets back into the car, clearly sensing a plan of action.

That night, a KGB security operative is lighting up a cigarette as he leans against Pushkin's Pullmann limousine outside the hotel. He looks across as a group of guests leave the main entrance of the building. The camera then pans up to better establish the upmarket hotel's exterior, before cutting to an interior shot of a hallway within. A couple are waiting patiently for an elevator to arrive on the floor, which it does a few moments later. Stepping out of the elevator carriage are Pushkin, looking rather upbeat, and a KGB minder (Alan Talbot) who is carrying a bunch of flowers and a small wicker basket of treats. Suddenly no-nonsense, Pushkin turns to the minder and – without a word – takes possession of the gifts that are in his hands. He then strides along the corridor to room 17, while the minder remains vigilant in the hallway nearby. Pushkin raps gently on the door, while the minder takes a seat on a guest couch across from the room. When there is no response, Pushkin looks puzzled and tries the door's handle, which is unlocked. Curious, he enters to discover Rubavitch sitting at a small dining table, set for two. Her expression is apprehensive in the extreme. Pushkin is concerned and asks why she appears so nervous, but while his attention is focused on his beautiful companion he is momentarily distracted from the room's door gently closing behind him. Pushkin turns to see Bond pointing his silenced pistol directly at him. He immediately recognises the British agent. Without looking around, Bond locks the door behind him and orders Pushkin to move towards the table without making any other unexpected motions. Pushkin does as he is told, stretching out his arms (while still holding his gifts for Rubavitch) as Bond quickly frisks his clothing for concealed weapons. Walking to the table with the utmost care, and never taking his eyes from Pushkin for a moment, Bond pulls out a dining chair and asks the KGB chief to sit down. When he does so, however, Bond violently tips him backwards onto the room's king-size bed which lies behind it. Startled, Rubavitch moves to assist Pushkin, but Bond immediately trains his handgun on her. Requiring no more persuasion, she returns to her seat. Deeply mystified, yet not daring to move from the bed, Pushkin tells Bond that he presumes that their meeting has been motivated more by business than pleasure. Bond responds in the affirmative, telling the General that his choice of flowers was ill-advised – he should have bought lilies instead. When Pushkin asks Bond the purpose behind his aggressive actions, Bond replies 'smiert spionam', which causes the General to react with mild amazement. He tells Bond that he is referring to ancient history; the *smiert spionam* operation had been ordered by Lavrenti Beria during the Stalin years of the Soviet Union, but has been shut down since the 1960s. Bond looks unconvinced, and tells Pushkin that two British agents are dead as a result of this so-called ancient history. Still baffled, Pushkin responds – with some irony – that while he mourns Bond's loss, the KGB had no part in the demise of his colleagues. Rubavitch is beginning to look restive, glancing around as though searching for an opportunity to escape. Bond starts to look as though he is taking Pushkin's account at face value. Still not lowering his gun, he enquires as to the location of Koskov. The General replies that his errant subordinate disappeared without a trace two weeks previously. At any rate, he adds, he was on the verge of having Koskov apprehended due to his misuse of state funds. When Bond probes the issue further, Pushkin irritably tells him that it is a matter of Soviet security and that he is not at liberty to discuss it any further. Surreptitiously, he moves his hand over to a wristwatch on his opposite wrist, furtively pressing its adjustment dial which triggers an alarm. Immediately hearing the watch bleeping, Bond moves over to discover the source. Angered by Pushkin's action in summoning help, he tells the General that he has acted foolishly and frustratedly punches him in the stomach.

As Pushkin is recoiling in pain, the KGB minder in the hall is responding to the signal that has been transmitted by Pushkin's watch. In Rubavitch's room, Bond tears the personal assistant's bathrobe off – much to her distress. Outside the room, the minder has now drawn a handgun of his own and is attempting to answer Pushkin's summons. Discovering that the door is locked, he forces it open by ramming it with his shoulder. As he enters the room, he is momentarily startled by the sight of the topless Rubavitch who is directly facing him. This transitory distraction is the only opening that Bond needs to attack the unwitting minder, pistol-whipping him into unconsciousness. Without skipping a beat, his gun is again trained on Pushkin and Rubavitch. Bond closes the door once again and then throws Rubavitch her bathrobe, telling her to go into the en-suite bathroom and lock the door behind her. Alarmed at the violence of Bond's actions, she needs no second bidding to do as he asks.

Once Rubavitch has departed, Bond – who still has his handgun pointed unwaveringly at Pushkin – demands that the Russian remain in his current position on the bed. Pushkin is cradling his abdomen, clearly still suffering the ill effects of Bond's earlier assault. Bond then tells him to get onto his knees on the floor. Now looking genuinely concerned for the first time since their encounter began, Pushkin does as he is told. Bond then demands that Pushkin put his hands behind his back. As he does so, Pushkin asks why Bond would want to kill him – he knows that the British agent is a consummate professional, who would only kill because of a reasonable motivation. Bond responds coldly that two of his fellow operatives are dead because of Pushkin – according to Koskov's testimony, at least. The increasingly agitated Pushkin assures him that he is just as oblivious to the facts behind the death of 004 and Saunders as Bond is. The KGB director tells Bond that there is only one way to break this stalemate: he must ask himself whether he trusts Koskov's accusations, or Pushkin's denial. Bond replies that if he had believed Koskov's story, Pushkin would be unable to even ask that question on account of the fact that he would already be dead. But, he adds, there is no way of knowing what Koskov is really planning as long as Pushkin remains alive. In that case, Pushkin replies with conviction, it is clearly necessary that his own life must be traded for Koskov's secrets.

Few sequences in *The Living Daylights* illustrate the darker, more ruthless nature of Dalton's Bond than this one. Whereas the Moore films had portrayed a largely convivial relationship between 007 and General Anatol Gogol, the head of the KGB, Bond's direct confrontation with Pushkin is stark, succinct and often outright brutal. Not only does he physically assault the high-ranking Russian spymaster, but for a time it really does seem as though Bond is entirely willing to take the Soviet's life – even although his doubts surrounding Koskov's story had been well established by this point. His forced stripping of Rubavitch to distract the attention of a KGB minder, much to her obvious distress, also seems much more bleakly vicious than anything that had appeared in the Roger Moore entries in the series, and forms an interesting counterpoint to the courtesy and consideration with which Bond has treated Kara. If anything in the film emphasised just how far Eon Productions were willing to go to realign the cinematic Bond with the cold professionalism and complex morality of Ian Fleming's literary character, these scenes were the clearest possible example of their artistic intentions.

At the conference centre the next day, a lavish banquet is being enjoyed by a selection of gathered delegates. A master of ceremonies (Richard Cubison) introduces Pushkin and invites him to address the conference. Pushkin rises from his chair, where he is seated next to Rubavitch, to appreciative applause from the other delegates around him. High on a balcony, while Pushkin enjoys the positive reception of his peers, we become aware that Necros has knocked one of the building's lighting technicians unconscious and is currently training a large lamp onto Pushkin's location. The KGB chief is now at the podium, and issuing warm greetings from the U.S.S.R. to all who are in attendance. Necros unzips his jacket and produces a handgun, taking aim at Pushkin as he stands on the stage. Before he can fire, however, several shots ring out from the other side of the room. Amid screams from the audience, Pushkin staggers backwards, three bullet-holes clearly visible on the breast of his suit jacket. Necros is momentarily startled at this turn of events, but quickly recovers and trains the lamp on the press gallery, where Bond can clearly be seen with his Walther PPK drawn. Although he immediately shoots the bulb out of Necros's lamp, Bond's location is now obvious to the Moroccan authorities. Wasting no time, he shoves past several confused reporters in his haste to escape from his balcony location. On the other side of the room, Necros is removing his jacket, revealing a grey lounge suit beneath.

Total chaos is breaking out in the main conference area. Pushkin's bloodied body lies prone behind the podium while delegates scramble to leave the room. Quickly holstering his gun, Bond is heading up a flight of stairs, leaving the other guests watching his hasty departure with surprise. Back on the stage, Rubavitch is inconsolable, crying in obvious grief as a KGB operative pulls her away from Pushkin's location before she can get too close to him. Several armed security officers are now in hot pursuit of Bond, who is still tearing up flight after flight of stairs. At the conference centre's main door, a Moroccan security chief (Nadim Sawalha) is ordering the building sealed, allowing no-one to enter or leave until the assassin has been apprehended. Bond emerges on the centre's roof, where he locks the access doorway behind him. Urgently looking around, he runs off across the top of other adjacent buildings, ploughing headlong into several lines of laundry as he does so. This proves to be a fortuitous course of action, as seconds later the pursuing security officers break through the access door and begin firing indiscriminately in all directions with machine guns. The drying laundry provides Bond with a few seconds of cover, which he uses to jump onto a large broadcast aerial and swing over onto the roof of another building close by. The Moroccan authorities on the ground watch in shock as Bond makes the daring jump and then releases the aerial, which springs back to hit one of the pursuing security men, knocking him to the ground. His colleague then immediately spots Bond and begins firing with a pistol, though his aim is insufficient to hit the fleeing agent. Bond jumps off the edge of the roof and runs along the top of another nearby building, attracting the attention of other armed officers who then begin firing at his location.

A number of bathing women watch in surprise as Bond races along the roof above their location on an elevated area. Not even stopping to acknowledge their presence, Bond then makes a difficult jump up onto another rooftop area, where he fights his way through more laundry lines while simultaneously being set upon by a woman who is still in the process of putting her washing out to dry. As Bond fights his way around her heavy wicker laundry basket, another security officer – still on top of the lofty conference centre – is hurriedly making a report into his walkie-talkie as he traces Bond's rapid escape across the city's rooftops. But 007 appears to have evaded his pursuers' attention, at least temporarily, as he picks up his pace without the sound of gunfire echoing after him.

Back in the centre, Pushkin's body is being stretchered away from the main conference area while the distraught Rubavitch follows on. Several press photographers are rapidly taking snapshots of the fallen KGB director, and – between the delegates, security staff and Russian operatives – the situation seems chaotic. Watching from nearby, Necros looks carefully at Pushkin as the stretchered body passes him in the corridor. He seems thoughtful. The two dark-suited KGB staff who are bearing the stretcher pass through a doorway into a private area, where they lay their superior's prone body on the floor. They then quietly withdraw, closing the door's curtains behind them in order to leave Rubavitch to grieve privately. As soon as they have gone, however, Pushkin's eyes snap open. Blood still seeping from the edges of his mouth, he sits up and looks around matter-of-factly, much to the amazement of his incredulous personal assistant.

Bond is weaving his way through a busy Tangier market-place, when his progress is spotted by two women (Catherine Rabett and Dulice Liecier) watching from a red Chevrolet Impala convertible. Bond continues along the street for a moment until he spots a cluster of armed officers who are obviously still searching for him. He ducks into a tourist shop, stealthily stealing a pair of dark sunglasses, when the red sports car smoothly pulls up alongside his location. One of the women asks Bond if he is 'looking for a party'. Seeing the means for a fast getaway, Bond concurs with enthusiasm and jumps into the convertible with them. Meanwhile, at the conference centre Pushkin is struggling out of a bulletproof vest which has been festooned with bags of fake blood concealed beneath his shirt. Apologising to Rubavitch for having distressed her by not informing her of his simulated assassination (presumably her genuine grief aided in maintaining the deception), Pushkin ruefully admits that this has been the first occasion in his life where he has been thankful that Bond's infamous accuracy with a handgun has such a well-deserved reputation.

These sequences are useful in emphasising the scale and double-edged nature of Koskov's chicanery. Bond's insistence to M that Pushkin was of good character is vindicated by his collaboration with the Soviet General, their alliance proving to be an effective bulwark against a common threat. Pushkin's improvised 'assassination' not only persuades Koskov and Whitaker that MI6 had taken Koskov's fabricated testimony seriously, but also underscores the fact that Whitaker's own suspicions concerning Koskov's slickly-delivered assurances had won out in the end – Necros had indeed been dispatched to murder Pushkin if Bond had not done so. Also of interest is Pushkin's admission that the Soviet authorities had lost track of Koskov more than a week before his hoax defection, which of course also highlights the point that his 'recovery' by the U.S.S.R. had been equally bogus.

As has been widely noted by many commentators, Bond's escape through Tangier was originally intended to have been a much lengthier sequence, including some humorous touches such as a 'magic carpet' ride over the rooftops (where Bond throws a mat over some wires and then climbs onto it in order to slide from building to building, briefly simulating a flying rug in midair) and a cameo from well-known motorbike stunt performer Eddie Kidd in disguise as a goods trader. Whether for reasons of timing or the fact that the visual comedy of these incidents would almost certainly have jarred badly with the surrounding scenes, the sequences were ultimately cut from the film when it went on cinematic release, though some of the excised footage has since been made available by Eon Productions on subsequent DVD releases.

In the front passenger seat of the Chevrolet, Bond asks the woman in the driver's seat to drop him off in the street that they are currently passing through. Pulling out his wallet, he makes it clear that he intends to recompense them for the inconvenience. In response, the driver's friend – in the back seat – withdraws a pistol and jams it into Bond's neck. Unruffled, Bond tells her that if his monetary offer was not generous enough, she should feel free to help herself to the entire wallet. But with a tight smile, the woman makes it clear that cash is not her objective. As a bewildered Bond returns the wallet to his jacket, she frisks his upper body, retrieving the Walther PPK. Bond looks mildly intrigued as she tells him to relax and enjoy the journey.

Eventually, the convertible pulls up at a busy dock. The wharf is bustling with shipping workers and various members of the public milling around a range of docked ships. A stylish modern yacht is moored nearby. (The ship is recognisable as the one which was earlier sailing offshore – while receiving footage from the hidden camera in the pigeon loft across from Whitaker's compound – during earlier scenes in Tangier.) Bond is ushered out of the car and directed towards the yacht; the woman from the back seat of the Chevrolet is following him closely, her gun covered by a cloth to avoid unwanted attention. He is then led onto the ship's deserted bridge, where he is directed downwards into a lower cabin. There, surrounded by cutting-edge electronic surveillance equipment, is Bond's old friend Felix Leiter (John Terry), a long-standing colleague from the CIA. Obviously curious about Bond's recent incendiary actions, a bemused Leiter asks what his friend's intentions are. But Bond replies with another question – what exactly is the CIA's interest in his current mission? The two women, now revealed to be Leiter's colleagues, withdraw on good terms with Bond, their search-and-retrieve mission successfully accomplished.

THE
LIVING DAYLIGHTS

This page and over from The Living Daylights (1987)

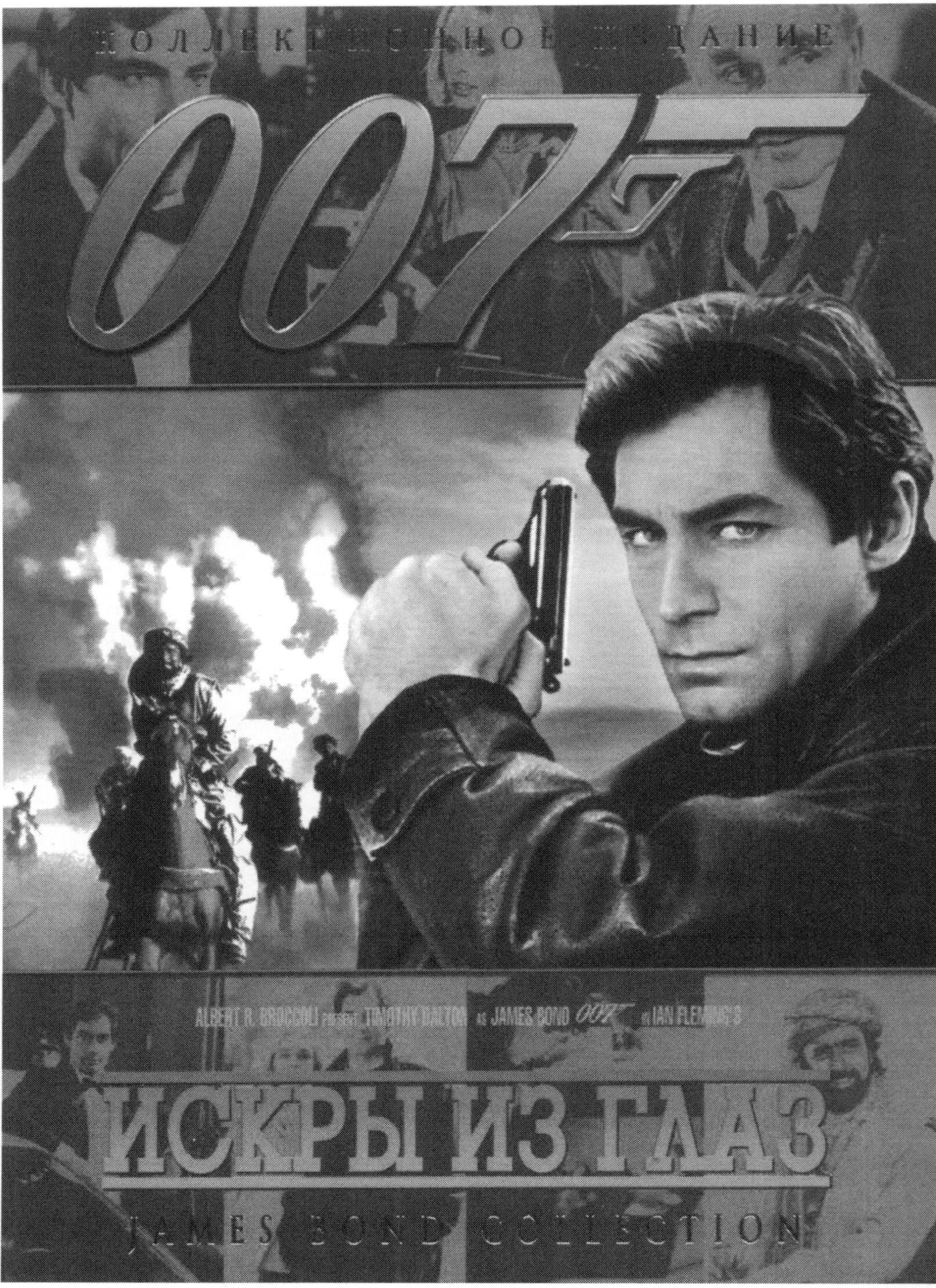
007
ИСКРЫ ИЗ ГЛАЗ
JAMES BOND COLLECTION

As Leiter closes the door to the cabin, Bond confesses that rumours of Pushkin's death will eventually prove to have been greatly exaggerated. Grumpily returning Bond's Walther PPK, Leiter seems annoyed at having been left out of the loop – and hoodwinked by his MI6 counterpart's trickery into the bargain. When Bond enquires about all the surveillance monitors, Leiter explains that the CIA have been keeping a close eye on Pushkin ever since he had met with Whitaker at his Tangier compound a few days beforehand. Bond asks if Pushkin has been instigating a secret arms deal with Whitaker, but Leiter explains that the situation remains puzzling – although Whitaker has sourced a few samples of the hi-tech weapons systems that are on offer, he has yet to order the large quantities that the Russians would require for combat. Even more attentive than usual, Bond tells Leiter that it seems as though their respective investigations – though at face value very different – should prove to have more common ground than might at first appear to be the case. He suggests that the two of them would benefit from comparing notes.

James Bond's onscreen friendship with Felix Leiter has lasted as long as the Eon film series itself. From his first appearance in *Dr No* (1962), the CIA agent has proven to be a stalwart support to Bond during his missions, and shares both Bond's dry wit and deadly proficiency. Their close camaraderie parallels the strong relationship which existed between British and American intelligence services during the Cold War, with both agents providing cooperation and key aid to one another during many films in the cycle including *Goldfinger* (1964), *Thunderball* (1965), *Diamonds Are Forever* (1971) and *Live and Let Die* (1973). Although Leiter's appearance in *The Living Daylights* is a comparatively brief one, amounting to little more than an extended cameo, this was to change dramatically for the next film in the series, *Licence to Kill*, where Bond's personal relationship with Leiter and his wife sparks the errand of vengeance which would underpin the feature's entire narrative.

At Whitaker's compound, the arms dealer and a well-dressed

Koskov are sitting cordially on a couch sharing a drink when the 'sergeant' arrives – with his requisite salute – to announce the return of Necros. Whitaker is elated to see the assassin return, given the news of Pushkin's 'demise'. Koskov embraces Necros warmly and congratulates him, the news of his successful mission having been heard on the radio news. But Necros informs them that Pushkin had died as a result of Bond's actions, not his own. Whitaker looks stunned, but Koskov is ecstatic, gleefully telling them that he always knew that the British would take his falsified story at face value. While the smug Koskov remains in a self-congratulatory mood, Whitaker's cordless telephone is ringing. It is answered by the 'sergeant', who speaks to an unheard caller on the other end of the line. Whitaker, pleased with developments, tells Necros and Koskov that in the wake of Pushkin's death he will now send word to Amsterdam so that they can begin moving 'the diamonds'. The 'sergeant' passes the phone to Whitaker, who answers it in typically gregarious fashion. However, on hearing the voice of the caller (still unknown to the audience), he quickly starts to look displeased. Briskly, he proffers the handset to Koskov – his expression far from happy – and tells the General that he has a call. Koskov initially seems quizzical but, upon speaking into the phone, immediately looks anxious as soon as the caller's identity becomes apparent to him. Nervously, he begins to finger his collar in apprehension.

A night shot of the Tangier coastline pans over to the sprawling city as the sound of Kara's cello playing can be heard. We then cut to a nicely-decorated apartment, where Bond is letting himself in through the door. Kara, wearing a dressing gown, is deep in concentration on the far side of the room as she reads music from a stand while playing a challenging piece on her instrument. (The battered case, seemingly none the worse for its use as a defection getaway vehicle, stands nearby.) As Bond closes the door behind him, the sound startles Kara, who springs to her feet. Seeming worried at his absence, she asks him why he has been gone for so long – and where, in fact, he has been. Bond deflects her questions, though not unkindly. As Kara lays down her cello, Bond tells her that he has heard nothing from Koskov. He assures her that she should feel free to keep on playing, but instead she stiffly suggests that they have a drink together. Bond appears confused at the sudden formality of her manner. Kara moves across to a nearby table and begins to mix a drink in a metal shaker. Bond is impressed that she had recalled his preference for his vodka martini to be shaken and not stirred. He proposes a toast to the two of them as he takes the glass from her, but as their respective glasses make contact Kara's expression seems inscrutable. She responds to his toast in her own language, then seems eager to know if she had mixed the drink to Bond's satisfaction. He answers that he has no complaints but, noticing again her new sense of remoteness, asks her why her manner has changed. When Kara offers no reply, Bond admits to her that he has not been entirely honest with her as regards his identity and motives. The contempt in her expression is impossible to conceal.

Bond tells Kara that not only is he no friend of Koskov's, but that he is working for British Intelligence to investigate her lover's dealings, adding that Koskov has not only betrayed the United Kingdom but also his own government, and even Kara herself. He adds that if British Intelligence had acted upon the tip-off that Koskov had given MI6 during his defection, Kara would have been killed on the assumption that she was a KGB sniper; her murder had been Koskov's intention all along, given that she could attest to the false nature of his flight to the West from the Soviet Union. Kara seems momentarily thoughtful at Bond's words, then rounds on him angrily. Accusing him of a campaign of deceit, she tells him that she has recently spoken with Koskov after phoning Whitaker's residence, and that the General had told her 'the truth' about the situation. Koskov has convinced Kara that Bond is in fact an undercover KGB agent who is using her in order to track the Russian down and assassinate him. Bond vehemently insists that it is Koskov who is lying, not him, but as he does so he suddenly discovers that he is becoming woozy.

Realising (too late) that Kara has spiked his drink with chloryl hydrate, and continuing to feel disoriented, Bond pushes Kara onto a couch near the table and pulls at the arm of her dressing gown. Kara shouts out in alarm, believing that the delirious Bond intends to attack her. Bond succeeds in tearing the fabric of her sleeve, exposing the wound on her forearm caused by his shot at her rifle back at the Bratislava Conservatoire. Fighting unconsciousness, he tells Kara that he can prove that he is with British Intelligence because he knows that she had suffered the injury at his own hand – he was the agent sent to kill her that night. Suddenly troubled by the credibility of Bond's account, she desperately asks him why he hadn't carried out his orders, but the agent is now slumped against the table and barely able to stay awake. Necros enters the room, dressed in a medic's tunic, and Bond struggles to pull his Walther PPK from his holster. Unable to focus on the assassin, however, Bond finally pitches over onto the carpet, having lost his battle against the knockout drug. As Kara eyes the prone Bond with growing concern, the truth of his words obviously beginning to play on her mind, Koskov enters the room after Necros, a white lab coat draped over his usual sharp suit. Praising her performance, he kisses Kara tenderly (if briefly) and passes a black medical bag to her, emphasising that time is of the essence. As he does so, Necros is hurriedly wheeling a stretcher into the room.

Early the next morning, a Red Crescent ambulance is speeding out of a Moroccan airport terminal towards a Russian cargo plane. A variety of security personnel halt the progress of the ambulance and shepherd Necros out of the driver's seat. Koskov, still dressed as a medical doctor, also leaves the vehicle and walks around to join Necros. The officers subject the front of the ambulance to a visual inspection before opening the side entry hatch. Inside, Kara – now dressed as a nurse – is tending to the still-unconscious Bond, who is lying on a stretcher surrounded by medical equipment. Standing prominently in front of them is a large organ transplant transportation box. One of the officers checks Bond's ID, and finds a Soviet passport (complete with identification photo) in the name of 'Jerzy Bondov', with a 1986-96 validity period. It bears an official U.S.S.R. stamp. The security officer thanks Koskov and returns Bond's 'passport' to the General. As he leaves, however, one of his colleagues approaches the organ transport box, which makes Koskov appear suddenly edgy. The other security man demands that the box be opened, and Koskov signals to Necros to do as he is asked. Within the box is a beating heart, packed with ice and surrounded by electronic monitoring equipment. Koskov warns him not to touch the organ, as it must be kept germ-free prior to the transplant operation taking place. Squeamish at the sight of the bloody organ, the officer withdraws, telling them that they are now free to go. Koskov jumps in beside Kara, while Necros closes the ambulance's sliding side door and returns to the driver's seat. He then drives the ambulance onto the cargo plane, Koskov's ruse to leave the country successful.

As the film now reaches the conclusion of its second act, Koskov's labyrinthine scheming is finally coming into focus. With Pushkin presumed dead, Whitaker's sudden eagerness to start transporting diamonds purchased from Amsterdam (itself a subtle reference to 1971's *Diamonds Are Forever*) sets up the last, as-yet-undescribed element of Koskov's outlandish plot, which in turn will eventually clarify all of his previous, seemingly-inexplicable actions – not least his attempts to convince the British to assassinate his KGB superior. But these sequences are also significant in the way that they continue to flesh out the complicated relationship between Kara and Bond. Although Kara had not been seen since Bond's arrival in Tangier, her actions in contacting Koskov and Whitaker unwittingly sets in motion the third act of the film, and the hurt at her palpable sense of betrayal – when she believes that Bond has been lying all along – quickly turns to trepidation when she realises, at the last moment, that it is her lover who has actually been deceiving her. The depth of her anger at Bond's assumed treachery, and indeed her later discomfort at Koskov's embrace, further emphasise the strength of her growing feelings for 007, and the intensity of her emotional attachment to him even when reunited with her Russian partner.

The Soviet cargo plane (actually a Transport Allianz C-160 Transall) is in flight over a large expanse of ocean. Moving to an interior shot of the plane's passenger area, Bond remains unconscious in one of the seats, Kara sleeping nearby across the aisle. Necros, who is sitting next to the organ transplant box – vigilant as ever – gets up and checks to make sure that Bond is still unresponsive. We then see that Bond's wrists are restrained by a set of handcuffs, securing him to the aircraft's seating in the event of his recovery. Satisfied with the situation, Necros withdraws through an internal doorway to an onboard lavatory. It then becomes apparent that Bond has been faking his apparent unconsciousness, as he opens his eyes and turns around as soon as Necros has retreated to a safe distance. Bond reaches across the aisle and, stretching out his arm, struggles to unclip the lid of the organ transport box. However, as his movements are restricted by the handcuffs, he can only reach the safety clip on one side. But as he fights to open it, another pair of hands appear from nearby to release the clip on the other side of the box – it is Kara, seeming both anxious and contrite. She tells Bond that she now realises how wrong she was about Koskov, but the agent holds her hand in mutual understanding, assuring her that she is certainly not the first person to have been fooled by the devious Russian – he has likewise been lied to as part of the General's internecine machinations. Bond asks Kara to open the lid for him – he is unable to reach it himself – and she recoils in shock when she sees the beating heart within. But Bond quickly reassures her that there is no need to worry; the heart is not human in origin, but instead belongs to an animal of some kind. As the plane's overhead lights shine on the interior of the box, however, Bond and Kara are both stunned when they realise that Koskov has hidden diamonds amongst the ice – the characteristic shimmer of the precious stones is unmistakeable. A toilet can be heard flushing in the near distance, and Bond realises that Necros's return is imminent. Kara urges him to tell her how he may assist her, and Bond responds hurriedly that she must get his keyring to him as soon as possible. Necros returns to the seating area, and Bond realises to his alarm that one of the transplant box's clips hasn't been closed properly. He feigns disorientation, draping himself over the arm of his chair and groaning, in order to distract Necros. When the assassin moves to shove Bond back into a sitting position, Bond surreptitiously signals to Kara, urging her to close the clip properly. She understands his meaning at the last moment and does as he asks, missing Necros's gaze by only seconds. Necros seems mildly suspicious, but – back in her seat before he could notice her actions – Kara merely smiles at him from behind a magazine. Appearing unconcerned, Necros then heads into the plane's cockpit, where Koskov – now dressed in a Soviet General's uniform – can briefly be glimpsed.

Later, the cargo plane is flying past mountainous terrain. Koskov emerges from the cockpit, copious medals and other decorations shining from where they hang on his uniform jacket. Genially, he asks Kara to make Bond a cup of black coffee to aid in reviving him. Smiling as she passes him to head for the beverage-making facilities, Koskov remarks patronisingly that she is a woman of many talents. Bond, however, seeks to cut through the pleasantries and asks Koskov why he has been allowed to live. The very picture of conceited satisfaction, Koskov takes the window seat beside Bond and tells him that he intends to turn the British agent over to the KGB so that he can stand trial for the assassination of Pushkin. Bond cannot help but be impressed by Koskov's affrontery – having murdered the KGB chief due to the falsified briefing (or so Koskov believes, at least), Bond is now to be apprehended while Koskov takes the credit for 007's capture. Genuinely curious, Bond then enquires exactly what Koskov expects in return for handing him over to the Soviets – immunity from prosecution, or permission to emigrate out of the Eastern Bloc. After all, he adds, they are unlikely to forgive the betrayal of Koskov's defection. Sneeringly, Koskov replies that as far as the Russians are concerned there has, in fact, been no defection to answer for: he will simply convince the authorities that Pushkin had ordered him on a covert mission to feed false information to the British government. After all, Pushkin is no longer alive to vouch for the story. He tells Bond that although he has admittedly become fond of the British agent, friendship counts for nothing when duty calls. But Bond subtly responds to the effect that Koskov's silver-tongued demeanour can't disguise a common confidence trickster. Kara smiles secretly at Bond as she passes him his promised cup of coffee.

This expository scene, coupled with the earlier discovery of the smuggled diamonds, further develops the endgame of Koskov's plan. While the presence of the precious stones was presaged by Whitaker's seemingly off-the-cuff comment following Pushkin's assassination, the intrigue is now being built around what purpose they will eventually serve. Meanwhile, the mystery surrounding Bond's continued existence is also explained; Koskov intends to use 007 as a bargaining chip on returning to his paymasters in the U.S.S.R. (There is a hidden irony here too, in that *Bond* films have become famous for their villains often concocting vastly complex methods of dispatching Bond when far more direct means of execution would be eminently more convenient. On this occasion, Bond's continued survival is actually of benefit to the antagonist.) Although Kara's loyalties have once again switched to Bond, they both know that her survival depends on Koskov – or, more immediately, his fate at the hands of the Russian authorities. With her exchange of allegiances back to Bond's cause, Kara also proves herself to be much more adaptable and self-determined than the rather misogynistic Koskov would ever have given her credit for. Although he treats her with condescending fondness, Kara appears deeply uncomfortable around Koskov, and she (along with the audience) already appears to be anticipating the inevitable betrayal that is to come. But while Koskov appears entirely assured about the security of his future, Bond alone knows that General Pushkin's clandestine survival may yet have a part to play in the disruption of Koskov's schemes at a later point.

The cargo plane is coming in to land at a Soviet military base in Afghanistan; a tracking shot taken from an air traffic control tower follows the aircraft as it heads for a runway. The plane taxis to a standstill, several Russian troops standing to attention as it approaches the complex which lies just beyond the runway. Koskov is putting a peaked uniform cap onto his head, telling Kara to join him as Necros retrieves the still-handcuffed Bond. While a technical crew are heading towards the plane with a set of debarkation steps, Kara is rifling through an overhead luggage compartment. She retrieves what looks like Bond's keyring from the storage area before an impatient Koskov, still presenting a benevolent facade, returns to the passenger area to hurry her on. On the runway, a well-groomed Soviet officer (John Bowe) is approaching the plane just as its passengers are disembarking. Koskov amiably embraces the man and introduces him as Colonel Feyador, the camp commandant and an old colleague of his. Feyador welcomes the General to Afghanistan. With no small amount of satisfaction, Koskov then presents Bond, who – he informs Feyador – is the British agent responsible for the murder of Pushkin in Tangier. He emphasises that Bond must be sent to Moscow at the earliest possible opportunity so that justice can be served upon him. While Koskov speaks, he seems oblivious to the fact that Kara is checking her bag, revealing that she has indeed retrieved Bond's keyring as asked. But just as Bond is being hustled away by security personnel, Koskov adds that Kara will be accompanying 007 to prison – she is a defector, after all, and must be punished accordingly. Outraged, Kara slaps him in the face, but Koskov is totally unmoved. Mockingly, he tells her that he intends to urge mercy in her trial, and will be sure to recommend that she be assigned to the Siberian Philharmonic Orchestra. Given that her testimony is unlikely to be taken seriously given her escape from the Eastern Bloc with Bond,

Koskov thus succeeds in burying the true story behind his own defection. He watches smugly as his former lover and 007 are both bundled into the distance by military police. (A large microphone with a grey cover can briefly be seen retreating from the shot as Kara is pulled away by the Soviets – almost certainly the most visibly obvious production error in the entire film.) Returning his attention to Feyador, Koskov tells his old comrade that he is currently on a top secret government mission, and will be requiring the use of several trucks as well as a detachment of soldiers. As Feyador smiles his assent, Koskov heads off towards the compound's main military complex.

Meanwhile, Bond and Kara are being strong-armed into the camp's prison block. The row of cells inside, though obviously grim in nature, appears orderly enough and seems to be mostly empty. The sadistic, muscle-bound Russian jailer (Ken Sharrock) in charge of the building is eyeing his new prey with great interest. He asks the accompanying military policemen the reason why these prisoners are being incarcerated, and seems quite interested when the reply is a murder charge. The jailer is especially fascinated by Kara, intoning sinisterly that he hasn't overseen a female prisoner in many years. He and the officers laugh menacingly at Kara's obvious discomfort at their attention towards her. The jailer then pushes Bond towards a cell, but is momentarily distracted when an Afghan prisoner in unkempt clothing (Art Malik) desperately asks him if Colonel Feyador has given consideration to his appeal. Jovially, the jailer replies that the good news is that the prisoner won't be hung the following morning as planned. The bad news, from the Afghan's point of view, is that he will be shot instead. This leads to further hilarity from the assembled security men.

As the prisoner continues to loudly protest his innocence, the jailer throws open the door of a cell and bluntly orders Kara to strip off. When she makes it clear that she has no intention of doing so, he grabs her blouse, leading to a string of angry Czech invective in response. Threateningly, the jailer tells her that shouts of protest will do her no good – the entire cell block is soundproofed. But his intimidating behaviour diverts his attention from Kara throwing Bond's keyring towards him. Noticing it, Bond bends down to retrieve it from the floor, but is struck with force by the jailer's truncheon. Falling to the ground painfully, Bond activates the still-unseen keyring as the jailer snarls that he did not give the agent permission to lie down. As Bond attempts to rise again, he is thumped a second time – even more agonisingly – as the jailer points out that he didn't order 007 to pick himself up either. He is wrestled from his knees by the jailer, who shouts that he should get onto his feet and move into the cell. As he does so, the jailer takes note of the keyring and wrests it from him. Shoved into the cell, Bond whistles, and the keyring beeps in response. Easily amused, the jailer and one of the security detachment laugh at the gadget's novelty value. The jailer whistles himself, and the keyring responds again. Bond then whistles the opening bars of 'Rule Britannia', and the device responds immediately with a cloud of knockout gas. The jailer and nearby security man both instantly collapse to the ground as soon as they inhale the vapour. The other remaining military policeman, who is still guarding Kara, races over to Bond, but is knocked off balance and cuffed in the face by the British agent. Bond then kicks the other security operative, knocking him out a little more permanently than before. The jailer is now beginning to regain consciousness and, infuriated but still disoriented, races at Bond, shoving him hard against a desk where the agent only narrowly misses being impaled by a correspondence spike. Incandescent at Bond's trickery, the jailer forces 007's head closer to the metal prong. Desperately, Bond kicks out his left leg, making sharp contact with the jailer's groin. The jailer cries out in pain, but his determination is undiminished. Bond turns around, his back to the desk, but is pinned down as the jailer tries to suffocate the agent by crushing 007's neck with his truncheon.

Desperately, Bond grabs his assailant's head and pushes his handcuffs hard against his nose, obviously paining him. One of the security men is starting to rouse; Kara, noticing his movement, quickly removes his helmet and strikes him over the head with a metal bucket, promptly silencing him again. Bond continues to push against the jailer's nostrils with the handcuffs, to the point where he is impeding his enemy's ability to breathe. Eventually the Russian is forced to momentarily break off his assault, angrily pushing Bond away with force towards the bars of an adjacent cell. Now free, he picks up the letter spike from his desk and races at Bond with the obvious intention of impaling him. With his other hand, he raises his baton to strike 007, but is surprised when his intended blow is impeded by the Afghan prisoner inside the cell. Enraged, the jailer begins to struggle with the incarcerated prisoner, which is all the opportunity that Bond needs to lift a nearby wooden chair and strike the jailer across the back. While this would be more than ample to knock most average people unconscious, the jailer proves to be so well-built that the chair falls apart on impact, leaving him apparently unharmed. He breaks off from his attack on the prisoner and repeatedly strikes against what remains of the chair, which Bond is still holding, breaking it apart piece by piece. When the chair has gone completely, he races to clout Bond himself, but the agent dodges his attack and causes the jailer to career into one of his own cells. The prisoner watches with rapt attention as Bond slams the heavy cell door shut just as the jailer is trying to escape, closing it on his arm and causing him to yelp in pain. Bond then jumps up, grabbing the barred metal framework above the cell door, and kicks the jailer square in the chest. This causes the Russian to fly backwards onto the cell's grubby bed, smashing his head against the metal frame as he does so. Bond hurriedly locks the door as the jailer groans in pain, the nearby prisoner applauding gleefully as he does so.

Kara drags one of the security men into another of the cells, while Bond retrieves his colleague. When they are both safely ensconced, Bond throws the prison keys to Kara and asks her to lock the cell securely while he gingerly retrieves his keyring from the floor. As Bond extracts the set of masterkeys from the keyring and begins to work on his handcuffs, Kara hugs him in elation and tells him that thanks to his ingenuity they are now free to go. Bond, however, does not seem to share her optimism – he points out that they are, after all, still trapped in the middle of a Russian military base at the heart of occupied Afghanistan. But at least it's a start; as Bond asks for Kara's assistance in unlocking his handcuffs, she points out that they have one major advantage in that the Russians didn't separate them before they were imprisoned. Unable to resist her wide-eyed enthusiasm, and now freed from his shackles, Bond leads her over to a selection of uniform jackets hanging on pegs nearby. Searching for the closest fit, they move towards the prison's entrance when the prisoner beseechingly asks Bond to throw him the cell keys. Bond has no hesitation in doing so, and the prisoner can barely contain his delight as he catches them, escaping from the imminent death sentence that awaits him.

Having broken out of the prison block, Bond and Kara are desperately sneaking around the Soviet base in search of a way to elude their Russian captors. Hearing an approaching vehicle, Bond quickly grabs Kara and pulls her around to the far side of the prison building. They then take refuge behind some wooden crates as they watch an armoured tank passing by, followed by Necros emerging from an office block carrying the organ trans-plant box. Although Bond's vision is impeded by the necessity of ducking in and out of view to avoid detection, it appears that Necros is loading the box onto a heavy armoured car of some kind. The Red Crescent ambulance that was used to transport the box in Morocco is parked nearby. Koskov, sauntering along at a leisurely pace behind Necros, has his hands in his pockets and looks even more immensely self-satisfied than before. Bond then hears a tow-truck approaching which is attached to a set of aircraft embarkation steps. Sensing a possible escape route, he ducks out of his hiding place behind the crates, pulling Kara behind him at a safe distance by her hand. Once he is sure that it's safe to move, he drags her around the back of the prison block.

Still wearing his Soviet uniform jacket and fighting to maintain a low profile, Bond is driving the tow truck – and the attached steps – away from the prison block. Kara is in the passenger seat beside him. We next cut to a high wire fence surrounding the military compound. A large warning sign, its wording in Russian, is hanging ominously from the fence; its emblem suggests an electrocution warning. Back at the prison block, however, the tow truck's driver is just discovering to his distress that his vehicle is no longer where he parked it. He rushes off, and soon after – back at Bond and Kara's location – orders can be heard being barked in Russian nearby as the security alarm is raised. A loud warning klaxon begins to sound as Kara and Bond race up the flight of stationary embarkation stairs. As the camera's angle changes, we realise that Bond has parked the steps right next to the perimeter fence. With some unease at the height required from his leap Bond jumps from the top of the stairs, landing heavily on the sandy ground on the other side of the fence. Quickly getting to his feet, he urgently signals Kara to join him. She lands more gracefully than 007 had done, and together they race off into the bleak, mountainous landscape. They have barely managed to make it a few steps away from the compound, however, when a group of armed freedom fighters suddenly appear, having concealed themselves under blankets to disguise their presence among the rocks. The men immediately pull knives, aiming to cut short the escape of Bond and Kara. Before they can make good on their attack, a sudden cry in Pushtu can be heard, stopping them in their tracks. The prisoner from the Russian cell block, who seems to have been following Bond and Kara, jumps from the top of the parked stairs to join his countrymen. Quickly issuing orders in their native language, the prisoner moves further towards the group, who quickly break ranks to leave Kara and Bond unharmed. Taken aback by the sudden activity, Bond asks the prisoner what is going on. The prisoner tells him in reply that he has assured his compatriots that Bond and Kara are not Russians, which has ensured their safety – for the moment. With some trepidation, Kara wonders aloud how long their protection from harm will last. Bond tries to buoy her confidence – where there's life, there's hope – as they race towards the freedom fighters' horses, which are waiting near their position.

With the details of the final phase of Koskov's plan still unknown, Bond and Kara's flight from Soviet incarceration proves to be an effective contrast to the lengthy exposition aboard Koskov's cargo plane. Given his previous form, it is almost inevitable that the rogue General will prove disloyal to Feyador, just as he has been towards virtually everyone else that he has encountered throughout the film. However, as he and Necros load their diamonds onto an armoured vehicle in order to head for an unidentified destination, it seems certain that the last elements of Koskov's grand scheme will soon be uncovered. Additionally, during the prison fight Bond makes use of two of the functions of the keyring which was supplied to him by Q – the short-term anaesthetic gas, and the set of masterkeys. But as Q's gadgets often tend to adhere to the Chekhov's Gun principle – explaining in great detail their function so as to foreshadow their later use in the film – it appears virtually guaranteed that as Bond recovers the keyring after his vicious fight with the jailer, its explosive capabilities have been saved for use at a further point in the narrative.

Day has now dawned in the Afghan desert. As Bond, Kara and their new allies gallop past a rocky outcropping, they pass a bombed-out Russian convoy. The corpses of fallen Soviet soldiers are currently being rifled for clothing and other useful items by the locals. Several armoured vehicles, now very much the worse for wear, lie abandoned near a selection of torched buildings. Kara, riding with Bond on one of the horses, looks around at the carnage evident in this bleak scene. Bond tells her that she is seeing the result of an attack by the Mujahedeen, resistance fighters who are working to overcome and repel the Soviet occupation of Afghanistan (which had begun in 1979). The camera pans up to some snow-covered mountains, indicating that Bond and Kara's journey still has a way to go.

Later, the freedom fighters arrive at a settlement and immediately pick up their pace. The leading horseman fires several rounds from his rifle in celebration of their arrival. As men and women rush forward from a sparse woodland area to herald the return of the fighters, cries of salutation can be heard from all around. The horsemen are heading for what appears to be a fortified stronghold at the top of a steep hill. Led by the freed prisoner, they proceed along a well-defended trench, galloping along to the sound of rapt jubilation. Bond is watching the scene very carefully, alert for any sign of threat to his or Kara's safety. As they get closer to the citadel, they pass a variety of livestock and further cheering locals before passing through a large archway into the main fortress beyond. Bond, Kara and the freedom fighters dismount from their horses in the courtyard of the stronghold as heavy doors are closed behind them, shutting off the fortress's entrance. Bond and Kara are then ushered through an internal doorway by some of their new-found collaborators. Outside the fortress's walls, further freedom fighters are arriving on horseback, emphasising just how heavily secured the area is.

Bond and Kara are being escorted through a hallway in the bastion, which is full of armed militiamen. They are shepherded through another door, in a manner which brooks no compromise, into a comfortable anteroom. In contrast with the practicality of the rest of the building, this area is well decorated and inviting, with plush cushions on the floor and a small table stocked with fresh fruit. Kara removes her Russian Army hat, looking around the room in quiet approval. Meanwhile, out in the citadel's courtyard the late-arriving freedom fighters are entering the area, a camel burdened with supplies being brought along behind them. Joining Kara in removing his Soviet military jacket, Bond opens the shutters of a window which overlooks the courtyard and peers outside. Kara moves alongside to join him. Outside, they see further camels arriving, similarly carrying goods, as they are led into the courtyard. One of the workmen charged with guiding the camels is toppled to the ground by an armed supervisor, who kicks him in the midriff and subjects his subordinate to an elaborate Pushtu diatribe. From inside the building, Bond remarks sardonically that he hopes that the supervisor won't be joining them for social occasions any time soon. Just as he says so, the door to the anteroom swings open once more, this time to admit another armed freedom fighter. He signals that Bond and Kara should follow him out of the room, and they readily comply with his request. Out in the courtyard, yet more camels are arriving – many of them laden down with Red Cross supplies, suggesting that their burden actually contains the fruits of a Mujahedeen raid.

Bond and Kara are being led into the stronghold's impressive main chamber. It is lushly appointed, and contains a number of freedom fighters. At the centre of the room, however, is the mysterious Afghan prisoner from the Russian jail block, currently trimming his newly-neatened beard with the aid of a cut-throat razor and a hand-mirror. Now in fresh clothes, he looks like a different man entirely. Seeing the arrival of his two fellow escapees, he gets to his feet and throws the cell keys back to Bond, mirroring the agent's own motion when he freed the prisoner at the compound. Speaking in a cut-glass Received Pronunciation accent which is far removed from his earlier, heavily-accented broken English, the man thanks Bond for his assistance at the Soviet base and apologises for his subterfuge in assuming a false identity – a remnant, he assures him, from his experiences at an amateur dramatics society he had frequented during his time at Oxford University. He now introduces himself as Kamran Shah and passes Bond a bundle of fresh clothing, telling him that he is free to clean himself up. Sensing an opportunity to find out more about his current situation, Bond instead hands the pile of garments to Kara and suggests that she go on ahead without him.

Kara is clearly uncertain, but Bond gently urges her to do as he suggests.

Once Kara has left the room, Bond decides to get straight to the point and asks Kamran to assist him in returning to the Soviet military compound. Kamran reacts with hilarity, as do his gathered associates, and tells Bond that this would be a massively unwise course of action – after all, the Russians will be on high alert and actively searching for the British agent after his escape. Wearily, Bond requests that if Kamran is unwilling to help, might he instead consider putting him in touch with the Mujahedeen directly. But all is not as it seems, he discovers, for Kamran is himself the Mujahedeen's Eastern District deputy commander. He explains that the Soviets discovered him during a reconnaissance mission at the airbase, but fortunately had no idea of his seniority within the Mujahedeen – if they had, he would have been unlikely to survive long enough to be imprisoned in the cell block where Bond found him. Gruffly, he then asks Bond to explain his own presence in Afghanistan. 007 tells Kamran that he works for British Intelligence (prompting another round of laughter from the nearby freedom fighters), and describes his investigation into Koskov's attempts to procure large quantities of Whitaker's advanced weapons technology – armaments which could prove disastrous for the Mujahedeen if deployed against them. Kamran regards Bond's words dourly, and tells the agent that he must report his findings to his superior, a Mujahedeen commander who is based in the Khyber Pass. Bond protests that such a journey would take too long – days at least on horseback – and implores Kamran to aid him in returning to the military base before Koskov has a chance to depart once again. Trying to offer a compromise, Kamran suggests that Bond and Kara accompany him and his associates on a mission the following day, and that he will then reflect on a further course of action. But Bond complains that this will also take too long. As 007 moves closer to Kamran, urging his assistance, one of the freedom fighters decides that Bond's proximity has become too great and snaps round, pointing his rifle straight at the agent's chest. Bond, requiring no further persuasion, doesn't move any further. He does, however, tell Kamran that all he needs is a gun and some guides – the rest he will do himself. But Kamran is now rapidly losing his patience, and tells Bond that even this approach will not be feasible; he is already short on operatives and horses for his existing operations as it is. Making it clear that the discussion is over, he tells Bond that he should go and rest; he and Kara will be needed at dawn the next day. Realising that there is no further point in debating the issue any further, Bond withdraws.

The Soviet occupation of Afghanistan was a hugely relevant issue in the area of foreign affairs during the eighties, and had immense ramifications for global geopolitics as well as the Cold War theory of containment. Mujahedeen resistance strikes against the country's U.S.S.R. occupiers were well-reported in the media, and their inclusion within the film brought a heightened topicality to its action. Whereas Bond's usual interactions with the Soviet Union often seemed to be faintly generic in their emphasis on maintaining the status quo of the international balance of power, by situating events within an Afghan context *The Living Daylights* was to achieve an explicitly contemporary political edge which few other entries in the series had done up to this point. Along with the inevitable parallels between the international arms trade, personified in Whitaker's stealthy undercover dealings, and the Iran-Contra scandal (which admittedly broke some time after *The Living Daylights* had gone into production), this film retains a deserved reputation as one of the most socio-politically pertinent entries in the entire *Bond* cycle.

Bond is being ushered through the crowded citadel hallway back into the anteroom which has been set aside for Kara and himself. As soon as he enters, Kara – who is now garbed in the Afghan clothing that Kamran had set aside for her – runs across to greet Bond, embracing him with fervour. She tells him that she was worried by his absence, given their rarefied surroundings. Bond is clearly touched by her compassion. She asks him what will happen to them next, obviously concerned due to the precarious nature of their situation, to which he replies distantly that he cannot help but notice how beautiful she looks. Appearing awkward at the fact that he has not yet offered her a frank explanation, 007 wanders over to the window to take a covert look outside as he admits to Kara that they are currently in a local headquarters of the Mujahedeen. Bond tells her that they will be heading out on an operation of some kind the following day (though he is unsure of the details surrounding it), but that she will instead be heading for the Khyber Pass. Rushing to the agent's side, Kara seems rattled by the news that he won't be joining her; when Bond replies that he will reunite with her at a later point, she immediately deduces that he intends to go after Koskov instead. Bond's silence reveals that this is, in fact, his true intent. Kara pleads with him not to pursue the General, but to stay with her instead. Bond tells her that he can't simply stand by and let Koskov carry out his schemes, but Kara protests that this plan of retaliatory action will almost certainly lead to his death. Angrily, she remonstrates that if Bond won't join her on the journey to the Khyber Pass, she will refuse to wait for his return when she gets there. In that case, Bond responds, he will ask Kamran to send her directly to London instead, in order to ensure her safety. Infuriated at Bond's apparent determination to make her decisions for her, Kara's temper finally boils over and she attacks him with one of the room's large floor cushions. Her assault catches Bond completely unaware, and he teeters over onto a bed while still clutching a glass and drink shaker. Amusedly asking for a translation of her indignant diatribe, which is largely in Czech, Kara tells him that she has just called him a horse's arse. Bond can't help but laugh at the absurdity of their situation, and eventually she joins him in his sudden burst of mirth. They hold each other tenderly. A tearful Kara tells Bond that she worries that if they are separated they may never be reunited, but Bond disagrees, giving her his word that he will return as promised. They kiss tenderly.

This scene emphasises the new-found vigour of the relationship which has now been forged between Kara and Bond. Following Koskov's explicit betrayal of his former lover at the Russian airbase, there is no longer any conflict in her romantic sentiments, and the shared sense of adversity which exists between Bond and Kara during their flight from captivity – in addition to their previous exploits in Czechoslovakia, Austria and Morocco – helps to forge between them a believable bond of attraction through mutual hardship. That she seems to elevate Bond's safety even over her regard for her own wellbeing, in spite of the obvious danger that they find themselves in, lends further weight to Kara's feelings for Bond, and even the prospect of exacting retribution upon Koskov – thwarting his plans and also revenging his treachery – is insufficient to risk the emotional bond that she discovers has grown between the two of them.

The following morning, a group of freedom fighters on horseback are moving swiftly through an austere region of desert. Bond and Kara, now more properly attired for the terrain, are with the group. Kamran is leading the operation, and is currently looking rather buoyant as they set out. At the Russian military compound, Feyador is bidding Koskov farewell as the General departs on board a heavily armoured all-terrain vehicle. The base commander signals to the driver, who accelerates away. Out in the desert, Kamran approaches a procession of Afghans which is being brought to a halt near an oasis. A large number of camels, many of them carrying the sackcloth Red Cross bags that had been seen back at the Mujahedeen stronghold, are being brought to rest. Bond, curious at the sheer number of sacks on display, wraps his headscarf around his face and surreptitiously blends in with the camels and the adjacent, bustling array of Afghans. As members of the Mujahedeen debate loudly with other Afghans in their native language, a crouching Bond pulls out a knife and slices into one of the Red Cross bags. He withdraws it, noticing a film of sticky residue on the blade, just as one of the Afghans spots him and eyes his actions curiously. Seeking no conflict, Bond quickly pulls back. As the Afghans continue their discussion, Bond returns to Kara, unfurls his scarf, and tastes the residue that is clinging to his knife. 007 finds that the taste is unmistakeable – raw opium. He tells Kara that the quantity of narcotics on display would likely fetch a street value of half a billion dollars in the United States.

Distant gunfire is then heard, with two Afghans on horseback racing towards the oasis as a line of Soviet armoured vehicles begin approaching the Mujahedeen's position. Bond angrily rounds on Kamran, who is still on horseback, and demands to know why he is trading in illegal drugs. Kamran indicates that he has been negotiating with the Snow Leopard Brotherhood; the leader of the group (Tony Cyrus) has employed the Mujahedeen's services occasionally. When Kara seems puzzled, Bond explains that the Brotherhood is the most prominent dealer of opium in the entire Golden Crescent. Kamran notes that he is unconcerned whether the Soviet occupiers are killed by force of arms or a drug overdose – the important thing, as far as he is concerned, is that they die. At any rate, he adds, the money from the sale of the narcotics is essential to purchase weapons for the Mujahedeen's continued operations against the Russians.

Kara spots Necros and Koskov in the near distance; Necros is currently setting down the transplant box full of diamonds onto a makeshift table near the Soviet armoured vehicles. When she points this out to Bond, he explains the reason for the presence of the precious stones – before Koskov's defection, the General had made arrangements for the Russian government to purchase a large shipment of advanced armaments from Whitaker, but he and the arms dealer had actually used the Soviets' deposit to buy the diamonds which are now being used to acquire the Afghan opium from the Snow Leopard Brotherhood. Bond adds that Koskov will almost certainly use the drugs to turn a vast profit for his own personal gain, while still retaining more than enough funds to provide the Soviets with their original order of weapons from Whitaker. But, 007 suggests, should the opium never leave

Afghanistan, Koskov's high-stakes plan will lie in ruins. Kamran is far from certain, warning Bond that disrupting the dealings of the Snow Leopard Brotherhood will have lethal consequences – especially given that their transaction with Koskov is their most profitable since the Russians invaded the country almost a decade beforehand. Not looking hopeful, Bond asks Kamran if he intends to help or not. With a wry smile, Kamran replies that he might be persuaded... though only if they attack after the Soviets have paid up in full and left the area. In that case, Bond responds, he will need access to some plastic explosives and a timer. Kamran nods soberly, promising to do his best, and withdraws with some of his men. After Kamran has ordered the Mujahedeen fighters in their native tongue, the horsemen eye Bond with a new sense of admiration as they head away.

With this scene, the full extent of Koskov's multifarious plan is finally unveiled. When Bond discovers the opium which is about to be traded, he is finally able to discern the last piece of the complex puzzle which at last defines Koskov's true intentions. This plot proves to be one of the most intricately complicated of all examples of villainy in the *Bond* series; with a scheme which has stretched from Soviet Russia to Western Europe via North Africa and the Asian subcontinent, Koskov's machinations are truly international in scope, and yet after all the elaborate chicanery they amount to only one thing – the criminal acquisition of money. That he is entirely willing to betray everyone from the British government to his own KGB superiors – and, quite possibly, eventually even Whitaker – in order to achieve his illicit aims is a quite breathtaking demonstration of an unerring confidence in his ability to accomplish this ultimate goal. Yet Koskov's arrogance – and his ready willingness to deceive anyone who stands in his way – may still be his undoing, given that Bond intends to ensure that the wayward General's disloyalty and unlawful dealings do not go unpunished.

Several Afghans are loading Red Cross sacks onto the back of one of the Russians' cargo trucks. Bond, glancing anxiously at

Kamran, covers his face with his scarf and carries one of the bags – on his shoulder – towards the open-backed truck. He passes Necros with only a few feet to spare. But Bond has only just passed the assassin when he calls the disguised 007 to a halt. Bond stops his motion, but retains his stance with the Red Cross sack perched on his shoulder. From a position nearby, Kamran watches the exchange apprehensively. Necros produces a sharp knife and, just as Bond had done earlier, slices into the bag. High on a hill, watching from a safe distance, Kara eyes Necros's motions warily. Tasting the opium on his blade, Necros seems satisfied at the bag's contents and orders Bond to continue on his way. Bond is naturally relieved that his disguise has passed muster; Kara also looks reassured at the agent's continued survival – for the time being, at least. Now having reached the truck, Bond loads his cargo on board and then jumps into the vehicle himself, hurriedly assisting an Afghan worker who is already labouring hard by stacking the bags into orderly columns. Necros, meanwhile, is beginning to load the Russians' fold-up tables back into the Soviet armoured vehicles, the transaction completed. With all of the bags now packed onto the back of the truck, the Afghans charged with loading the opium jump back onto the ground. Bond, however, has secretly remained onboard. Hidden behind rows and rows of Red Cross sacks, he surreptitiously withdraws an improvised explosive device that has been tied around his waist but hidden beneath his tunic. A Russian soldier clambers onto the back of the truck, causing Bond to withdraw further into the vehicle. The agent realises that he has no chance of escape, and that his plans must be altered accordingly. Kara watches with trepidation as Necros also jumps aboard and the truck's loading ramp is retracted, making it ready for transport. The leader of the Snow Leopard Brotherhood, satisfied that their business has been concluded satisfactorily, throws a bag of currency at Kamran. The Mujahedeen leader, though, barely notices the arrival of his remuneration; he is watching with concern as the Russians begin to leave, taking Bond with them.

Aboard the cargo truck, several of the Red Cross sacks tumble over as the vehicle judders over the rocky desert terrain. Bond presses himself back still further, trying desperately to evade the attention of Necros but rapidly running out of hiding space. As the Soviet vehicles continue to retreat from the oasis, the Mujahedeen fighters cheer at the successful operation. Kara, deeply worried about Bond's fate, rides over to Kamran and exhorts him to mount a rescue attempt. When Kamran points out that Bond is now essentially on his own, Kara angrily reminds him that he would still be in a cell – or more likely executed – if it had not been for the British agent's altruistic actions. Subdued, Kamran assures her that he has no options left, but Kara disagrees. Grabbing a rifle from a saddle-bag on Kamran's horse, she urges her horse forward, galloping towards the departing Russians. Sighing, Kamran watches the stubborn but brave cellist race off in pursuit of the Soviets, but makes no attempt to follow her. His assembled freedom fighters, curious at Kamran's next move, watch him attentively. Seeming conflicted, but realising that he has no real choice if he is to avoid losing face, Kamran orders them onwards. Cheering rapturously, the horsemen set off at pace across the rough landscape.

Here Kara's loyalty to Bond is demonstrated unambiguously; having once been deceived by Koskov into doubting the agent's motives, she now seems determined to repay her earlier error of character judgement by fighting to save 007 even in the face of overwhelming odds. Though Kamran knows that the chances of an assault on the Russian military – much less on their airbase in the region – is virtually suicidal, his natural caution is eventually overcome by Kara's inspiring display of courage, and also her pointed reminder that he remains in Bond's debt. Keen to retain the respect of the Afghans under his command, his eventual decision to accompany Kara on her improbably dangerous rescue mission seems a rational one even considering that he had only met the British agent the day beforehand, and that he has had to take Bond's word concerning Koskov's elaborate treachery (and the Russian's intention to procure advanced armaments to subdue the resistance movement).

The four Russian vehicles are continuing to travel at speed across the desert. Inside the cargo truck, Bond is wrestling with one of the Red Cross sacks, pulling out its contents – several plastic bags stuffed with opium. Necros continues to look out of the truck, watching the receding track behind the vehicle. As the Soviet convoy moves onward, Bond crams the plastic explosives into the now-empty bag. While he does so, the truck is nearing the perimeter fence of the military base. Several heavy vehicles of numerous different types are parked outside the compound's boundary. While the convoy begins to move through the main gate, Bond is rapidly sewing up the neck of the sack, ensuring that it will remain unobserved in the event of all but the closest inspection. At the rear of the vehicle, Necros watches as Soviet soldiers disembark from the convoy's troop carrier. The truck then swings around to park close to a cargo plane with Russian markings – one which is quite different from the one that Koskov had used to travel from Morocco. (Although supposedly a Soviet aircraft, it is – in truth – a Lockheed Hercules C-130 cargo plane which has been repainted and given an appropriate set of Russian decals.) As the truck's ramp is lowered, Necros jumps off only to be replaced on board by several Afghan workers. They begin to unload the opium bags, gradually uncovering Bond's hiding position. As the number of Afghans on the truck increases, however, Bond decides to attempt to blend in and starts passing the bags to the workers who are – in turn – handing them to further members of the workforce who are standing on the runway. Some of them seem mildly puzzled at Bond's sudden appearance, but say nothing. As the human production line continues to shift the opium from the truck over to the cargo plane, Colonel Feyador arrives in a jeep. Disembarking, he is cordially met by a grinning Koskov, who now looks to be the very acme of self-congratulation. From the truck, the disguised

Bond is watching the exchange with interest.

Outside the perimeter, another jeep is fast approaching the compound. The vehicle is waved through by the duty officer, and advances through the main gate checkpoint. A Russian sentry remains on guard, and spots movement nearby which he attempts to investigate. Emerging from the side of a parked truck is Kara, guiding her horse. Her blonde hair now flowing freely, she smiles sweetly at the soldier. Momentarily taken aback by her appearance, the trooper has barely enough time to acknowledge her presence before Kamran emerges from the side of the stationary vehicle and pulls the Russian's uniform helmet back, allowing another Mujahedeen fighter to knock the Soviet unconscious. As two of the Afghan fighters jog on towards the airbase, Kamran stops to tell Kara that she should wait for them outside the perimeter where it will be (relatively) safe. He assures her that he will return for her after the operation, but Kara looks doubtful nonetheless.

In the back of the cargo truck, Bond is checking through the opium bags until he finds the one that is packed with explosives. Deciding to carry this particular package himself, he jumps off the truck and walks across the runway towards the plane, passing Feyador, Koskov and Necros and he does so. Heading up the plane's cargo ramp, a Soviet officer is barking orders in Russian, indicating where the various bags should be placed. Moving to the end of a column of Red Cross sacks, he rapidly swings into a crouching position out of the sight of the nearby Russians. Bond then opens the mouth of his sackcloth bag slightly, exposing a digital detonation timer. Working quickly, he activates the timer and adjusts it to set off the explosives after ten minutes and thirty seconds. Once he has set it going, he adds it to the pile of other bags just as the plane's ramp begins to rise, having allowed the last few Afghan workers time to depart. Bond looks alarmed, clearly believing that he has been discovered, but a Russian soldier – spotting him – briskly orders him off the plane, gesturing with his rifle. Relieved, 007 heads towards the plane's passenger doorway instead, but reaches it only to come face to face with Koskov and Necros. This time, however, his scarf is not covering his features, meaning that Koskov recognises him straight away. The General is stunned at Bond's presence. Necros immediately reacts, but not quite as quickly as Bond, who grabs the machine gun of the soldier nearest to him and clobbers him with it, sending the trooper careening off the plane. The hapless Soviet flies over the steps parked at the side of the cargo aircraft, crashing into Necros and Koskov and knocking both men to the ground. The plane's pilot and co-pilot watch these developments in shock. Bond then fires the gun into the air, scattering Russian troops and officers in every direction. Koskov and Necros, unwilling to risk their lives to Bond's caprices, race for cover. The two pilots decide to make a run for it and, while Bond is busily firing towards the runway, they dive over the closing cargo ramp to safety. Bond snaps round to cover them, but quickly discovers that the pair have already gone. He then returns to his original firing position and looses off several more rounds of ammunition – this time towards Feyador's jeep. The Colonel only narrowly manages to avoid being hit himself. 007 then sweeps a hail of bullets over a nearby troop carrier... only to discover that the gun has run out of ammunition. Sensing that Bond's luck has run out, Feyador pulls a handgun, but Koskov agitatedly tells him not to fire – given its expensive cargo, they can't risk damaging the plane.

A few tense moments pass as Bond and the Russians contemplate their stalemate. An armed Russian soldier covertly sneaks around the side of the troop carrier, but Feyador gestures for him to stay back. Bond, the empty gun in his hands, hides out of range next to the plane's passenger door. The sound of a vehicle can be heard emerging from the distance; a large mechanical bulldozer comes bursting through the compound's wire perimeter fence at speed. Sparks from the electrified barrier fly off in all directions. The Russians react in stunned disbelief at this latest turn of events. Kamran, in the driver's seat of the bulldozer, laughs at their consternation. With the path now clear, the Mujahedeen horsemen rush the military base, streaming through the gap in the fence as well as the main gateway. Russian soldiers on gate duty attempt to hold their position, but are knocked from their feet by the rapidly advancing freedom fighters. One horseman flings a grenade into the gate checkpoint, destroying it in a ball of flame. As the Russian soldiers scramble in disarray, Bond carefully peeks around the plane door to see Kamran gleefully demolishing a Russian habitation block with his bulldozer, and then another which runs parallel to it. One of the buildings appears to be a shower block; after he has ploughed through it with the construction vehicle, two naked Russian soldiers – suddenly exposed in more ways than one – are forced to flee as the Afghan fighters continue to advance. Koskov, Necros and Feyador are still hiding behind the Colonel's jeep, though they have now switched sides around the vehicle and are shielding themselves from the oncoming Mujahedeen attack. Bond, seeing that Kamran's audacious attack has diverted the Russians' attention from his own endeavours, kicks away the plane's external stairs and heads further into the plane. Ditching his empty gun and headscarf, he hurriedly moves through the cockpit door.

As the horsemen move closer to the plane, gunshots ringing out in every direction, Koskov, Feyador and Necros are racing from the side of the jeep over to the cover of the troop transport. They desperately scramble underneath the vehicle, minimising their profile on the battlefield, while Bond is getting into the pilot's seat of the cargo plane. The Mujahedeen fighters do not slacken in their assault; one of them releases a rocket from a launcher which causes an explosion not far from the cargo plane. Bond gauges the resulting fireball's proximity with concern as he prepares the aircraft for flight. Its propellers begin to turn with increasing speed as the Afghans keep up their offensive, forming a cordon around the aircraft's position. Kara is watching the carnage with rapt attention. Kamran, still in the bulldozer, is heading towards a nest of machine guns. Raising the vehicle's metal shovel, he deflects the Russians' bullets as he ploughs towards the emplacement. One trooper desperately flings a hand-grenade at the oncoming vehicle. Kamran watches for its approach, and seconds later it lands neatly onto the shovel of the bulldozer. Knowing that the grenade's detonation will be only moments away, he jumps out of the driver's cabin onto a horse which one of his men has brought alongside. The Soviet gunners, seeing the bulldozer continuing to speed towards their position, hasten out of the emplacement mere seconds before the construction vehicle collides with it, creating a huge explosion as the grenade sets off the remaining ammunition.

With the cargo plane's propellers now turning at full speed, Bond attempts to taxi the aircraft but soon discovers that its progress is impeded – a wooden chock down on the runway is obstructing the wheels. Koskov, Necros and Feyador, remaining under the troop transport, watch as total chaos reigns all across the base. One Mujahedeen fighter is thrown from his horse by gunfire from a Russian soldier. Then a spray of bullets collide with the side of the transport vehicle, causing Koskov and his allies to flinch momentarily. With the cargo plane still unable to overcome the wooden chock, Bond decides to put it into reverse to give himself a chance to pick up some speed. Kara, still outside the complex, continues to watch as explosions rock the area; fires now rage all around. Seeing the plane heading backwards, Koskov frantically tells Feyador to blockade the runway, thus preventing the aircraft from reaching take-off speed. The Colonel rolls away from the jeep in an attempt to do as Koskov asks. Bond, now having taken the plane some distance back from the wooden chock, accelerates sharply and is – this time – able to move over the impediments. He then steers the aircraft rapidly, turning it away from the pandemonium that is engulfing the area nearby.

As it taxis, Feyador is struggling to fight his way towards his military subordinates; Afghan horsemen continue to gallop around their position, keeping Koskov and Necros pinned down.

A sudden hail of bullets kills another two Russian soldiers in a jeep with a mounted gun, almost as quickly as they arrive. Feyador is thrown backwards against the passenger-side door of the troop transport, only narrowly avoiding being shot himself. Three other armed Russian troopers then arrive to support the Colonel, looking around wildly at the rapidly-shifting combat scene.

Kamran is ordering his Mujahedeen fighters, gesturing for them to divide their attack. Bond smiles grimly from the plane's cockpit as he watches the continuing confrontation. Finally sensing a lull in the assault, Koskov and Necros quickly pull themselves free from their hiding place beneath the troop transport. Also seeing an opening, Feyador barks instructions to his soldiers, urging them to head away from their position of cover. One Soviet trooper falls into a firing position and uses his machine gun to emit a hail of bullets towards an oncoming Afghan fighter, who quickly falls to the ground along with his horse. As the cargo plane picks up its pace, Koskov and Necros are racing after it, desperate to regain control. Bond pushes the aircraft to maximum acceleration, immediately resulting in a burst of speed. Koskov, running as fast as he can, only just manages to grab hold of the passenger doorway which Bond had left open following his earlier shooting spree. However, he is unable to keep pace with the plane and falls painfully to the runway as it continues to taxi. Necros is following close behind him, but both are forced to rethink as the battle intensifies once again.

Outside the compound, Kara – who is still watching the bloodshed from a distance – is taken by surprise by a Russian trooper, who sneaks behind her and tries to topple her from her horse. The horse rears in panic, however, which momentarily startles the soldier and gives Kara sufficient opportunity to repeatedly punch him in the face, kicking the Soviet backwards and leaving him unconscious. Knowing that she is no longer safe in her current position, Kara spurs her horse forward. Kamran, meanwhile, looks on as Bond gives him a thumbs-up from the plane's cockpit. He grins, raising his rifle to return the acknow-ledgement. But his relief is to be short-lived. Moments later, he notices a group of Russian soldiers – led by Feyador – racing towards a petrol tanker. Subjecting the vehicle's driver to a fevered tirade in Russian, the frantic Colonel drags him out of his seat. Instantly noting the coming danger, Kamran orders his men to head towards the tanker immediately. Another wave of Afghan bullets startles the Soviets, sending Necros and Koskov pitching towards a truck. One horseman lets off another rocket, further adding to the turmoil. Koskov, now looking increasingly fraught, joins Necros at the front of the stationary truck as they watch the cargo plane speeding away from them.

Kara is riding into the combat zone, watching carefully as the battle unfolds around her. The wreckage of Russian military buildings lies all around her. On the runway, Mujahedeen horsemen are riding in front of the cargo plane, clearing the way for Bond by scattering the oncoming Soviets. Kara calls out to Bond, but up in the cockpit he is unable to hear her cries. In the petrol tanker, Feyador is discovering – much to his frustration – that he is unable to turn over the engine with the ignition. He turns around momentarily to pick off an attacking freedom fighter with his handgun, then resumes his efforts. Perceiving an opening, Kamran pulls the pin from a hand-grenade and hurls it at the tanker; it lands squarely beneath its chassis. He then pulls his men back, only seconds before Feyador discovers what has happened. From the cockpit, Bond notices the Afghan fighters suddenly fleeing in the opposite direction from his own trajectory. As Feyador yells helplessly, the tanker explodes in a massive ball of flame. Fire bursts out everywhere, leaping towards the rapidly-retreating Russian soldiers and causing Koskov and Necros to flinch from the ferocity of the detonation. From the safety of the plane's cockpit Bond notices the violent eruption of debris, but also realises that it has cleared the way for him to leave the runway. Kara watches as the Afghans regroup, while Necros quietly slinks – out of sight – behind another parked vehicle. As the Russians also begin to reform their ranks, Kara decides to make a dash for the retreating plane. Just as she urges her horse forward, though, a Russian armoured tank fires a missile which only narrowly misses her. The resulting shockwave knocks her from her horse, and she lands heavily on the ground. Kara quickly recovers to see the Mujahedeen fighters racing away in the opposite direction. Kamran, having pulled back, is looking around urgently for Kara but is unable to find her at the expected rendezvous point. Unknown to the Afghans, she has reached a jeep and is currently easing herself into its driver's seat. Koskov is watching the plane's seemingly-unstoppable progress and rages to Necros that they have to find some way of halting Bond before time runs out. As he does so, Kara's jeep races at them from behind, causing Necros to pull Koskov out of its path. But when he recognises the driver of the speeding military vehicle, Koskov soon becomes even more incensed.

John Glen was no stranger to action sequences throughout his directorial career, and *The Living Daylights*'s depiction of the Afghan attack on the Soviet airbase was arguably his most impressive display of battle choreography of all five films that he was to helm in the *Bond* series. From Kamran's gleeful demolition of the Russian occupiers' buildings to the striking array of pyrotechnics that are on offer, the sequence presents a satisfyingly bullet-ridden climax to the film, with the endgame of Koskov's calculating treachery spilling over – much to his horror – into fiery disaster. As the Soviets' installation falls into blazing ruin, we can also observe Koskov's demeanour changing by degrees as his viewpoint changes from arrogant superiority to near-total desolation as Bond and his allies sabotage his plans at the last minute. Yet even this carefully orchestrated display of carnage was, of course, only to set the scene for Bond's final victory over Koskov and his nefarious collaborators that was still to come.

Kara doesn't slacken the pace of her jeep, scattering Russian troops left and right as she forges a path towards the cargo plane. In an attempt to commandeer the vehicle, one of the Soviets jumps forward onto the engine and grabs hold of the windshield. Koskov, meanwhile, is getting into the driver's seat of another jeep – but this one is fitted with a mounted machine gun, which Necros jumps up in order to control. Dispassionately, he kicks the corpse of a dead Russian soldier out of the way as he moves into a firing position. Kara feverishly fights off the Soviet soldier who is attacking her; after a violent scuffle she activates the vehicle's windscreen wipers, which painfully rake across the bloodied trooper's features. When he raises his head above the windshield to avoid further contact, Kara punches him hard in the face, causing the soldier to topple from the jeep while Kara continues to accelerate towards the escaping cargo plane. Koskov's countenance is the very picture of determination as he remains in hot pursuit of Kara; Necros fires the jeep's machine gun, spraying the fleeing Czech's vehicle with bullets and causing her to take sharp evasive manoeuvres. By the time that Necros's initial hail of gunfire has ceased, Kara's jeep has made it to the runway. Attempting to draw alongside the nose of the aircraft, Kara signals urgently as she tries to catch Bond's attention. At first 007 is too intent on steering the plane to notice her, but eventually she catches his eye and the agent reacts with shock. As Kara smiles at his recognition, he gestures insistently towards the rear of the aircraft.

Necros continues to fire as Koskov's jeep joins Kara's vehicle on the runway. Suddenly anxious, Koskov slides open the driver's hatch to the exterior of the jeep and tells Necros to cease firing: just one stray bullet has the potential to cause disaster if it were to hit the plane's fuel tanks. Bond is currently hitting the cockpit control to extract the aircraft's cargo ramp. Turning to Kara, still steering alongside, Bond repeats his hand signal for her to decelerate behind the plane and then move the jeep up onto the ramp in order to gain access. He looks frustrated at her failure to understand his rapid gestures, but just then she sees what he is indicating and nods in response. Relieved, Bond returns to the controls as Kara moves behind the plane as instructed and then accelerates sharply towards its now fully descended ramp. Necros spots her strategy and begins to clamber around the top of Koskov's jeep as the Russian manoeuvres just behind Kara's position. Intensely focused, Kara hits the accelerator hard one final time, sending the vehicle forward over the ramp and sharply projecting it into the hold of the cargo plane. Restraining bolts snap up into place, keeping the jeep secure on either side. As the plane's ramp then closes once more, Kara wastes no time in clambering out of the jeep and heading for the cockpit. She does not notice that Koskov is now accelerating alongside the still-open passenger door of the aircraft. Reunited with Bond, Kara affectionately embraces him; though Bond is relieved to see her too, he is momentarily alarmed when she inadvertently pulls his gaze away from the aircraft's controls. Kara gasps in shock at the sudden arrival of another Russian plane which is currently coming in to land. The pilots of the other Soviet aircraft react with alarm at the unexpected position of Bond's cargo plane (an unscheduled flight, to say the least). As the newly-arrived plane touches down, Bond's aircraft continues to taxi relentlessly towards it. Koskov, now as close to the passenger door as he dare steer the jeep, yells for Necros to jump onto the plane. In the cockpit, Bond is wrestling with the controls, eventually pulling hard on the joystick to coax the plane into the air just as the other aircraft looks certain to collide. The ascending cargo plane misses the fuselage of the just-landed Russian aeroplane by just a few feet. But the Soviet pilots react in shock nonetheless, for their narrowly-avoided crash with Bond is followed by an actual collision with Koskov's jeep. The General screams in panic as his vehicle tears through the Russian plane's wing, causing it to explode in a ferocious burst of flame. Bond and Kara look down from the airborne cockpit to witness the aftermath of the blast. Miraculously, Koskov survives the impact, though both he and the jeep look much the worse for the incident. He desperately flings himself free of the burning vehicle, pitching himself onto the rocky ground as the jeep – still entwined with the remnants of the aircraft's wing –

trundles a few metres further before violently tearing itself apart. Bruised and blooded, his uniform battered, Koskov spits out a mouthful of dirt and watches helplessly as Bond flies off in the cargo plane.

Back in the cockpit, Kara and Bond share a sigh of relief... albeit one which is short-lived, as Bond tells Kara that she must fly the plane in his absence. Kara is shocked by his request, but Bond instructs her to keep the joystick level and keep navigating straight ahead. When she asks him why he must leave the cockpit, Bond replies that he has to disarm the detonator of the bomb that he had planted in the plane before the Mujahedeen attack. Bond moves into the cargo hold from the cockpit and, bracing himself as the plane is buffeted by turbulence, pulls himself towards the passenger door, which he draws closed. An exterior shot displays the plane cruising through the mountainous terrains of Afghanistan. Bond is hurriedly searching through a column of familiar-looking Red Cross sacks when – without warning – Necros flings a cargo net around his face in an attempt to choke him. Taken completely by surprise at the assassin's presence, Bond struggles desperately as he tries to avoid suffocation. Kara hears the altercation, but as she looks over her shoulder the cockpit door swings closed, obscuring her view of the fight. Bond reaches around Necros's back and withdraws the assassin's knife from its sheath. Necros anticipates the move and hammers Bond's hand – still clutching the blade – against a pile of opium bags, squeezing his wrist with all his might. Bond, still choking under the strain of the cargo net, is clearly just clinging to consciousness and looks pained in the extreme. Edging the blade just a little further, he succeeds in cutting a restraining cord, causing the bags to spring free. They are flung all across the cargo hold, as are Necros and Bond. Necros's hold on Bond never slackens, however. Perturbed, Kara looks over her shoulder again, hearing the struggle but powerless to intervene due to the fact that she is the only one in control of the plane. Back in the cargo hold, Necros is viciously hitting Bond's arm against another bank of opium sacks. Kara is now beginning to seem openly apprehensive. Suddenly breaking free, Bond tears the net away from his face at the same time as he fiercely elbows Necros in the midriff. The assassin recoils at the impact. The plane banks slightly in midair. In the cockpit, Kara desperately searches the control panel, eventually finding a lever with a 'down' function which she decides to operate. She little realises that this is, in fact, the activation switch for the cargo ramp, which begins to lower at the rear of the aircraft. Necros kicks Bond forcefully, sending the agent flying to the back of the plane – and perilously close to the still-dropping hydraulic ramp. Kara then pulls back sharply on the joystick, causing the plane's nose to rise into the air. This action suddenly increases the gradient in the cargo hold; as Necros staggers towards Bond, both men are suddenly flung out into mid-air, clinging for dear life to the cargo netting which is now the only thing which is still connecting them to the plane.

Kara pushes forward on the joystick, causing the plane to rapidly even out its altitude but having the unintended side effect of causing the cargo netting to swing violently, along with Bond and Necros. Inside the aircraft, one of the metal clips which are holding the netting in place is starting to strain the supporting cord due to the tension that is being placed on it. Kara looks over again, seemingly unaware that the detonator attached to Bond's plastic explosives is still ticking down; its digital display can be seen in operation, still partially hidden within the Red Cross sack. Out on the cargo net, Necros is kicking Bond violently, causing 007 to fight hard merely to retain his grip. He slips to the bottom of the net, only just holding on. Bond then scrambles up the netting on the opposite side to Necros as both men struggle to reach the top – and the plane's cargo ramp – first. Appearing unexpectedly from the underside of the net, Bond surprises Necros with a punch to the face, causing the assassin to yelp in pain and swing further down as he reacts to the blow. Bond then redoubles his efforts to climb to the ramp before Necros, little realising that the netting's attachment to the metal clip is becoming more frayed by the second. Fighting desperately to reach the top of the net, Bond keeps climbing while Necros, who seems to have recovered quickly from 007's attack, withdraws his knife. He slashes forward in the hope of cutting Bond, but misses and stabs one of the opium bags instead. Bond kicks the assassin hard in the head and, retrieving the knife, lashes out at him with his boot a second time for good measure. In the cargo hold, the detonator has now reached one minute and forty seconds... and is continuing to count down.

As Necros watches helplessly, Bond uses the knife to cut through several strands of the netting, causing the sacks of opium to fly unrestrained out into the open air. Necros has to hold on for all that he is worth while the heavy sackcloth bags buffet him in all directions as they leave the net. The detonator has now reached one minute and thirteen seconds. Kara, still in the cockpit, is becoming increasingly fretful. With the cargo netting now holding only a few remaining bags of opium, Bond is struggling back towards the ramp when Necros reaches out to grab the agent's leg. The digital detonator display now reads one minute and nine seconds. Bond hangs on desperately as Necros attempts to cling on to his thigh. The rope is now looking extremely ragged, and seems liable to give way at any moment. The agent struggles with Necros, causing the assassin to wince in discomfort as 007 attempts to twist free from his grasp. Only fifty-one seconds remain on the bomb's countdown. Necros is clinging by his fingertips to Bond's right boot. Knowing that this is his last chance to dispense with the murderer, Bond reaches down with the knife and begins to cut through his laces. Necros watches with horror, and – uncharacteristically for such a coldly efficient killer – pleads with the agent for his life. But Bond has had enough, and continues to sever the last remaining laces. This causes the boot to fly off, and Necros with it. With a bloodcurdling scream, the assassin is hurled through the air towards a certain death far below.

His progress now unimpeded, Bond continues his fight to

reach the top of the netting. A sudden buffeting in the plane's motion causes the net – and Bond – to pitch forward onto the cargo ramp, where 007 lands heavily mere seconds before the supporting clip finally gives way. Bond fights to free himself from the heavy netting and then, realising that time is of the essence, activates a nearby control switch to retract the ramp. Utterly exhausted, he slumps back against the hold... that is, until he hears a familiar bleeping noise. Realising almost too late that the timer still has to be defused, he races frantically through the remaining Red Cross sacks until he finds the detonator, which he rapidly deactivates with only two seconds to spare. Realising just how close he and Kara have come to annihilation, he exhales deeply.

Bond struggles back to the cockpit, where a fearful Kara asks what has happened to Necros. 007 barely has time to deliver one of his customary puns – along the lines that the assassin has finally been given the boot – when he notices that the plane is headed straight towards a mountain range which they are approaching at high speed. Rushing into the pilot's seat, he desperately pulls on the joystick, sending the plane into a rapid ascent which only narrowly manages to avoid the aircraft striking the summit. Another disaster averted by the skin of his teeth, Bond sighs in relief. He and Kara then notice their Mujahedeen allies on the ground, who are being closely pursued by a variety of Russian armoured vehicles. The Soviets have clearly managed to regroup after the attack on their airbase; they are now firing relentlessly on Kamran and his men, attacking with bullets and rockets. The Afghan horsemen race away from their pursuers, heading for a road bridge just as the cargo plane passes above their position. A Russian rocket knocks one of the freedom fighters from their horses, causing Kamran to turn back in an attempt to rescue him. In spite of a hail of Soviet bullets, Kamran waits while the man clambers onto his own horse before beating a hasty retreat. Bond, meanwhile, turns the plane around and tells Kara to keep steering the aircraft as steadily as possible. When she asks what he intends to do this time, 007 responds that having succeeded in defusing the plastic explosives, it's now time to put them to good use.

As the Russian armoured column moves onto the bridge in pursuit of the Mujahedeen, the cargo plane flies low over their position once again. Most of the horsemen are now safely on the far side of the crossing; Kamran raises his hand by way of a greeting. Bond is quickly resetting the detonator, this time for a countdown of only nine seconds. He throws it, still within its Red Cross sack, out of the passenger door. A Soviet gunner on the back of one of the armoured vehicles watches curiously as the bag lands hard on the bridge below. The plastic explosives then finally ignite, causing a massive fireball which tears through the midsection of the bridge – and the passing armoured vehicle. The metal framework of the bridge quickly gives way, shattering and falling into the river beneath. Flames from the explosion also spread to one of the proximate structural supports. Kamran and his men cheer, knowing that Bond has ensured that they will fight another day. 007 grins down from the passenger door of the cargo plane, closing it just as the bridge's central support falls to pieces under the destructive power of the explosion. Another large section of the structure collapses, followed by further secondary detonations which rock other nearby sections of the bridge. The plane continues on its course as Bond returns to the cockpit, his expression one of great satisfaction. On the ground, the Mujahedeen fighters continue to celebrate, saluting Bond as the aircraft passes close overhead.

The destruction of the road bridge forms a visually spectacular conclusion to the long, climactic action sequence of *The Living Daylights*. It is a chain of scenes which reinforce Kara's bravery and resourcefulness, the utter ruination of Koskov's elaborate schemes, and the end of the sadistic Necros – a heartlessly professional murderer whose forlorn dying pleas to Bond make his demise seem slightly more poignant than is usual for the average henchman in other entries in the series. Bond's actions here appear to have more in common with eighties icon John Rambo than the damaged military intelligence officer of the Fleming novels; he seems capable of taking on what at times seems like the entire Soviet occupation force in Afghanistan with only a small, experienced Mujahedeen fighting force and a Czechoslovakian classical musician to aid his efforts. The whole operation is expertly structured by Maibaum and Wilson from start to finish, with Bond's desperate fight to deactivate the explosive detonator appearing even more satisfying when we later discover that – unlike many previous *Bond* films – he later finds a worthwhile use for the explosives.

Bond and Kara share a brief look of approval at the culmination of their efforts before peril faces them once again. The plane's fuel warning light is flashing red, and the gauge shows that the tank is very nearly empty. As Bond flicks various switches, Kara asks him what the problem is, to which he replies that the plane is running out of fuel at an alarming rate. He looks out of the cockpit, and notices that one of the engines has been ruptured by the impact of several Soviet bullet-holes. Fuel from the tank is haemorrhaging out into the air. Putting a folded geographical chart on top of the cabin's instruments, Bond grimly comments that he hopes that there may just be enough fuel left in reserve to get the plane over the border to Pakistan. Mere seconds after he has said this, however, the propellers come to an abrupt halt – first on the left wing, then on the right. Bond begins to look uncertain; with such mountainous terrain nearby it will be impossible to attempt even a crash landing. Stressing the urgency of their situation, he tells Kara to get into the jeep that is still parked in the cargo hold. Clearly unsure of his intentions, she does as he asks and quickly moves out of the cockpit. Bond then lowers the cargo ramp one last time. Joining Kara out in the hold, he tells her to fasten herself in before racing to the back of the jeep and engaging an emergency parachute system. As the plane comes ever closer to ground level, the parachute darts out of the rear cargo hatch, pulling the jeep behind it on a metal support platform. Bond barks to Kara to hold on tight as the support platform hits the ground and then pitches forward at speed, the parachute unable to slow it down sufficiently. They continue ahead until the platform collides with a low wall, which flings the jeep free of the parachute and ahead onto the rough terrain beyond. Driving to a standstill near a roadway, Bond and Kara look over their shoulder as the cargo plane cruises towards a mountainside. They hold hands as, a few seconds later, the plane collides with the rocky crag, bursting into flame as its last remaining fuel reserves ignite. The pair share another glance as they realise that once again they have only just managed to cheat death. Noticing a road sign nearby, pointing towards Islamabad in one direction and Karachi in the other, Bond suggests that they head for the latter destination; not only does he know a good eating place in Karachi, which is shown to be only 200km away, but if they hurry then they may even be able to get there in time for an evening meal. (While the road sign is an indication that Bond did indeed make it over the border to Pakistan, it does raise an interesting geographical quandary: it shows Islamabad to be 325km in one direction and Karachi as 200km in the other, whereas in reality the two cities are situated nearly one and a half thousand kilometres apart.) Without further ado, Bond hits the accelerator and heads off onto the long road ahead.

This final section of Bond's escape from Afghanistan gives another good example of the relevance of *The Living Daylights* to eighties popular film culture; whereas the attack on the Russian airbase would have definite resonance with Peter MacDonald's action epic *Rambo III* (1988) which was released the following year, Bond and Kara's knife-edge evasion of death when departing the cargo plane has undeniable similarities with the opening sequence of Steven Spielberg's *Indiana Jones and the Temple of Doom* (1984), with the parallels even stretching to their last-minute getaway (substituting a parachute-assisted jeep for an inflatable life-raft). Yet interestingly, the screenwriters' skilful use of foreshadowing – which was in evidence throughout most of the

Bond films upon which Wilson and Maibaum had collaborated – is employed particularly well here, where Bond's last-minute parachute jump to pull clear of the burning Land Rover in the pre-titles sequence presages the means of his later razor's-edge escape from the doomed cargo plane (with the latter incident admittedly proving to be somewhat larger and more impressive in scale).

Some time later, and thousands of miles away, night has fallen in Tangier. A sentry keeps watch outside Whitaker's residence, while a Muslim call to prayer can be heard in the distance. The camera pans across to a familiar-looking house with a pigeon loft, just across the street from Whitaker's compound. Felix Leiter's voice can be heard over a communication system as he informs an as-yet-unseen Bond that Whitaker is currently on the ground floor of his residence, whereas Koskov is in a bedroom upstairs. Switching to the deck of surveillance cameras on the CIA yacht, we can now see one of Whitaker's security operatives patrolling the large outdoor pool as Leiter informs Bond on the radio that the guard is nearby. Leiter and his two female colleagues from earlier in the film are then shown in the yacht control room, as the American agent informs Bond that it is now clear to proceed. Back at the complex, Bond is now revealed, hiding in a leafy area near the poolside. He is dressed all in black, as befits a stealth mission. As he steps forward at Leiter's urging, he disturbs a pigeon which flutters around his head, momentarily surprising him. (This is the film's obligatory demonstration of Glen's directorial trademark – a startled pigeon emerging into shot – which was to make an appearance at some point in all of his *Bond* films.) Leiter watches pensively as Bond continues his progress. As 007 moves midway along the length of a high hedge, passing a small statue as he does so, his CIA counterpart tells him to halt his progress. The American warns Bond that the guard is returning to his previous position, causing Bond to acknowledge the advice by signalling electronically with his earpiece. Leiter radios Bond again to let him know that the guard is in range, just as Bond punches the hapless security operative when he emerges through a gap in the hedge next to the pool. Caught completely unaware by the intruder, the unconscious guard topples over. Bond grabs him before he can hit the ground and drags his prone form away from the opening in the hedge. Sipping from a mug of coffee, a satisfied Leiter remarks to his colleagues that Bond has now successfully penetrated the defences of Whitaker's compound… and that the rest of the mission depends on 007 from thereon in.

Bond is now moving through Whitaker's historical hall of fame, his Walther PPK in his hand. He seems nonplussed by the seemingly endless array of military mannequins, all of them wearing the arms dealer's features. 007's dark clothing assists him in blending into the background successfully. As he paces silently along the hallway, the sound of a battlefield can be heard nearby – as can the mildly deranged laughter of Whitaker himself. Bond emerges into the private military museum to see his adversary enthusiastically replaying the American Civil War's Battle of Gettysburg with the aid of models and simulated sound effects. He quietly closes the internal doors behind him as tiny flashes and puffs of smoke emanate from the miniature battlefield. While the arms dealer remains enraptured by the carnage of his re-enactment, Bond softly but firmly tells him that Pickett's Charge had taken place at Cemetery Ridge, rather than Little Round Top (where Whitaker's strategy has shown it). Whitaker appears totally unfazed by Bond's sudden appearance. Refusing to remove his attention from the model, he tells Bond that he is replaying the conflict by his own rules – in his opinion, Union General George Meade may have been a determined officer, but his tactics were overly wary. Had he pressed his advantage, Whitaker reasons, he could have achieved an overwhelming victory over Confederate General Robert E. Lee by the end of the battle, concluding the American Civil War rather than simply providing its turning point. Tired of martial small-talk, Bond bluntly tells Whitaker that his presence is simple: he wants

Koskov handed over. This finally captures the arms dealer's attention. Raising his gaze from the battle simulation, Whitaker smiles sinisterly and tells Bond that he is more than welcome to the seditious Russian General... but only when the opium has been handed over. With the greatest of satisfaction, Bond tells him that this will be impossible – the narcotics have all been destroyed. Incredulous, Whitaker asks him to confirm that he has, genuinely, disposed of half a billion dollars' worth of illegal drugs – an enquiry which Bond is only too happy to agree to. Strangely calm, Whitaker remarks that this is an unfortunate turn of events: Bond could have left his compound a wealthy man, rather than as a corpse. His pistol never wavering as he retains his aim at Whitaker, Bond seems unmoved by the blatant threat.

Calmly, 007 tells Whitaker that his game is over: both the Russians and the Americans are now after him for his part in Koskov's schemes. But the arms dealer brushes aside the comment. Returning his gaze to the model battlefield, he coolly reflects that Meade should have been willing to risk the lives of many tens of thousands more soldiers than he had actually done during the conflict at Gettysburg; if he had been bolder, Whitaker believes, he could have ended the Civil War a whole year earlier than history records had been the case. As he makes these observations, he moves model figures around the board, and ends by stabbing a miniature cavalry figure onto a hitherto-unnoticed remote control unit which is lying close by on the tabletop. Just as he remarks that Ulysses S. Grant would likely have achieved what George Meade didn't, an electronic drawer shoots out of the simulator's table in response to the signal from the remote control, hitting Bond hard in the knees and knocking him backwards into a smaller table clustered with ornaments. As 007 grunts in pain, another drawer opens on the opposite side of the table, granting Whitaker access to a powerful sub-machine gun.

Clearly expert in its use, the arms dealer lets rip with round after round of bullets, shattering glass cases and sending Bond racing for cover further into the museum. With another flick of the remote control, Whitaker silences the simulated battle sounds, plunging the room into silence.

Bond is now crawling out from underneath another simulation table – this one showing the Battle of Agincourt – as he takes aim at Whitaker. The arms dealer is emerging from behind a pillar; he is carrying an advanced-looking machine gun of some kind, complete with a toughened face shield. Bond fires three rounds from his Walther PPK, but each shot is deflected harmlessly by the transparent shield. Whitaker grins smugly at the ineffectiveness of Bond's time-honoured pistol. Carefully taking aim, Bond fires another five bullets at his adversary, but once again the shots are ineffective. Whitaker laughs, telling Bond that he is more than aware that the agent's handgun is now empty... but that he, on the other hand, is just getting started. Stabbing the remote control again, flashing lights begin to emit from around the room as more battlefield simulations come online. Then he starts firing with the machine gun, causing severe damage to the area around the Agincourt simulation. As Bond dives for cover once again, Whitaker laughs psychotically at the destructive power of his weaponry, taunting 007 as he reflects on how outmoded the agent's trusted Walther gun has proven to be. Whitaker hits the remote control yet again, suddenly vigilant as he realises that he has lost track of Bond's location. Cautiously, he edges around another pillar, the shielding around his gun now looking rather battered as a result of Bond's well-aimed bullets. Spotting the agent standing near a model of an eighteenth-century cannon, complete with a life-sized replica gunner in period uniform, Whitaker presses another button on his control. This causes the gunner to lower a burning taper into position onto the cannon's fuse. His eyes widening at this sudden, unexpected development, Bond dives for cover as a cannonball blasts past, only narrowly missing him. Having succeeded in flushing 007 out of his hiding place, Whitaker then starts firing with the machine gun again, blasting more of his exhibits in the process. The arms dealer's eyes are drawn to a large metal bust of the Duke of

Wellington, victor of the Battle of Waterloo. Correctly sensing that Bond is hiding behind the heavy pillar supporting the bust, Whitaker mocks him by calling the British historical figure a mere 'vulture'. Bond, meanwhile, is covertly attaching his magnetic keyring to the back of the bust, still out of his enemy's line of sight. Whitaker goads Bond by saying that he believes Wellington's victory over Napoleon was only made possible by him employing German mercenaries to bolster his own troops on the battlefield. (Typically for Whitaker, this is an inaccurate assessment – the King's German Legion were actually under Wellington's direct command at Waterloo, while no other Germans involved in the battle were specifically aligned to the British Army – officially or otherwise.) In response to his comment, Bond gives a wolf-whistle, activating the explosives within the keyring. Whitaker laughs, thinking that the agent was reacting to his needling, but his mirth is short-lived when the keyring detonates, sending the pillar – and the heavy bust – toppling down onto him. Crushed to death by the metal sculpture, Whitaker is pinned down against a tabletop simulation of (ironically enough) the Battle of Waterloo, his face blooded by the shards of glass lying around from his earlier shooting spree. Bond looks down at the fallen would-be military genius, touching his arm gently as he checks that he is, in fact, dead.

Seconds later, Whitaker's 'sergeant' comes racing into the museum through the internal doors; although too late to save his employer, he takes aim at Bond with a machine gun... only to be shot himself by an unknown assailant out in the hallway. Bond is stunned at the suddenness of the whole incident. Having recoiled in the face of the expected attack, he picks himself up just as Whitaker's ill-fated member of staff falls dead to the ground. General Pushkin, gun in hand, emerges from the hall, flanked by three black-clad KGB operatives. The Russian security men quickly scout the room for dangers, one of them efficiently taking Pushkin's firearm for him. Pushkin notes that he had an unsettled debt with Bond which has now been repaid. As the Russian looks down with disdain on Whitaker's corpse, Bond remarks that – just had been the case for Napoleon before him – Waterloo had not gone well for the malign arms dealer. Seeing the humour in his observation, Pushkin smiles appreciatively.

Moments later, the KGB operatives – joined by several colleagues – begin to herd up Whitaker's security staff and frogmarch them into the museum. First to be shoved into the room, however, is Koskov, now back in civilian clothing. Seeming shocked at this unexpected situation, the rogue General appears momentarily lost for words as he sees his presumed-dead KGB superior. But he quickly recovers and feigns relief, throwing his arms around the (totally unresponsive) Pushkin and telling him how reassured he is by the intelligence chief's presence in Tangier. Clearly thinking on his feet, Koskov tells Pushkin that he has been held captive at the compound for weeks by Whitaker, all the while eyeing Bond – who naturally knows otherwise – with considerable trepidation, as though begging him to stay silent. Now it is Pushkin's turn for some acting. Pretending to be overjoyed at finding Koskov (who then gives Bond an odiously smug glance), Pushkin tells one of his black-clad subordinates to book his scheming colleague onto a plane to Moscow. Koskov is jubilant at this news, believing that he has actually managed to hoodwink the KGB director... until Pushkin dryly adds that he will be travelling back to Russia in the diplomatic bag. His expression immediately changing to one of stunned perplexity, Koskov is led off by Pushkin's KGB minders before he can comment further on his fate. Now that the two men are left alone, Bond retrieves his Walther PPK and asks Pushkin what will happen to Kara now that the mission is over. Reflectively, Pushkin notes that there is no ignoring the fact that like Koskov, she is a defector. Putting an avuncular arm around the British agent, the KGB chief suggests that they should discuss a way that her situation can be resolved.

In this sequence of scenes, we see justice being delivered upon Bond's two antagonists in the established tradition of the series. Whitaker effectively lays the groundwork for his own downfall, suffering a violent death in a private museum which glories in carnage and bloodshed. (The demise of Whitaker did not mark the end of Joe Don Baker's participation with the *Bond* series, however – he would later return alongside Pierce Brosnan's Bond as CIA agent Jack Wade in *GoldenEye*, 1995, and *Tomorrow Never Dies*, 1997). That the arms dealer should perish as a result of his own grandiose collection is ironic in itself, but it is certainly less surprising than Koskov's fate. The Soviet General is one of very few Bond villains who manage to survive the conclusion of the film without their nefarious schemes leading to their death – although from Pushkin's tone, it is heavily suggested that Koskov's life may not extend much beyond his return to Russia. (Indeed, the fact that he was already earmarked for arrest due to his embezzlement prior to his defection suggests that Pushkin was already well aware of his plans, and that Koskov's labyrinthine chicanery has merely been delaying the inevitable.) Jeroen Krabbé delivers a masterclass of comic timing in Koskov's final scene, lurching from the astonishment of seeing Pushkin after presuming him long since dead through to grovelling sycophancy as he tries to convince him of his innocence – all the while maintaining a totally different, entirely unspoken interaction with Bond all the way throughout his multifaceted discourse with the KGB chief – and ending with a priceless expression of shock as he realises that his tortuously convoluted network of deception has finally collapsed in on itself. Although it is never explained how Koskov was able to return to the West from Afghanistan after the crippling Mujahedeen attack on the Soviet military base, his demeanour as he is led away by the Russian authorities suggests that – as he knew that Bond was still at large – returning to Whitaker's compound may not have been his wisest course of action in hindsight. The interaction between the American arms dealer Whitaker and the rogue Russian strategist Koskov is an interesting one in Cold War terms, for it emphasises an unconventional kind of international co-operation in the pursuit of enlightened self-interest. Yet it is mirrored by the later collaboration between the British agent Bond, American operative Leiter and KGB director Pushkin, all of whom indirectly pool their efforts in order to shut down the conspiracy between Whitaker and Koskov and neutralise the threat that they pose to the geopolitical status quo.

We next cut to a very familiar looking cello which proudly bears a similarly recognisable bullet-hole. The string instrument is currently being played by a formally-dressed Kara, her expression completely intent on the music. She – and the rest of the orchestra that she is part of – is midway through performing Tchaikovsky's Rococo Variations. As the camera switches viewpoints, we realise that her dream has been realised: she is playing the Lady Rose at New York's famous Carnegie Hall. (Although his role is uncredited, the musicians are being conducted by none other than long-running Bond composer John Barry.) While Kara continues to perform the challenging piece, she looks out at the vast audience with both awe and ill-concealed happiness. She smiles beatifically as the music comes to an end, rising to her feet on the stage as the audience explodes into vigorous applause.

At a reception after the performance, champagne is being poured by attendants in Regency attire. Kara is being flanked by press journalists, photographers and well-wishers; she smiles graciously as questions are fired at her relentlessly, but she seems uncomfortable by the crowd's close proximity and the intensity of the situation. Appearing suddenly, M eases his way through the gathering and asks Kara to join him. Carrying a large bouquet of flowers, she is guided away politely by the MI6 director, who gently but firmly asks the assembled group to excuse them. Ushering her to a quieter part of the room, M introduces Kara to Soviet General Anatol Gogol (Walter Gotell), the one-time KGB leader – and Pushkin's predecessor – who now works for the U.S.S.R.'s foreign office. Gogol expresses heartfelt approval of Kara's exquisite musical skills, and tells her that he hopes that she will soon be playing in Moscow to delight the audiences there. Kara begins to look panicked, clearly believing that Gogol intends to return her to the other side of the Iron Curtain, but M quickly reassures her: Gogol hasn't come to New York to apprehend Kara, but to grant her an immigration visa. The elderly General smiles at her with genuine benevolence, confirming M's account of the situation. Kara's immense relief is tangible; she will now be able to freely move from East to West – and back again – without fear of detention by the Soviets.

There is sudden commotion near the reception hall's entranceway; two doormen are swept aside as a group of instantly-recognisable Mujahedeen fighters swarm into the room. Intrigued by their surprise appearance, Kara politely excuses herself and heads towards them. Entering the room last is the distinguished Kamran Shah, immaculately dressed in regal Afghan garments. He apologises profusely to Kara for having missed her performance: unfortunately he and his men had been delayed by airport officials upon entering the country. M, sardonically noting that he had no idea why this might be (given that the freedom fighters are all swathed in seemingly-endless strings of bullets), introduces Kamran to Gogol. In spite of the deep animosity which exists between their respective countries, the two men greet each other cordially. Kamran then asks M if Bond is present. The British Intelligence chief replies that unfortunately Bond is overseas on a mission and was thus unable to make the concert. Kara, upset by the news, respectfully withdraws from the group, leaving Kamran watching with concern as she heads for her dressing room. She enters and closes the door behind her, revealing a large poster advertising her world tour as she does so. Still holding her flowers, she closes her eyes and takes a deep, regretful sigh... until she notices two glasses and a mixer placed on a silver tray in front of her. Carefully putting the bouquet down on a nearby table, Kara whistles only to discover – seconds later – that a certain familiar beeping can be heard. Slowly, a hand emerges from behind a dressing screen holding an immediately-identifiable keyring. Kara laughs as she realises that Bond is not really abroad on a mission, but only a few feet away. Moving to snatch the keyring from his hand, Kara is gently grabbed by Bond and pulled behind the screen. Embracing her lovingly, Bond gently asks if she honestly thought that he would fail to attend this of all performances. They kiss passionately as the camera pulls back, leaving the pair behind the dressing screen as Kara moans Bond's name appreciatively. Cutting to an exterior shot of Carnegie Hall, the Pretenders' song 'If There Was a Man' can be heard as the end credits roll. Closing on a shot of the two glasses and shaker in Kara's dressing room, a superimposed caption promises that 'James Bond Will Return' as the screen eventually fades to black.

The closing sequence of the film ties up the last remaining threads of *The Living Daylights*'s narrative. The audience discovers that not only has Kara achieved her crowning ambition of performing at the world-famous Carnegie Hall, but that it is seemingly only the first venue on a high-profile tour of the globe. Kamran and his men are shown to have survived the Russian counterattack in Afghanistan, and thanks to Bond have lived to continue their struggle against the Soviet occupation. And the legality of Kara's defection is made official by the intervention of General Gogol, presumably as a result of Bond's unofficial brokering with Pushkin at Whitaker's Moroccan residence. Walter Gotell's wily KGB director had been a recurring character in the *Bond* cycle since *The Spy Who Loved Me* in 1977. This was to be the actor's final appearance in a *Bond* film and, fittingly, it sees him promoted to a foreign office position, passing Gogol's baton over to Pushkin while similarly ensuring that the East-West amity that the character had so often personified continued to remain alive and well. The closing shots, where Bond and Kara are reunited away from the cellist's new-found admirers, seem more affecting than in many other *Bond* films due to the genuine sense of a deepening relationship between the pair. The characters' romance had been touchingly and realistically developed throughout the course of the film by d'Abo and Dalton, making the gentle, building rapport between Kara and Bond one of the most tenderly-rendered romantic pairings in the series. That said, of course, in the grand tradition of the *Bond* cycle there was to be no mention of her in the series' next film, where 007 would move on to a new partner who was to prove as different from Kara Milovy as it is possible to conceive.

The Living Daylights received its world premiere on 29 June 1987, in the highly-publicised presence of the Prince and Princess of Wales, at the London Odeon Leicester Square Theatre. A year after its release, the film would go on to win a Golden Screen Award in Germany as well as a BFI Film Music Award for John Barry's original score. It was also nominated for a Saturn Award by the Academy of Science Fiction, Fantasy and Horror Films, in the category of Best Fantasy Film. As the twenty-fifth anniversary entry in the series, the film succeeded in presenting Timothy Dalton as a very different kind of Bond – a darker, more intense character than had been presented by the cycle since the very early days of Sean Connery's portrayal. But it also reinforced the series' generic credentials by presenting a genuinely intriguing spy thriller as well as an action adventure, complete with the narrative complexity that this generic distinction implies, without neglecting the familiar and firmly-established tropes of the Eon cycle. Although the film's geopolitical topicality was to prove relevant to many critics at the time, *The Living Daylights* has aged surprisingly well, and today remains among the most narratively sophisticated of *Bond* films. When placed in the wider context of the *Bond* series it is difficult to deny that the film came to form a highlight of the decade, as well as proving to be one of John Glen's most accomplished features for Eon Productions.

Some James Bond merchandizing
(mainly linked to the 1980s movies).

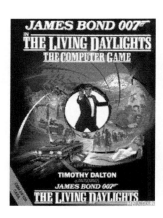

The romance of Kara Milovy and James Bond is
touchingly and realistically developed throughout
the course of The Living Daylights by Maryam d'Abo
and Timothy Dalton, making the gentle, building
rapport between Kara and Bond one of the most
tenderly-rendered romantic pairings in the
James Bond series.

APPENDIX I

THE FILMOGRAPHY OF JOHN GLEN

The Third Man. Dir. Carol Reed. British Lion/ London Films. 1949. [as Assistant Sound Editor]

The Wooden Horse. Dir. Jack Lee. British Lion/ Wessex/ London Films. 1950. [as Second Assistant Editor]

The Long Dark Hall. Dir. Anthony Bushell, Reginald Beck. British Lion/ Five Oceans. 1951. [as Second Assistant Editor]

There Was a Young Lady. Dir. Lawrence Huntingdon. Ellis Films/ Butcher's Film Service. 1953. [as Second Assistant Editor]

Make Me an Offer. Dir. Cyril Frankel. Group Three. 1954. [as Assistant Editor]

John and Julie. Dir. William Fairchild. Group Three. 1955. [as Assistant Editor]

The Extra Day. Dir. William Fairchild. British Lion. 1956. [as Assistant Editor]

The Green Man. Dir. Robert Day. British Lion/ Grenadier. 1956. [as Sound Editor]

Three Men in a Boat. Dir. Ken Annakin. Romulus. 1956. [as Assembly Editor/ Sound Editor]

The Admirable Crichton. Dir. Lewis Gilbert. Columbia/ Modern Screenplays. 1957. [as Sound Editor]

The Scamp. Dir. Wolf Rilla. Minter/ Renown. 1957. [as Sound Editor]

A Cry from the Streets. Dir. Lewis Gilbert. Film Traders. 1958. [as Sound Editor]

Life is a Circus. Dir. Val Guest. Vale Films. 1958. [as Sound Editor]

Dentist in the Chair. Dir. Don Chaffey. Briand. 1960. [as Sound Editor]

Foxhole in Cairo. Dir. John Moxey. Omnia. 1960. [as Sound Editor]

Buona Sera, Mrs Campbell. Dir. Melvin Frank. United Artists/ Connaught. 1968. [as Additional Sound Editor]

Baby Love. Dir. Alastair Reid. Avco/ Avton. 1968. [as Editor]

The Italian Job. Dir. Peter Collinson. Paramount/ Oakhurst. 1969. [as Additional Sound Editor]

On Her Majesty's Secret Service. Dir. Peter Hunt. United Artists/ Eon Productions. 1969. [as Editor/ Second Unit Director]

Murphy's War. Dir. Peter Yates. Hemdale. 1971. [as Co-Editor/ Second Unit

Director]

Catlow. Dir. Sam Wanamaker. MGM. 1971. [as Supervising Editor/ Second Unit Director]

Pulp. Dir. Mike Hodges. United Artists. 1972. [as Editor]

Sitting Target. Dir. Douglas Hickox. MGM. 1972. [as Editor]

A Doll's House. Dir. Patrick Garland. Elkins/ Freeward. 1973. [as Editor]

Gold. Dir. Peter Hunt. Hemdale/ Avton. 1974. [as Editor/ Second Unit Director]

Dead Cert. Dir. Tony Richardson. United Artists/ Woodfall. 1974. [as Editor]

Conduct Unbecoming. Dir. Michael Anderson. British Lion/ Crown. 1975. [as Editor]

Shout at the Devil. Dir. Peter Hunt. Tonav. 1976. [as Second Unit Director]

Seven Nights in Japan. Dir. Lewis Gilbert. EMI/ Marianne. 1976. [as Editor]

The Spy Who Loved Me. Dir. Lewis Gilbert. United Artists/ Eon Productions. 1977. [as Editor/ Co-Second Unit Director]

The Wild Geese. Dir. Andrew V McLaglen. Rank/ Richmond. 1978. [as Editor/ Second Unit Director]

Superman. Dir. Richard Donner. Warner. 1978. [as Second Unit Director]

Moonraker. Dir. Lewis Gilbert. United Artists/ Eon Productions. 1979. [as Editor/ Co-Second Unit Director]

The Sea Wolves. Dir. Andrew V McLaglen. Richmond/ Lorimar/ Varius. 1980. [as Editor]

For Your Eyes Only. Dir. John Glen. United Artists/ Eon Productions. 1981.

Octopussy. Dir. John Glen. MGM/ United Artists/ Eon Productions. 1983.

A View to a Kill. Dir. John Glen. MGM/ United Artists/ Eon Productions. 1985.

The Living Daylights. Dir. John Glen. MGM/ United Artists/ Eon Productions. 1987.

Licence to Kill. Dir. John Glen. MGM/ United Artists/ Eon Productions. 1989.

Aces: Iron Eagle III. Dir. John Glen. New Line/ 7 Arts. 1992.

Christopher Columbus: The Discovery. Dir. John Glen. Rank/ Peel Enterprises. 1992.

The Point Men. Dir. John Glen. Columbia TriStar/ Black Magic. 2001.

APPENDIX II

THE FILMOGRAPHY OF ROGER MOORE

Honeymoon Deferred. Dir. Mario Camerini. Vic Films. 1950. [in the role of 'Ornithologist']

The Last Time I Saw Paris. Dir. Richard Brooks. MGM. 1954. [in the role of 'Paul']

Interrupted Melody. Dir. Curtis Bernhardt. MGM. 1955. [in the role of 'Cyril Lawrence']

The King's Thief. Dir. Robert Z. Leonard. MGM. 1955. [in the role of 'Jack']

Diane. Dir. David Miller. MGM. 1956. [in the role of 'Prince Henri']

The Miracle. Dir. Irving Rapper. Warner. 1959. [in the role of 'Captain Michael Stuart']

The Sins of Rachel Cade. Dir. Gordon Douglas. Warner. 1961. [in the role of 'Paul Wilton']

Gold of the Seven Saints. Dir. Gordon Douglas. Warner. 1961. [in the role of 'Shaun Garrett']

Romulus and the Sabines. Dir. Richard Pottier. FICIT/ CIPRA/ Dubrava Film. 1961. [in the role of 'Romulus']

No Man's Land. Dir. Fabrizio Taglioni. FICIT/ Coliseum Film/ Contact Organisation. 1962. [in the role of 'Enzo Prati']

The Fiction Makers. Dir. Roy Ward Baker. ITC/ Bamore. 1968. [in the role of 'Simon Templar'/ 'The Saint']

Crossplot. Dir. Alvin Rakoff. United Artists/ Tribune. 1969. [in the role of 'Gary Fenn']

The Man Who Haunted Himself. Dir. Basil Dearden. ABP/ Excalibur. 1970. [in the role of 'Harold Pelham']

Live and Let Die. Dir. Guy Hamilton. United Artists/ Eon Productions. 1973. [in the role of 'James Bond']

Gold. Dir. Peter R. Hunt. Hemdale/ Avton. 1974. [in the role of 'Rod Slater']

The Man with the Golden Gun. Dir. Guy Hamilton. United Artists/ Eon Productions. 1974. [in the role of 'James Bond']

That Lucky Touch. Dir. Christopher Miles. Rank/ Gloria. 1975. [in the role of 'Michael Scott']

The Sicilian Cross. Dirs. Maurizio Lucidi and Guglielmo Garroni. Aetos. 1976. [in the role of 'Ulysses']

Shout at the Devil. Dir. Peter R. Hunt. Tonav. 1976. [in the role of 'Sebastian Oldsmith']

The Spy Who Loved Me. Dir. Lewis Gilbert. United Artists/ Eon Productions. 1977. [in the role of 'James Bond']

The Wild Geese. Dir. Andrew V. McLaglen. Rank/ Richmond. 1978. [in the role of Lieutenant Shawn Fynn]

Escape to Athena. Dir. George Pan Cosmatos. ITC/ Pimlico. 1979. [in the role of 'Major Otto Hecht']

Moonraker. Dir. Lewis Gilbert. United Artists/ Eon Productions. 1979. [in the role of 'James Bond']

Ffolkes (a.k.a. *North Sea Hijack*). Dir. Andrew V. McLaglen. Universal/ Cinema Seven. 1980. [in the role of 'Ffolkes']

The Sea Wolves. Dir. Andrew V. McLaglen. Richmond/ Lorimar/ Varius. 1980. [in the role of 'Captain Gavin Stewart']

Sunday Lovers. Dirs. Bryan Forbes, Edouard Molinaro, Dino Risi and Gene Wilder. Medusa Productions/ Viaduc Productions. 1980. [in the role of 'Harry Lindon']

The Cannonball Run. Dir. Hal Needham. Golden Harvest. 1981. [in the role of 'Seymour Goldfarb, Junior']

For Your Eyes Only. Dir. John Glen. United Artists/ Eon Productions. 1981. [in the role of 'James Bond']

Octopussy. Dir. John Glen. MGM/ United Artists/ Eon Productions. 1983. [in the role of 'James Bond']

Curse of the Pink Panther. Dir. Blake Edwards. MGM/ United Artists/ Titan/ Jewel. 1983. [in the role of 'Chief Inspector Jacques Clouseau']

The Naked Face. Dir. Bryan Forbes. Cannon. 1984. [in the role of 'Dr Judd Stevens']

A View to a Kill. Dir. John Glen. MGM/ United Artists/ Eon Productions. 1985. [in the role of 'James Bond']

The Magic Snowman. Dirs. Stanko Crnobrnja and C. Stanner. Pavlina Ltd./ TRZ Ton i Film. 1987. [in the role of 'voice of Lumi Ukko the Snowman']

Fire, Ice and Dynamite. Dir. Willy Bogner. Willy Bogner Film. 1990. [in the role of 'Sir George']

Bullseye! Dir. Michael Winner. Castle Premiere/ 21st Century. 1990. [in the role of 'Garald Bradley-Smith'/ 'Sir John Bevistock']

Bed and Breakfast. Dir. Robert Ellis Miller. Hemdale. 1991. [in the role of 'Adam']

The Quest. Dir. Jean-Claude Van Damme. Universal/ MDP. 1996. [in the role of 'Lord Edgar Dobbs']

The Saint. Dir. Phillip Noyce. Paramount/ Rysher. 1997. [in the role of 'Voice on Car Radio']

Spice World. Dir. Bob Spiers. Polygram/ Icon/ Fragile. 1997. [in the role of 'Chief']

The Enemy. Dir. Tom Kinninmont. Carousel Picture Company/ Enemy Films U.K. Ltd./ Promark Entertainment Group/ UFA International/ Videal. 2001. [in the role of 'Superintendent Robert Ogilvie']

Boat Trip. Dir. Mort Nathan. MPCA/ IWP/ ApolloMedia/ Boat Trip/ Erste Productions/ Gemini Film. 2002. [in the role of 'Lloyd Faversham']

Agent Crush. Dir. Sean Robinson. Crush Productions. 2008. [in the role of 'voice of Burt Gasket']

The Wild Swans. Dirs. Peter Flinth and Ghita Nørby. JJ Film. 2009. [in the role of 'voice of Archbishop']

Gnomes and Trolls: The Forest Trial. Dir. Robert Rhodin. White Shark. 2010. [in the role of 'voice of Leif']

Cats and Dogs: The Revenge of Kitty Galore. Dir. Brad Peyton. CD2 Films/ Mad Chance/ Polymorphic Pictures/ Village Roadshow Pictures. 2010. [in the role of 'voice of Tab Lazenby']

A Princess for Castlebury. Dir. Michael Damian. Media Pro Pictures/ MPCA/ Riviera Films. 2011. [in the role of 'Edward, Duke of Castlebury']

APPENDIX III

THE FILMOGRAPHY OF TIMOTHY DALTON

The Lion in Winter. Dir. Anthony Harvey. Avco Embassy. 1968. [in the role of 'Philip II']

Wuthering Heights. Dir. Robert Fuest. American International Pictures. 1970. [in the role of 'Heathcliff']

Cromwell. Dir. Ken Hughes. Irving Allen Productions. 1970.[in the role of 'Prince Rupert']

The Voyeur. Dir. Franco Indovina. PIC/ Ultra Film/ PECF. 1970. [in the role of 'Mark']

Mary, Queen of Scots. Dir. Charles Jarrott. Univeral Pictures. 1971. [in the role of 'Henry, Lord Darnley']

Permission to Kill (a.k.a. *The Executioner*). Dir. Cyril Frankel. Sascha-Verleih. 1975. [in the role of 'Charles Lord']

Sextette. Dir. Ken Hughes. Briggs and Sullivan. 1978. [in the role of 'Sir Michael Barrington']

The Man Who Knew Love. Dir. Miguel Picazo. General Films Corporation. 1978. [in the role of 'Juan de Dios']

Agatha. Dir. Michael Apted. Sweetwall Productions/ The First Artists Production Co. Ltd./ Warner Bros. 1979. [in the role of 'Colonel Archibald Christie']

Flash Gordon. Dir. Mike Hodges. Starling Productions Ltd. 1980. [in the role of 'Prince Barin']

Chanel Solitaire. Dir. George Kaczender. Larry G. Spangler Production. 1981. [in the role of 'Boy Capel']

The Doctor and the Devils. Dir. Freddie Francis. Brooksfilms/ Twentieth Century Fox. 1985. [in the role of 'Dr Thomas Rock']

The Living Daylights. Dir. John Glen. MGM/ United Artists/ Eon Productions. 1987. [in the role of 'James Bond']

Hawks. Dir. Robert Ellis Miller. Producers Representative Organization. 1988. [in the role of 'Walter Bancroft']

Brenda Starr. Dir. Robert Ellis Miller. AM/ PM Entertainment/ New World Pictures/ Tribune Entertainment. 1989. [in the role of 'Basil St. John']

Licence to Kill. Dir. John Glen. MGM/ United Artists/ Eon Productions. 1989. [in the role of 'James Bond']

The King's Whore. Dir. Axel Corti. AFC/ Cinecittà/ Cinema & Cinema/ Cofimage/ France 3 Cinéma/ Images Investissements/ Invest-image/ Ministero del Turismo e dello Spettacolo/ Radiotelevisione Italiana/ Slav Productions/ Sofinergie 1/ Umbrella Films. 1990. [in the role of 'King Vittorio Amadeo']

The Rocketeer. Dir. Joe Johnston. Walt Disney Pictures/ Touchstone Pictures/ Silver Screen Partners IV/ Gordon Company. 1991. [in the role of 'Neville Sinclair']

Naked in New York. Dir. Daniel Algrant. Fine Line/ Pandora. 1993. [in the role of 'Elliot Price']

Salt Water Moose. Dir. Stuart Margolin. FUND/ TMN/ The Ontario Film Development Corporation/ Showtime Networks/ Téléfilm Canada. 1996. [in the role of 'Lester Parnell']

The Beautician and the Beast. Dir. Ken Kwapis. High School Sweethearts/ Koch Company/ Paramount Pictures. 1997. [in the role of 'Boris Pochenko']

The Informant. Dir. Jim McBride. Hallmark Entertainment/ Johnny Loves Suzie Productions/ Showtime Networks. 1997. [in the role of 'Detective Chief Inspector Rennie']

Made Men. Dir. Louis Morneau. Decade Pictures/ Made Men Productions/ Hallmark Entertainment/ Johnny Loves Suzie Productions/ Showtime Networks. 1999. [in the role of 'Sheriff Dex Drier']

The Reef (a.k.a. *Passion's Way*). Dir. Robert Allan Ackerman. Freyda Rothstein Productions/ Hearst Entertainment Productions/ Stillking Films/ Zweites Deutsches Fernsehen. 1999 [in the role of 'Charles Darrow']

Bitter Suite. Dir. Sharon von Wietersheim. B&H Entertainment/ Constantin Film Production. 2000. [in the role of 'Matt Farragher']

American Outlaws. Dir. Les Mayfield. Morgan Creek Productions. 2001. [in the role of 'Allan Pinkerton']

Looney Tunes: Back in Action. Dir. Joe Dante. Warner Bros./ Baltimore Spring Creek Productions/ Goldmann Pictures/ Lonely Film Productions. 2003. [in the role of 'Damien Drake']

Tales from Earthsea. Dir. Goro Miyazaki. Buena Vista Home Entertainment/ DENTSU/ Hakuhodo DY Media Partners/ GNDHDDT/ Mitsubishi/ Nibariki/ NTV/ Studio Ghibli/ Toho Company. 2006. [in the role of 'voice of Ged'/ 'voice of Sparrowhawk']

Hot Fuzz. Dir. Edgar Wright. Universal Pictures/ StudioCanal/ Working Title Films/ Big Talk Productions/ Ingenious Film Partners. 2007. [in the role of 'Simon Skinner']

Toy Story 3. Dir Lee Unkrich. Pixar Animation Studios/ Walt Disney Pictures. 2010. [in the role of 'voice of Mr Pricklepants']

The Tourist. Dir. Florian Henckel von Donnersmarck. GK Films/ Columbia Pictures/ Spyglass Entertainment/ StudioCanal/ Birnbaum/ Barber. 2010. [in the role of 'Chief Inspector Jones']

Clean Out. Dir. Barthélémy Grossmann. Dädalus Film/ Frantic Films Live Action Productions/ Mind's Eye Entertainment. 2011. [in the role of 'Kupfer']

APPENDIX IV

A CHRONOLOGICAL FILMOGRAPHY OF EON PRODUCTIONS' *JAMES BOND* FILM SERIES

Dr No. Dir. Terence Young. United Artists/ Eon Productions. 1962.

From Russia with Love. Dir. Terence Young. United Artists/ Eon Productions. 1963.

Goldfinger. Dir. Guy Hamilton. United Artists/ Eon Productions. 1964.

Thunderball. Dir. Terence Young. United Artists/ Eon Productions. 1965.

You Only Live Twice. Dir. Lewis Gilbert. United Artists/ Eon Productions. 1967.

On Her Majesty's Secret Service. Dir. Peter Hunt. United Artists/ Eon Productions. 1969.

Diamonds Are Forever. Dir. Guy Hamilton. United Artists/ Eon Productions. 1971.

Live and Let Die. Dir. Guy Hamilton. United Artists/ Eon Productions. 1973.

The Man with the Golden Gun. Dir. Guy Hamilton. United Artists/ Eon Productions. 1974.

The Spy Who Loved Me. Dir. Lewis Gilbert. United Artists/ Eon Productions. 1977.

Moonraker. Dir. Lewis Gilbert. United Artists/ Eon Productions. 1979.

For Your Eyes Only. Dir. John Glen. United Artists/ Eon Productions. 1981.

Octopussy. Dir. John Glen. MGM/ United Artists/ Eon Productions. 1983.

A View to a Kill. Dir. John Glen. MGM/ United Artists/ Eon Productions. 1985.

The Living Daylights. Dir. John Glen. MGM/ United Artists/ Eon Productions. 1987.

Licence to Kill. Dir. John Glen. MGM/ United Artists/ Eon Productions. 1989.

GoldenEye. Dir. Martin Campbell. MGM/ United Artists/ Eon Productions. 1995.

Tomorrow Never Dies. Dir. Roger Spottiswoode. MGM/ United Artists/ Eon Productions. 1997.

The World is Not Enough. Dir. Michael Apted. MGM/ United Artists/ Eon Productions. 1999.

Die Another Day. Dir. Lee Tamahori. MGM/ United Artists/ Eon Productions. 2002.

Casino Royale. Dir. Martin Campbell. MGM/ Columbia Pictures/ Eon Productions. 2006.

Quantum of Solace. Dir. Marc Forster. MGM/ Columbia Pictures/ Eon Productions. 2008.

Skyfall. Dir. Sam Mendes. MGM/ Columbia Pictures/ Eon Productions. 2012.

APPENDIX V

MAIN PRODUCTION AND CAST CREDITS FOR THE *JAMES BOND* FILMS OF THE 1980s

FOR YOUR EYES ONLY (1981)

Production Company: Eon Productions Ltd.
Distributors: United Artists Entertainment.
Director: John Glen.
Screenwriters: Richard Maibaum and Michael G. Wilson.
Producer: Albert R. Broccoli.
Associate Producer: Tom Pevsner.
Executive Producer: Michael G. Wilson.
Original Score: Bill Conti.
Director of Photography: Alan Hume.
Film Editor: John Grover.
Production Design: Peter Lamont.
Art Direction: John Fenner.
Casting: Deborah McWilliams and Maude Spector.
Set Decoration: Vernon Dixon.
Costume Design: Elizabeth Waller.
Running Time: 127 minutes.

Main Cast: Roger Moore (James Bond), Carole Bouquet (Melina Havelock), Topol (Columbo), Lynn-Holly Johnson (Bibi Dahl), Julian Glover (Kristatos), Cassandra Harris (Countess Lisl), Jill Bennett (Brink), Michael Gothard (Locque), John Wyman (Kriegler), Jack Hedley (Havelock), Lois Maxwell (Moneypenny), Desmond Llewelyn (Q), Geoffrey Keen (Minister of Defence), Walter Gotell (General Gogol), James Villiers (Tanner), John Moreno (Ferrara), Charles Dance (Claus), Paul Angelis (Karageorge), Toby Robins (Iona Havelock), Jack Klaff (Apostis), Alkis Kritikos (Santos), Stag Theodore (Nikos), Stefan Kalipha (Gonzales), Graham Crowden (First Sea Lord), Noel Johnson

(Vice Admiral), William Hoyland (McGregor), Paul Brooke (Bunky), Eva Rueber-Staier (Rublevich), Fred Bryant (Vicar), Robbin Young (Girl in Flower Shop), Graham Hawkes (Mantis Man), Janet Brown (Prime Minister), John Wells (Denis).

OCTOPUSSY (1983)

Production Companies: Eon Productions Ltd.
Distributors: MGM/ UA Entertainment Co.
Director: John Glen.
Screenwriters: Richard Maibaum, Michael G. Wilson and George MacDonald Fraser.
Producer: Albert R. Broccoli.
Associate Producer: Thomas Pevsner.
Executive Producer: Michael G. Wilson.
Original Score: John Barry.
Director of Photography: Alan Hume.
Film Editors: Peter Davies and Henry Richardson.
Production Design: Peter Lamont.
Art Direction: John Fenner.
Set Decoration: Jack Stephens.
Casting: Debbie McWilliams.
Costume Design: Emma Porteous.
Running Time: 131 minutes.

Main Cast: Roger Moore (James Bond), Maud Adams (Octopussy), Louis Jourdan (Prince Kamal Khan), Kristina Wayborn (Magda), Kabir Bedi (Gobinda), Steven Berkoff (General Orlov), David Meyer (Mischka), Anthony Meyer (Grischka), Desmond Llewelyn (Q), Robert Brown (M), Lois Maxwell (Miss Moneypenny), Michaela Clavell (Penelope Smallbone), Walter Gotell (General Anatol Gogol), Vijay Amritraj (Vijay), Albert Moses (Sadruddin), Geoffrey Keen (Minister of Defence), Douglas Wilmer (Jim Fanning), Andy Bradford (009), Philip Voss (Auctioneer), Bruce Boa (U.S. General), Richard Parmentier (U.S. Aide), Paul Hardwick (Soviet Chairman), Suzanne Jerome (Gwendoline), Cherry Gillespie (Midge), Dermot Crowley (Kamp), Peter Porteous (Lenkin), Eva Rueber-Staier (Rublevitch), Jeremy Bullock (Smithers), Tina Hudson (Bianca), William Derrick (Thug with Yo-yo), Stuart Saunders (Major Clive), Patrick Barr (British Ambassador), Gabor Vernon (Borchoi), Hugo Bower (Karl), Ken Norris (Colonel Luis Toro), Tony Arjuna (Mufti), Gertan Klauber (Bubi), Brenda Cowling (Schatzi), David Grahame (Petrol Pump Attendant), Brian Coburn (South American V.I.P.), Michael Halphie (South American Officer), Richard Graydon (Francisco the Fearless).

A VIEW TO A KILL (1985)

Production Company: Eon Productions Ltd.
Distributor: MGM/ UA Entertainment Co.
Director: John Glen.
Screenwriters: Richard Maibaum and Michael G. Wilson.
Producers: Albert R. Broccoli and Michael G. Wilson.
Associate Producer: Thomas Pevsner.
Original Score: John Barry.
Director of Photography: Alan Hume.
Film Editor: Peter Davies.
Production Design: Peter Lamont.
Art Direction: John Fenner.
Casting: Debbie McWilliams.
Set Decoration: Crispian Sallis.
Costume Design: Emma Porteous.
Running Time: 121 minutes.

> Main Cast: Roger Moore (James Bond), Christopher Walken (Max Zorin), Tanya Roberts (Stacey Sutton), Grace Jones (May Day), Patrick Macnee (Sir Godfrey Tibbett), Patrick Bauchau (Scarpine), David Yip (Chuck Lee), Fiona Fullerton (Pola Ivanova), Manning Redwood (Bob Conley), Alison Doody (Jenny Flex), Willoughby Gray (Dr Carl Mortner/ Hans Glaub), Desmond Llewelyn (Q), Robert Brown (M), Lois Maxwell (Miss Moneypenny), Walter Gotell (General Anatol Gogol), Geoffrey Keen (Sir Frederick Gray), Jean Rougerie (Achille Aubergine), Daniel Benzali (W.G. Howe), Bogdan Kominowski (Klotkoff), Papillon Soo Soo (Pan Ho), Mary Stavin (Kimberley Jones), Dominique Risbourg (Butterfly Act Compere), Carole Ashby (Whistling Girl), Anthony Chin (Taiwanese), Lucien Jerome (Paris Taxi Driver), Joe Flood (U.S. Police Captain), Gérard Bühr (Auctioneer), Dolph Lundgren (Venz), Tony Sibbald (Mine Foreman), Bill Ackridge (O'Rourke), Peter Ensor (Tycoon).

THE LIVING DAYLIGHTS (1987)

Production Company: Eon Productions Ltd.
Distributor: MGM/ UA Communications Co.
Director: John Glen.
Screenwriters: Richard Maibaum and Michael G. Wilson.
Producers: Albert R. Broccoli and Michael G. Wilson.
Associate Producers: Barbara Broccoli and Tom Pevsner.
Original Score: John Barry.
Director of Photography: Alec Mills.
Film Editors: Peter Davies and John Grover.
Production Design: Peter Lamont.

Art Direction: Terry Ackland-Snow.
Casting: Debbie McWilliams.
Set Decoration: Michael Ford.
Costume Design: Emma Porteous.
Running Time: 130 minutes.

Main Cast: Timothy Dalton (James Bond), Maryam d'Abo (Kara Milovy), Jeroen Krabbé (General Georgi Koskov), Joe Don Baker (Brad Whitaker), John Rhys-Davies (General Leonid Pushkin), Art Malik (Kamran Shah), Andreas Wisniewski (Necros), Thomas Wheatley (Saunders), Desmond Llewelyn (Q), Robert Brown (M), Geoffrey Keen (Minister of Defence), Walter Gotell (General Anatol Gogol), Caroline Bliss (Miss Moneypenny), John Terry (Felix Leiter), Virginia Hey (Rubavitch), John Bowe (Colonel Feyador), Julie T. Wallace (Rosika Miklos), Kell Tyler (Linda), Catherine Rabett (Liz), Dulice Liecier (Ava), Nadim Sawalha (Tangier Chief of Security), Alan Talbot (Koskov's KGB Minder), Carl Rigg (Imposter), Tony Cyrus (Chief of Snow Leopard Brotherhood), Atik Mohamed (Achmed), Ken Sharrock (Jailer), Peter Porteous (Gasworks Supervisor), Antony Carrick (Blayden Male Secretary), Frederick Warder (004), Glyn Baker (002), Derek Hoxby (Sergeant Stagg), Bill Weston (Blayden Butler), Richard Cubison (Trade Centre Toastmaster).

LICENCE TO KILL (1989)

Production Company: Eon Productions Ltd.
Distributor: MGM/ UA Distribution Company.
Director: John Glen.
Screenwriters: Michael G Wilson and Richard Maibaum.
Producers: Albert R Broccoli and Michael G Wilson.
Associate Producers: Tom Pevsner and Barbara Broccoli.
Original Score: Michael Kamen.
Director of Photography: Alec Mills.
Film Editor: John Grover.
Production Design: Peter Lamont.
Art Direction: Dennis Bosher and Michael Lamont.
Set Decoration: Michael Ford.
Casting: Janet Hirshenson and Jane Jenkins.
Costume Design: Jodie Tillen.
Running Time: 133 minutes.

Main Cast: Timothy Dalton (James Bond), Carey Lowell (Pam Bouvier), Robert Davi (Franz Sanchez), Talisa Soto (Lupe Lamora), Anthony Zerbe (Milton Krest), Frank McRae (Sharkey), David Hedison (Felix Leiter), Wayne Newton (Professor Joe Butcher), Benicio Del Toro (Dario), Anthony Starke (Truman-Lodge), Everett McGill (Ed Killifer), Desmond Llewelyn (Q), Pedro Armendariz (President Hector Lopez), Robert Brown (M), Priscilla Barnes

(Della Churchill Leiter), Don Stroud (Heller), Caroline Bliss (Miss Money-penny), Cary-Hiroyuki Tagawa (Kwang), Grand L. Bush (Hawkins), Alejandro Bracho (Perez), Guy De Saint Cyr (Braun), Rafer Johnson (Mullens), Diana Lee-Hsu (Loti), Christopher Neame (Fallon), Jeannine Bisignano (Stripper), Claudio Brook (Montelongo), Cynthia Fallon (Consuelo), Enrique Novi (Rasmussen), Osami Kawawo (Oriental), George Belanger (Doctor), Roger Cudney (Wavekrest Captain).

NEVER SAY NEVER AGAIN (1983)

Production Company: Warner Brothers Pictures/ Taliafilm/ Woodcote Productions, in association with Producers Sales Organisation.
Distributor: Warner Brothers Pictures.
Director: Irvin Kershner.
Screenwriter: Lorenzo Semple Jr., from a story by Kevin McClory, Jack Whittingham and Ian Fleming.
Producer: Jack Schwartzman.
Associate Producer: Michael Dryhurst.
Executive Producer: Kevin McClory.
Original Score: Michel Legrand.
Cinematographer: Douglas Slocombe.
Film Editor: Ian Crafford.
Production Design: Stephen Grimes and Philip Harrison.
Supervising Art Director: Leslie Dilley.
Art Direction: Roy Stannard and Michael White.
Set Decoration: Peter Howitt.
Casting: Maggie Cartier.
Costume Design: Charles Knode.
Running Time: 134 minutes.

Main Cast: Sean Connery (James Bond), Kim Basinger (Domino Petachi), Klaus Maria Brandauer (Maximilian Largo), Barbara Carrera (Fatima Blush), Max Von Sydow (Ernst Stavro Blofeld), Bernie Casey (Felix Leiter), Alec McCowen (Q/ Algy), Edward Fox (M), Pamela Salem (Miss Moneypenny), Rowan Atkinson (Nigel Small-Fawcett), Valerie Leon (Lady in Bahamas), Milow Kirek (Kovacs), Pat Roach (Lippe), Anthony Sharp (Lord Ambrose), Prunella Gee (Patricia), Gavan O'Herlihy (Jack Petachi), Ronald Pickup (Elliott), Robert Rietty (Italian Minister #1), Guido Adorni (Italian Minister #2), Vincent Marzello (Culpepper), Christopher Reich (Number 5), Billy J. Mitchell (Captain Pederson), Manning Redwood (General Miller), Anthony Van Laast (Kurt), Saskia Cohen Tanugi (Nicole), Sylvia Marriott (French Minister), Dan Meaden (Bouncer at Casino), John Stephen Hill (Communications Officer), Wendy Leech (Girl Hostage), Roy Bowe (Ship's Captain).

APPENDIX VI

STATISTICAL DATA AND
REPRESENTATIVE CRITICAL OPINION

FOR YOUR EYES ONLY (1981)

UK Release Date: 24 June 1981. USA Release Date: 26 June 1981. Budget: $28,000,000.

USA Total Gross: $54,812,802.

USA Total Admissions: 22.4 million.

USA Opening Weekend Revenue: $6,834,967 from 952 Theatres.

Global Box Office Total: $194.9 million.

Award Wins: Golden Screen Award, Germany (1982), ASCAP Award: Most Performed Feature Film Standards (1982).

Award Nominations: Academy Award for Best Music: Original Song (1982), Golden Globe Award: Best Original Song: Motion Picture (1982), Writers Guild of America Award (1982), Golden Satellite Award: Best Classic DVD Release (2004).

Representative Critical Opinion:

'Beneath his suave double-entendres and amplified body blows, one can hear the sound of expensive gears meshing – for [Roger] Moore is merely the best-oiled cog in this perpetual motion machine.'

Richard Corliss, *Time Magazine*, 29 June 1981.

'*For Your Eyes Only* is not the spaced-out fun that *Moonraker* was, but its tone is consistently comic even when the material is not.'

Vincent Canby, *The New York Times*, 26 June 1981.

'*For Your Eyes Only* is the most impersonal and mechanical of the James Bond pictures. If you like action, stunts and thrills, you may enjoy it – but most likely at a low level of involvement.' David Denby, *New York Magazine*, 29 June 1981.

'Roger Moore has crumpled his comic-strip good looks into something approaching world-weariness, and the newfound maturity in his expression is reflected in director John Glen's style, which goes for the measured and elegant over the flashy and excessive.'

Dave Kehr, *The Chicago Reader Online*, 13 October 2008.

'In many ways, *For Your Eyes Only* is the most Hitchcockian of the Bond movies, and I mean that as the highest of compliments. It is also the most like a European art film – which I mean more as a tease, since Glen superficially (yet effectively) adopts certain stylistic elements, including airy widescreen compositions and tense, wordless set pieces to give the proceedings a classier edge.'

Peter Debruge, *Variety Online*, 10 August 2012.

DVD/Blu-Ray Availability:

DVD:
MGM Home Entertainment, Catalogue Number: F1-SGB 1617201088
Blu-Ray:
MGM Home Entertainment, Catalogue Number: F1-BSGB 1617207088

OCTOPUSSY (1983)

UK Release Date: 6 June 1983. USA Release Date: 10 June 1983. Budget: $27,500,000.

USA Total Gross: $67,893,619.

USA Total Admissions: 21.5 million.

USA Opening Weekend Revenue: $8,902,564 from 1311 theatres.

Global Box Office Total: $183,700,000.

Award Wins: Golden Screen Award, Germany (1984), Golden Reel Award: Best Sound Editing (1984).

Award Nominations: Saturn Award: Best Fantasy Film (1984), Saturn Award: Best Actress (1984), Golden Satellite Award: Best Classic DVD Release (2004).

Representative Critical Opinion:

'Roger Moore, who plays Bond yet again, is not getting any younger, but neither is the character. The two have grown gracefully indivisible.'

Vincent Canby, *The New York Times*, 10 June 1983.

'*Octopussy* is one of the most inventive and satisfyingly preposterous of all the Bond movies. [...] In modern movies, action is fantasy, and in the race for the most enjoyably absurd effects, *Octopussy* comes out somewhere near the top.'

David Denby, *New York Magazine*, 20 June 1983.

'The old double-entendres could still raise a grimace, and with the help of his blessed stunt team, Bond would doubtless feel his way through tight spots until he was older than yesterday. [...] Another scrape, and no scratches. Another nuclear

holocaust averted, and now another woman – the good one, he guessed.'
Richard Corliss, *Time Magazine*, 27 June 1983.

'Though getting a little creaky in the role, Roger Moore takes the Bond franchise for an entertaining ride in *Octopussy* to exotic Indian locations with some of the most sensuous women in the series, perhaps to distract us from an overdone plot and his increasing tendency to excessive humor.'
Nicholas Sylvain, *DVD Verdict*, 27 October 2000.

'Don't forget that [*Octopussy*] showcased a reluctant-to-return Roger Moore still managing to go toe-to-toe with the original – and younger, though not that you'd notice it – Bond, Sean Connery, and, more importantly, coming out intact and on top.'
Cas Harlow, *AVForums*, 9 November 2012.

DVD/ Blu-Ray Availability:
DVD:
MGM Home Entertainment, Catalogue Number: F1-SGB 1620501088
Blu-Ray:
MGM Home Entertainment, Catalogue Number: WVJ-BSGB 1620507000

A VIEW TO A KILL (1985)

UK Release Date: 13 June 1985. USA Release Date: 24 May 1985. Budget: $30,000,000.
USA Total Gross: $50,327,960.
USA Total Admissions: 14.1 million.
USA Opening Weekend Revenue: $10,687,114 from 1583 theatres.
Global Box Office Total: $152,400,000.
Award Wins: Golden Screen Award, Germany (1986).
Award Nominations: Golden Globe Awards: Best Original Song: Motion Picture (1986), Saturn Award: Best Science Fiction Film (1986), Saturn Award: Best Supporting Actress (1986), Golden Satellite Award: Best Classic DVD Release (2004).

Representative Critical Opinion:

'In his seventh movie as James Bond, [Roger Moore] is looking less like a chap with a license to kill than a gent with an application to retire. Moore is an extremely engaging fellow and an admirable professional, but when he turns on that famous quizzical smile, his facial muscles look as if they're lifting weights.'
Jack Kroll, *Newsweek*, 27 May 1985.

'You go to a Bond picture expecting some style or, at least, some flash, some lift; you don't expect the dumb police-car crashes you get here. You do see some ingenious daredevil feats, but they're crowded together and, the way they're set

up, they don't give you the irresponsible, giddy tingle you're hoping for.'
Pauline Kael, *The New Yorker*, 3 June 1985.

'As lavishly escapist as they are, the latest James Bond films have become strenuous to watch, now that the business of maintaining Bond's casual *savoir-faire* looks like such a monumental chore. The effort involved in keeping Roger Moore's 007 impervious to age, changing times or sheer *deja-vu* seems overwhelming.'
Janet Maslin, *The New York Times*, 24 May 1985.

'But this jokey tone couldn't be more different from the relative self-seriousness of helmer John Glen's first 007 directing effort, *For Your Eyes Only,* and frankly, I yearn for more of that class. Certainly the real-life Roger Moore had it, which was part of the reason he made such a nice fit for the character a dozen years earlier.'
Peter Debruge, *Variety Online*, 14 September 2012.

'With production designer Ken Adam having deserted the series and Roger Moore all but checked into a nursing home, the Bond films hadn't much left to cover their threadbare formula. This one, directed by John Glen, just follows the numbers, plodding from one unimaginative set piece to the next.'
Dave Kehr, *Chicago Reader Online*, 13 October 2008.

DVD/ Blu-Ray Availability:

DVD:
MGM Home Entertainment, Catalogue Number: F1-SGB 1623401088
Blu-Ray:
MGM Home Entertainment, Catalogue Number: WVJ-BSGB 1623407000

THE LIVING DAYLIGHTS (1987)

UK Release Date: 29 June 1987. USA Release Date: 31 July 1987. Budget: $40,000,000.
USA Total Gross: $51,185,897.
USA Total Admissions: 14.1 million.
USA Opening Weekend Revenue: $11,051,284 from 1728 theatres.
Global Box Office Total: $191,200,000.
Award Wins: Golden Screen Award, Germany (1988), Golden Reel Award: Best Sound Editing: Foreign Feature (1988), BMI Film Music Award (1988).
Award Nominations: Saturn Award: Best Fantasy Film (1988), Golden Satellite Award: Best Classic DVD Release (2004).

Representative Critical Opinion:

'[Timothy] Dalton, the latest successor to the role of James Bond, is well

equipped for his new responsibilities. He has enough presence, the right debonair looks and the kind of energy that the Bond series has lately been lacking. If he radiates more thoughtfulness than the role requires, maybe that's just gravy.'
Janet Maslin, *The New York Times*, 31 July 1987.

'The raw materials of the James Bond films are so familiar by now that the series can be revived only through an injection of humor. That is, unfortunately, the one area in which the new Bond, Timothy Dalton, seems to be deficient. He's a strong actor, he holds the screen well, he's good in the serious scenes, but he never quite seems to understand that it's all a joke.'
Roger Ebert, *The Chicago Sun-Times*, 31 July 1987.

'In Timothy Dalton's interpretation of 007 in *The Living Daylights*, one finds some of the lethal charm of Sean Connery, along with a touch of crabby Harrison Ford. This Bond is as fast on his feet as with his wits; an ironic scowl creases his face; he's battle ready yet war-weary.'
Richard Corliss, *Time Magazine*, 10 August 1987.

'After Roger Moore's [...] increasingly campy take on the role, Dalton very intentionally tried to steer Bond closer to Ian Fleming's original intent, giving us a darker, more serious Bond. *The Living Daylights* is also notable as the last true Cold War adventure for James Bond.'
Erick Harper, *DVD Verdict*, 24 October 2000.

'*The Living Daylights* is so far the last Bond film to capture the feel of Fleming's novels so exactly. It's a true shame that the mixture of espionage and action has never been entwined again to such good effect. In a way Dalton is the most over-looked of all the Bonds [...] but this is a shame because Dalton has a strong case for best Bond ever. Underrated, undervalued and under-appreciated, *The Living Daylights* is the last Bond film that can genuinely lay claim to the title "classic".'
M.P. Bartley, *eFilmCritic.com*, 11 August 2004.

DVD/ Blu-Ray Availability:

DVD:
MGM Home Entertainment, Catalogue Number: F1-SGB 1619301088
Blu-Ray:
MGM Home Entertainment, Catalogue Number: WVJ-BSGB 1619307000

LICENCE TO KILL (1989)

UK Release Date: 13 June 1989. USA Release Date: 14 June 1989. Budget: $36,000,000.
USA Total Gross: $34,667,015.
USA Total Admissions: 8.7 million.

USA Opening Weekend Revenue: $8,774,776 from 1575 theatres.
Global Box Office Total: $156,200,000.
Award Nominations: Edgar Allan Poe Award: Best Motion Picture (1990).

Representative Critical Opinion:

'On the basis of this second performance as Bond, Dalton can have the role as long as he enjoys it. He makes an effective Bond – lacking Sean Connery's grace and humor, and Roger Moore's suave self-mockery, but with a lean tension and a toughness that is possibly more contemporary.'
Roger Ebert, *The Chicago Sun-Times*, 14 July 1989.

'In *Licence to Kill*, the bad guys' hideaway blows up real good [and] there are some great truck stunts. A pity nobody – not writers Michael G. Wilson and Richard Maibaum nor director John Glen – thought to give the humans anything very clever to do.'
Richard Corliss, *Time Magazine*, 24 July 1989.

'The film retains its familiar, effective mix of despicably powerful villains, suspiciously tantalizing women and ever-wilder special effects. But Mr Dalton's glowering presence adds a darker tone. The screenwriters Michael G. Wilson and Richard Maibaum have accommodated this moodier Bond, and have even created a script that makes him fit for the 90s.'
Caryn James, *The New York Times*, 14 July 1989.

'*Licence to Kill* is certainly a dramatic change from the gadget-filled and increasingly campy Bond films of the Roger Moore era, as it sets a more somber and gritty stage for the series. I appreciate the risks taken with this movie, both to keep the series fresh and to present a Bond that while less known to the audience is truer to the spirit of Fleming's Bond.'
Nicholas Sylvain, *DVD Verdict*, 22 October 1999.

'While the action is cool and tough and nasty in *Licence to Kill*, there's nothing remotely "Bondian" about the film. It could very well be an excellent episode of *Miami Vice*; Dalton can't make Bond his own, and *Licence to Kill* just becomes an anonymous, gritty actioner.'
Paul Mavis, *DVD Talk*, 7 November 2006.

DVD/ Blu-Ray Availability:

DVD:
MGM Home Entertainment, Catalogue Number: F1-SGB 1584701088
Blu-Ray:
MGM Home Entertainment, Catalogue Number: WVJ-BSGB 1584707000

NEVER SAY NEVER AGAIN (1983)

UK Release Date: 14 December 1983. USA Release Date: 7 October 1983. Budget: $36,000,000.

USA Total Gross: $55,432,841.

USA Total Admissions: 17.5 million.

USA Opening Weekend Revenue: $10,958,157 from 1550 theatres.

Global Box Office Total: $160,000,000.

Award Wins: Golden Screen Award, Germany (1984).

Award Nominations: Golden Globe Award: Best Supporting Actress (1984), Saturn Award: Best Fantasy Film (1984), Saturn Award: Best Special Effects (1984).

Representative Critical Opinion:

'In his post-Bond career, Mr Connery easily proved himself to be an actor of far more resourcefulness than his 007 films had indicated. In *Never Say Never Again*, the formula is broadened to accommodate an older, seasoned man of much greater stature, and Mr Connery expertly fills the bill.'

Janet Maslin, *The New York Times*, 7 October 1983.

'One of the best James Bond adventure thrillers ever made [...] this picture is likely to remain a cherished, savory example of commercial filmmaking at its most astute and accomplished.'

Gary Arnold, *The Washington Post*, 6 October 1983.

'The movie is called *Never Say Never Again*. The title has nothing to do with the movie – except why Connery made it – but never mind, nothing in this movie has much to do with anything else. It's another one of those Bond plots in which the basic ingredients are thrown together more or less in fancy.'

Roger Ebert, *The Chicago Sun-Times*, 7 October 1983.

'The absence of so many elements moviegoers had come to expect from a 007 movie – the gun barrel opening, "The James Bond Theme", appearances by Desmond Llewellyn and Lois Maxwell as "Q" and Miss Moneypenny – made for a decidedly off-kilter viewing experience. In the end, it's still an above-average Bond movie, better certainly as a swan song for the irreplaceable Sean Connery.'

Stuart Galbraith, *DVD Talk*, 30 March 2009.

'The primary question of this movie [...] becomes whether or not the Bond franchise benefits from being molded by a different pair of hands at its very core, and the answer the film presents to that query is a resounding Maybe.'

Deepayan Sengupta, *Sound on Sight*, 25 November 2012.

DVD/ Blu-Ray Availability:

DVD:
MGM Home Entertainment, Catalogue Number: 1988201000
Blu-Ray:

MGM Home Entertainment, Catalogue Number: 1988207000

Box office statistical data drawn from the MI6 website (www.mi6hq.com) and Box Office Mojo (www.boxofficemojo.com).

SELECT BIBLIOGRAPHY

Allen, Dennis W., 'Alimentary, Dr Leiter', in *Ian Fleming and James Bond: The Cultural Politics of 007*, ed. by Edward P. Comentale, Stephen Watt, and Skip Willman, (Bloomington: Indiana University Press, 2005), pp.24-41.

Allon, Yoram, Del Cullen and Hannah Patterson, eds, *Contemporary British and Irish Film Directors: A Wallflower Critical Guide* (London: Wallflower Press, 2001).

Altman, Mark A., 'Nobody Still Does It Better', in *Cinefantastique*, July 1989, pp.17-35; p.56; p.57; p.61.

Anon., 'Kevin McClory, Sony & Bond: A History Lesson', in *UniversalExports.net*, 2007. <www.universalexports.net/ 00Sony.shtml>

Arnold, Gordon B., *Conspiracy Theory in Film, Television and Politics* (Westport: Praeger Publishers, 2008).

Ashby, Justine, and Andrew Higson, eds, *British Cinema, Past and Present* (London: Routledge, 2000).

Banner, Simon, 'Of Inhuman Bondage', in *Time Out*, 26 April 1989, pp.14-15. Barber, Hoyt L., and Harry L. Barber, *The Book of Bond, James Bond* (Nipomo: Cyclone, 1999).

Barnes, Alan, and Marcus Hearn, *Kiss Kiss Bang Bang: The Unofficial James Bond Film Companion* (London: B.T. Batsford, 1997).

Bennett, Tony, 'The Bond Phenomenon: Theorising a Popular Hero', in *The Southern Review*, July 1983, pp.195-225.

—. & Janet Woollacott, *Bond and Beyond: The Political Career of a Popular Hero* (London: Palgrave McMillan, 1987).

—. & Janet Woollacott, 'The Moments of Bond', in *The James Bond Phenomenon: A Critical Reader*, ed. by Christoph Lindner (Manchester: Manchester University Press, 2003), pp.13-33.

Black, Jeremy, 'The Geopolitics of James Bond', in *Understanding Intelligence in the Twenty-First Century: Journeys in Shadows*, ed. by L.V. Scott and P.D. Jackson (Abingdon: Routledge, 2004), pp.135-46.

—. *The Politics of James Bond: From Fleming's Novels to the Big Screen* (London: Greenwood Press, 2001).

Boyd-Barrett, Oliver, David Herrera, and Jim Bauman, *Hollywood and the CIA: Cinema, Defense, and Subversion* (Abingdon: Routledge, 2011).

Canby, Richard, 'James Bond Meets *Octopussy*' in *The New York Times*, 10 June 1983. <http:// movies.nytimes.com/ movie/review?res=

9804E1D7123BF933A25755C0A965948260>

Caplen, Robert A., *Shaken and Stirred: The Feminism of James Bond* (Bloomington: Xlibris, 2010).

Cart, '*For Your Eyes Only*', in *Variety,* 24 June 1981, p.23.

Cawelti, John G., and Bruce A. Rosenberg, *The Spy Story* (Chicago: University of Chicago Press, 1987).

Chapman, James, 'A Licence to Thrill', in *The James Bond Phenomenon: A Critical Reader,* ed. by Christoph Lindner (Manchester: Manchester University Press, 2003), pp.91-98.

—. 'Bond and Britishness', in *Ian Fleming and James Bond: The Cultural Politics of 007,* ed. by Edward P. Comentale, Stephen Watt, and Skip Willman (Bloomington: Indiana University Press, 2005), pp.129-43.

—. *Licence to Thrill: A Cultural History of the James Bond Films* (London: I.B. Tauris, 1999).

Cockburn, Alexander, 'James Bond At 25', in *American Film,* Volume 12, Issue 9, 1987, pp.27-31; p.59.

Comentale, Edward P., Stephen Watt, and Skip Willman, *Ian Fleming and James Bond: The Cultural Politics of 007* (Bloomington: Indiana University Press, 2005).

Coop, '*Licence to Kill*', in *Variety,* 14 June 1989, p.7.

Cooper, Michael, '*Warhead 2000*: The Lost Bond Film', in *Alternative 007,* 2007. <www.alternative007.co.uk/ 73.htm>

Cork, John, and Bruce Scivally, *James Bond: The Legacy* (London: Boxtree, 2002).

—. & and Collin Stutz, *James Bond Encyclopedia,* rev. edn (London: Dorling Kindersley, 2009).

Corliss, Richard, 'Cinema: Bond Keeps Up His Silver Streak', in *Time Magazine,* 10 August 1987. <www.time.com/ time/ magazine/ article/ 0,9171,965173,00.html>

—. 'Cinema: Perpetual Motion Machine', in *Time Magazine,* 29 June 1981. <www.time.com/ time/ magazine/ article/ 0,9171,951750,00.html>

—. 'Cinema: Rushes a *View to a Kill*', in *Time Magazine,* 10 June 1985. <www.time.com/ time/ magazine/ article/ 0,9171,958516,00.html>

—. 'Cinema: The Bond Wagon Crawls Along', in *Time Magazine,* 27 June 1983. <www.time.com/ time/ magazine/ article/ 0,9171,953973,00.html>

—. 'Cinema: We Don't Need Another Heroid', in *Time Magazine,* 24 July 1989. <www.time.com/ time/ magazine/ article/ 0,9171,958214,00.html>

—. & Richard Schickel, 'Cinema: Raking Up the Autumn Leavings', in *Time Magazine,* 17 October 1989. <www.time.com/ time/ magazine/ article/ 0,9171,952223,00.html>

d'Abo, Maryam, and John Cork, *Bond Girls Are Forever: The Women of James Bond* (London: Boxtree, 2003).

Del Buono, Oreste, and Umberto Eco, eds, *The Bond Affair* (London: Macdonald, 1966).

Dempsey, Ray, 'What is the Best Bond Movie?: Bonding by the Numbers', in *James Bond in the 21st Century: Why We Still Need 007,* ed. by Glenn Yeffeth (Texas: BenBella Books, 2006), pp.49-72.

Denby, David, 'Movies: Sean is Back and the Shark Has Got Him', in *New York Magazine,* 7 November 1983, pp.100-01.

Di Leo, Michael, *The Spy Who Thrilled Us: A Guide to the Best of Cinematic James Bond* (New York: Limelight Editions, 2002).

DiMare, Philip C., ed., *Movies in American History: An Encyclopedia*, ed. by (Santa Barbara: ABC-CLIO, 2011).

Dipaolo, Marc, *War, Politics and Superheroes: Ethics and Propaganda in Comics and Film* (Jefferson: McFarland, 2011).

Dixon, Wheeler Winston, *Film Genre 2000: New Critical Essays* (Albany: State University of New York Press, 2000).

Dodds, Klaus, *Global Geopolitics: A Critical Introduction* (Harlow: Pearson, 2005).

—. 'Licensed to Stereotype: Geopolitics, James Bond and the Spectre of Balkanism', in *Geopolitics*, Volume 8, Issue 2, 2003, pp.125-56.

—. 'Popular Geopolitics and Audience Dispositions: James Bond and the Internet Movie Database', in *Transactions of the Institute of British Geographers*, Volume 31, Issue 2, June 2006, pp.116–130.

—. Screening Geopolitics: James Bond and the Early Cold War Films (1962-1967)', in *Geopolitics*, Volume 10, Issue 2, 2005, pp.266-89.

Dougall, Alastair, *Bond Girls* (London: Dorling Kindersley, 2010).

—. *The Book of Bond* (London: Dorling Kindersley, 2010).

Drummond, Lee, *American Dreamtime: A Cultural Analysis of Popular Movies and their Implications for a Science of Humanity* (London: Rowman and Littlefield, 1996).

Earnest, David C., and James N. Rosenau, 'The Spy Who Loved Globalization', in *Foreign Policy*, No. 120, September-October 2000, pp.88-90.

Ebert, Roger, *'For Your Eyes Only'*, in *The Chicago Sun-Times*, 29 June 1981. <http://rogerebert.suntimes.com/ apps/ pbcs.dll/ article?AID=/ 19810101/ REVIEWS/ 101010326/ 1023>

—. *'Licence to Kill'*, in *The Chicago Sun-Times*, 14 July 1989. <http://rogerebert.suntimes.com/ apps/ pbcs.dll/ article?AID=/ 19890714/ REVIEWS/ 907140301/ 1023>

—. *'Never Say Never Again'*, in *The Chicago Sun-Times*, 7 October 1983. <http://rogerebert.suntimes.com/ apps/ pbcs.dll/ article?AID=/ 19831007/ REVIEWS/ 310070301/ 1023>

—. *'The Living Daylights'*, in *The Chicago Sun-Times*, 31 July 1987. <http://rogerebert.suntimes.com/ apps/ pbcs.dll/ article?AID=/ 19870731/ REVIERE/ 707310304/ 1023>

Eco, Umberto, 'The Narrative Structure in Fleming', in *The Bond Affair*, ed. by Oreste Del Buono and Umberto Eco (London: Macdonald, 1966), pp.35-75.

Ffolkes, Sebastion, 'Timothy Dalton is James Bond', in *Starburst*, August 1987, pp.40-44.

Fishlock, Trevor, 'Russians Dismiss "Silly" Bond Film', in *The Daily Telegraph*, 8 August 1987, p.6.

Gerriga, Richard J., and Allan B.I. Bernardo, 'Readers as Problem-Solvers in the Experience of Suspense', in *Poetics*, Volume 22, Issue 6, December 1994, pp.459-72.

Giammarco, David, *For Your Eyes Only: Behind the Scenes of the Bond Films* (London: ECW Press, 2002).

Glen, John, *For My Eyes Only: My Life with James Bond* (London: Brassey's, 2001).

Hamblin, Cory, *Serket's Movies: Commentary and Trivia on 444 Movies* (Pittsburgh: RoseDog Books, 2009).

Hammond, Andrew, ed., *Cold War Literature: Writing the Global Conflict* (London: Routledge, 2006).

Hodgkinson, Tom, 'Bonding Experiences', in *The Guardian*, 16 November 1995, pp.10-11.

Hunter, Allan, ' *The Living Daylights*, in *Films and Filming,* August 1987, p.35.

James, Caryn, 'Review/ Film: Dalton as a Brooding Bond In*License to Kill*', in *The New York Times,* 14 July 1989. <http:// movies.nytimes.com/ movie/ review?res=950DEED8173DF937A25754C0A96F948260>

Jenkins, Tricia, 'James Bond's "Pussy" and Anglo-American Cold War Sexuality', in *The Journal of American Culture,* Volume 28, Issue 3, September 2005, pp.309-17.

Johnston, Sheila, 'James Bond: For Your Eyes Mainly', in*The Independent,* 2 July 1987, p.12.

Jütting, Kerstin, *'Grow Up, 007!': James Bond Over the Decades: Formula vs Innovation* (Norderstedt: Der Deutschen Bibliothek, 2005).

Lane, Andy, and Paul Simpson, *The Bond Files: The Unofficial Guide to Ian Fleming's James Bond* (London: Virgin Books, 1998).

Lindner, Christoph, ed., *The James Bond Phenomenon: A Critical Reader* (Manchester: Manchester University Press, 2003).

Lipschutz, Ronnie D., *Cold War Fantasies: Film, Fiction, and Foreign Policy* (Oxford: Rowman and Littlefield, 2001).

Lor, *'Octopussy'*, in *Variety,* 8 June 1981, p.23.

Marano, Michael, 'Who is the Best James Bond?: Dalton's Gang', in *James Bond in the 21st Century: Why We Still Need 007,* ed. by Glenn Yeffeth (Texas: BenBella Books, 2006), pp.101-12.

Maskell, Karl, 'No Moore Bond', in*Starburst,* Issue 100, 1986, pp.59-61.

Maslin, Janet, 'Film: *Living Daylights,* with the New Bond', in *The New York Times,* 31 July 1987. <http://movies.nytimes.com/ movie/ review?res=9B0DEEDB1630F932A05754C0A961948260>

Maslin, Janet, 'The Screen: James Bond', in *The New York Times,* 24 May 1985. <http:// movies.nytimes.com/ movie/ review?res=9C07EEDF103BF937A15756C0A963948260>

Mavis, Paul, *The Espionage Filmography: United States Releases, 1898 Through 1999* (Jefferson: McFarland, 2001).

McMahon, Robert J., *The Cold War: A Very Short Introduction* (Oxford: Oxford University Press, 2003).

Metz, Walter, *Engaging Film Criticism: Film History and Contemporary American Cinema* (New York: Peter Lang Publishing, 2004).

Morefield, David, 'So You Want to Be an Evil Genius?', in *James Bond in the 21st Century: Why We Still Need 007,* ed. by Glenn Yeffeth (Texas: BenBella Books, 2006), pp.135-44.

Müller, Jürgen, *Movies of the 80s* (London: Taschen, 2003).

Murray, Scott, 'The Bond Age', in *Cinema Papers,* Issue 66, 1987, pp.20-25.

Newkey-Burden, Chas, *Nuclear Paranoia* (Harpenden: Pocket Essentials, 2003).

Owen, Gareth, and Oliver Bayan, *Roger Moore: His Films and Career* (London: Robert Hale, 2002).

Packer, Jeremy, ed., *Secret Agents: Popular Icons Beyond James Bond* (New York: Peter Lang Publishing, 2009).

—. & Sarah Sharma, 'Postfeminism Galore: The Bond Girl as Weapon of Mass Consumption', in *Secret Agents: Popular Icons Beyond James Bond,* ed. by Jeremy Packer (New York: Peter Lang Publishing, 2009), pp.89-111.

Palmer, William J., *The Films of the Eighties: A Social History* (Carbondale: Southern Illinois University, 1993).

Parker, Barry R., *Death Rays, Jet Packs, Stunts, and Supercars: The Fantastic Physics of Film's Most Celebrated Secret Agent* (Baltimore: John Hopkins University Press, 2005).

Payne, Stephen, and Gary Russell, 'James Bond Returns', in *Starburst*, July 1987, pp.8-13.

Peachment, Chris, '*A View to a Kill*', in *Time Out*, Issue 773, 13 June 1985, p.37.

Pearson, John, *James Bond: The Authorized Biography of 007* (London: Sidgwick & Jackson, 1973).

Pfeiffer, Lee, and Philip Lisa, *The Films of Sean Connery* (New York: Citadel Press, 1997).

—. & Dave Worrall, *The Essential James Bond: The Revised Authorised Guide to the World of 007* (London: Boxtree, 2003).

Pomerance, Murray, ed., *Bad: Infamy, Darkness, Evil, and Slime on Screen* (Albany: State University of New York Press, 2004).

Pulleine, Tim, '*A View to a Kill*', in *Monthly Film Bulletin*, Volume 52, Issue 618, July 1985, pp.228-29.

QSF, '*The Living Daylights*', in *Screen International*, Issue 608, 4 July 1987, p.38.

Rissik, Andrew, 'Where Can James Bond Possibly Go From Here?', in *Films Illustrated*, Volume 10, Issue 119, 1981, pp.413-16.

Rivers, John, 'John Glen', in *Contemporary British and Irish Film Directors: A Wallflower Critical Guide*, ed. by Yoram Allon, Del Cullen and Hannah Patterson (London: Wallflower Press, 2001), pp.121-122.

Roberts, Van, 'The Bond Films', in *Movies in American History: An Encyclopedia*, ed. by Philip C. DiMare (Santa Barbara: ABC-CLIO, 2011), pp.51-54.

Rubin, Steven Jay, *The Complete James Bond Movie Encyclopaedia* (London: Contemporary Books, 2002).

Rubio, Steven, 'Who is the Best Bond Villain? If I Were a Villain, But Then Again, No', in *James Bond in the 21st Century: Why We Still Need 007*, ed. by Glenn Yeffeth (Texas: BenBella Books, 2006), pp.93-100.

Russell, Gary, 'Serious Bondage', in *Starburst*, July 1989, pp.40-43.

Santas, Constantine, *The Epic in Film: From Myth to Blockbuster* (Plymouth: Rowman and Littlefield, 2008).

Scott, L.V., and P.D. Jackson, eds, *Understanding Intelligence in the Twenty-First Century: Journeys in Shadows* (Abingdon: Routledge, 2004).

Setchfield, Nick, 'Heroes and Inspirations: John Landis', in *SFX*, Issue 217, February 2012, pp.78-81.

Shaw, Tony, *British Cinema and the Cold War: The State, Propaganda and Consensus* (London: I.B. Tauris, 2006).

Shaw, Tony, *Hollywood's Cold War* (Edinburgh: Edinburgh University Press, 2007).

Simpson, Paul, ed., *The Rough Guide to James Bond* (London: Penguin, 2002).

Sorlin, Pierre, 'From *The Third Man* to *Shakespeare in Love*: Fifty Years of British Success on Continental Screens', in *British Cinema, Past and Present*, ed. by Justine Ashby and Andrew Higson (London: Routledge, 2000), pp.80-92.

South, James B., and Jacob M. Held, eds, *James Bond and Philosophy: Questions Are Forever* (Chicago: Open Court, 2006).

Sprinker, Michael, 'We Lost It at the Movies', in *MLN*, Volume 112, Number 3, April 1997, pp.385-99.

Storry, Mike, and Peter Childs, *British Cultural Identities* (London: Routledge, 1997).

Street, Sarah, *British National Cinema* (London: Routledge, 1997).

Welsh, James M., 'Action Films: The Serious, the Ironic, The Postmodern', in *Film Genre 2000: New Critical Essays*, ed. by Wheeler Winston Dixon (Albany: State University of New York Press, 2000), pp.161-76.

Woodward, Steven, 'The Arch Archenemies of James Bond', in *Bad: Infamy, Darkness, Evil, and Slime on Screen*, ed. by Murray Pomerance (Albany: State University of New York Press, 2004), pp.173-86.

Woollacott, Janet, 'The James Bond Films: Conditions of Production', in *The James Bond Phenomenon: A Critical Reader*, ed. by Christoph Lindner (Manchester: Manchester University Press, 2003), pp.99-117.

Yeffeth, Glenn, ed., *James Bond in the 21st Century: Why We Still Need 007* (Texas: BenBella Books, 2006).

About the Author

Dr Thomas Christie has a life-long fascination with films
and the people who make them. A member of the Royal Society of
Literature and the Society of Authors, he holds an M.A. in Humanities
with British Cinema History from the Open University of Milton Keynes,
and a Ph.D. in Scottish Literature awarded by the University of Stirling.

Thomas Christie is the author of *Liv Tyler, Star in Ascendance:
Her First Decade in Film* (2007), *The Cinema of Richard Linklater* (2008),
John Hughes and Eighties Cinema (2009), *Ferris Bueller's Day Off: Pocket
Movie Guide* (2010) and *The Christmas Movie Book* (2011), all of which are
published by Crescent Moon Publishing. A study of Mel Brooks
is forthcoming.

For more information about Tom and his books, visit his website
at www.tomchristiebooks.co.uk.

CRESCENT MOON PUBLISHING

web: www.crmoon.com e-mail: cresmopub@yahoo.co.uk

ARTS, PAINTING, SCULPTURE

The Art of Andy Goldsworthy
Andy Goldsworthy: Touching Nature
Andy Goldsworthy in Close-Up
Andy Goldsworthy: Pocket Guide
Andy Goldsworthy In America
Land Art: A Complete Guide
The Art of Richard Long
Richard Long: Pocket Guide
Land Art In the UK
Land Art in Close-Up
Land Art In the U.S.A.
Land Art: Pocket Guide
Installation Art in Close-Up
Minimal Art and Artists In the 1960s and After
Colourfield Painting
Land Art DVD, TV documentary
Andy Goldsworthy DVD, TV documentary
The Erotic Object: Sexuality in Sculpture From Prehistory to the Present Day
Sex in Art: Pornography and Pleasure in Painting and Sculpture
Postwar Art
Sacred Gardens: The Garden in Myth, Religion and Art
Glorification: Religious Abstraction in Renaissance and 20th Century Art
Early Netherlandish Painting
Leonardo da Vinci
Piero della Francesca
Giovanni Bellini
Fra Angelico: Art and Religion in the Renaissance
Mark Rothko: The Art of Transcendence
Frank Stella: American Abstract Artist
Jasper Johns
Brice Marden
Alison Wilding: The Embrace of Sculpture
Vincent van Gogh: Visionary Landscapes
Eric Gill: Nuptials of God
Constantin Brancusi: Sculpting the Essence of Things
Max Beckmann
Caravaggio
Gustave Moreau
Egon Schiele: Sex and Death In Purple Stockings
Delizioso Fotografico Fervore: Works In Process 1
Sacro Cuore: Works In Process 2
The Light Eternal: J.M.W. Turner
The Madonna Glorified: Karen Arthurs

LITERATURE

J.R.R. Tolkien: The Books, The Films, The Whole Cultural Phenomenon
J.R.R. Tolkien: Pocket Guide
Tolkien's Heroic Quest
The *Earthsea* Books of Ursula Le Guin
Beauties, Beasts and Enchantment: Classic French Fairy Tales
German Popular Stories by the Brothers Grimm
Philip Pullman and *His Dark Materials*
Sexing Hardy: Thomas Hardy and Feminism
Thomas Hardy's *Tess of the d'Urbervilles*
Thomas Hardy's *Jude the Obscure*
Thomas Hardy: The Tragic Novels
Love and Tragedy: Thomas Hardy
The Poetry of Landscape in Hardy
Wessex Revisited: Thomas Hardy and John Cowper Powys
Wolfgang Iser: Essays and Interviews
Petrarch, Dante and the Troubadours
Maurice Sendak and the Art of Children's Book Illustration
Andrea Dworkin
Cixous, Irigaray, Kristeva: The *Jouissance* of French Feminism
Julia Kristeva: Art, Love, Melancholy, Philosophy, Semiotics and Psychoanalysis
Hélene Cixous I Love You: The *Jouissance* of Writing
Luce Irigaray: Lips, Kissing, and the Politics of Sexual Difference
Peter Redgrove: Here Comes the Flood
Peter Redgrove: Sex-Magic-Poetry-Cornwall
Lawrence Durrell: Between Love and Death, East and West
Love, Culture & Poetry: Lawrence Durrell
Cavafy: Anatomy of a Soul
German Romantic Poetry: Goethe, Novalis, Heine, Hölderlin
Feminism and Shakespeare
Shakespeare: Love, Poetry & Magic
The Passion of D.H. Lawrence
D.H. Lawrence: Symbolic Landscapes
D.H. Lawrence: Infinite Sensual Violence
Rimbaud: Arthur Rimbaud and the Magic of Poetry
The Ecstasies of John Cowper Powys
Sensualism and Mythology: The Wessex Novels of John Cowper Powys
Amorous Life: John Cowper Powys and the Manifestation of Affectivity (H.W. Fawkner)
Postmodern Powys: New Essays on John Cowper Powys (Joe Boulter)
Rethinking Powys: Critical Essays on John Cowper Powys
Paul Bowles & Bernardo Bertolucci
Rainer Maria Rilke
Joseph Conrad: *Heart of Darkness*
In the Dim Void: Samuel Beckett
Samuel Beckett Goes into the Silence
André Gide: Fiction and Fervour
Jackie Collins and the Blockbuster Novel
Blinded By Her Light: The Love-Poetry of Robert Graves
The Passion of Colours: Travels In Mediterranean Lands
Poetic Forms

POETRY

Ursula Le Guin: Walking In Cornwall
Peter Redgrove: Here Comes The Flood
Peter Redgrove: Sex-Magic-Poetry-Cornwall
Dante: Selections From the Vita Nuova
Petrarch, Dante and the Troubadours
William Shakespeare: Sonnets
William Shakespeare: Complete Poems
Blinded By Her Light: The Love-Poetry of Robert Graves
Emily Dickinson: Selected Poems
Emily Brontë: Poems
Thomas Hardy: Selected Poems
Percy Bysshe Shelley: Poems
John Keats: Selected Poems
Joh n Keats: Poems of 1820
D.H. Lawrence: Selected Poems
Edmund Spenser: Poems
Edmund Spenser: Amoretti
John Donne: Poems
Henry Vaughan: Poems
Sir Thomas Wyatt: Poems
Robert Herrick: Selected Poems
Rilke: Space, Essence and Angels in the Poetry of Rainer Maria Rilke
Rainer Maria Rilke: Selected Poems
Friedrich Hölderlin: Selected Poems
Arseny Tarkovsky: Selected Poems
Arthur Rimbaud: Selected Poems
Arthur Rimbaud: A Season in Hell
Arthur Rimbaud and the Magic of Poetry
Novalis: Hymns To the Night
German Romantic Poetry
Paul Verlaine: Selected Poems
Elizaethan Sonnet Cycles
D.J. Enright: By-Blows
Jeremy Reed: Brigitte's Blue Heart
Jeremy Reed: Claudia Schiffer's Red Shoes
Gorgeous Little Orpheus
Radiance: New Poems
Crescent Moon Book of Nature Poetry
Crescent Moon Book of Love Poetry
Crescent Moon Book of Mystical Poetry
Crescent Moon Book of Elizabethan Love Poetry
Crescent Moon Book of Metaphysical Poetry
Crescent Moon Book of Romantic Poetry
Pagan America: New American Poetry

MEDIA, CINEMA, FEMINISM and CULTURAL STUDIES

J.R.R. Tolkien: The Books, The Films, The Whole Cultural Phenomenon
J.R.R. Tolkien: Pocket Guide
The *Lord of the Rings* Movies: Pocket Guide
The Cinema of Hayao Miyazaki
Hayao Miyazaki: *Princess Mononoke*: Pocket Movie Guide
Hayao Miyazaki: *Spirited Away*: Pocket Movie Guide
Tim Burton : Hallowe'en For Hollywood
Ken Russell
Ken Russell: *Tommy*: Pocket Movie Guide
The Ghost Dance: The Origins of Religion
The Peyote Cult
Cixous, Irigaray, Kristeva: The *Jouissance* of French Feminism
Julia Kristeva: Art, Love, Melancholy, Philosophy, Semiotics and Psychoanalysis
Luce Irigaray: Lips, Kissing, and the Politics of Sexual Difference
Hélene Cixous I Love You: The *Jouissance* of Writing
Andrea Dworkin
'Cosmo Woman': The World of Women's Magazines
Women in Pop Music
HomeGround: The Kate Bush Anthology
Discovering the Goddess (Geoffrey Ashe)
The Poetry of Cinema
The Sacred Cinema of Andrei Tarkovsky
Andrei Tarkovsky: Pocket Guide
Andrei Tarkovsky: *Mirror*: Pocket Movie Guide
Andrei Tarkovsky: *The Sacrifice*: Pocket Movie Guide
Walerian Borowczyk: Cinema of Erotic Dreams
Jean-Luc Godard: The Passion of Cinema
Jean-Luc Godard: *Hail Mary*: Pocket Movie Guide
Jean-Luc Godard: *Contempt*: Pocket Movie Guide
Jean-Luc Godard: *Pierrot le Fou*: Pocket Movie Guide
John Hughes and Eighties Cinema
Ferris Bueller's Day Off: Pocket Movie Guide
Jean-Luc Godard: Pocket Guide
The Cinema of Richard Linklater
Liv Tyler: Star In Ascendance
Blade Runner and the Films of Philip K. Dick
Paul Bowles and Bernardo Bertolucci
Media Hell: Radio, TV and the Press
An Open Letter to the BBC
Detonation Britain: Nuclear War in the UK
Feminism and Shakespeare
Wild Zones: Pornography, Art and Feminism
Sex in Art: Pornography and Pleasure in Painting and Sculpture
Sexing Hardy: Thomas Hardy and Feminism

The Light Eternal is a model monograph, an exemplary job. The subject matter of the book is beautifully
organised and dead on beam. (Lawrence Durrell)
It is amazing for me to see my work treated with such passion and respect. (Andrea Dworkin)

CRESCENT MOON PUBLISHING
P.O. Box 1312, Maidstone, Kent, ME14 5XU, Great Britain. www.crmoon.com

cresmopub@yahoo.co.uk   www.crescentmoon.org.uk

21943653R00188

Printed in Great Britain
by Amazon